BEFORE CONFUCIUS

SUNY Series in Chinese Philosophy and Culture
Edited by David L. Hall and Roger T. Ames

BEFORE CONFUCIUS

*Studies in the Creation
of the Chinese Classics*

Edward L. Shaughnessy

STATE UNIVERSITY OF NEW YORK PRESS

Published by
State University of New York Press, Albany

Printed in the United States of America.

For information, address State University of New York Press,
State University Plaza, Albany, N.Y. 12246

Production by Cathleen Collins
Marketing by Anne Valentine

Library of Congress Cataloging-in-Publication Data

Shaughnessy, Edward L., 1952-
    Before Confucius : studies in the creation of the Chinese classics
/ Edward L. Shaughnessy.
        p.   cm. — (SUNY series in Chinese philosophy and culture)
    Includes bibliographical references and index.
    ISBN 0-7914-3377-3 (alk. paper). — ISBN 0-7914-3378-1 (pb. : alk
paper)
    1. Chinese classics—history and criticism.   2. China—
Civilization—To 22. B.C.   I. Title.   II. Series.
PL2461.Z6S46   1997
895.1'109—dc21   97–2449
                                                                CIP

10 9 8 7 6 5 4 3 2 1

To my parents

Contents

Illustrations

Introduction

The Master said: "As for the rites of Xia, I can speak about them but [the state of] Ji is not sufficient to attest to them. As for the rites of Yin, I can speak about them but [the state of] Song is not sufficient to attest to them. This is because the literary documents are insufficient. If they were sufficient, then I would be able to attest to them."

Analects 3/9

The Master said: "Zhou mirrored itself in the Two Dynasties. So manifold, indeed, in literature; I follow Zhou."

Analects 3/14

The Master said: "I transmit but do not create. I am faithful to and delight in antiquity, presuming even to compare myself to our Old Peng."

Analects 7/1

For two thousand years or more, China's received wisdom held that Confucius established the classical canon by selecting, editing, and, in some cases, commenting upon the literary legacy of the Xia, Shang, and especially the Western Zhou dynasties. The preeminence within the Chinese intellectual tradition of the *Zhouyi* or *Zhou Changes* (also known as the *Yijing* or *Classic of Changes*), the *Shangshu* or *Venerated Documents* (also known as the *Shujing* or *Classic of Documents*), and the *Shijing* or *Classic of Poetry* is due in some measure—apart from their own very considerable intrinsic virtues—to their presumed pedigree of having been created in the first place by the sages of the Three Dynasties of high antiquity and then subsequently having been transmitted by Confucius himself.

The first concerted assault on this received wisdom did not come until the dying days of China's imperial age, when nativist "New Text" scholars seeking a savior for China's traditions consolidated all of the creative effort in the single person of Confucius.[1] The great irony, of course, was that to gain a savior they had to sacrifice a good part of the tradition. It was not long before other scholars—infused with the iconoclastic spirit of the twentieth century—saw fit to sacrifice Confucius himself, not only rebuking the "New Text" critics for the naiveté of their scholarship, but even denying most if not all of Confucius's role even in transmitting the classics. Indeed, the most celebrated studies of the *Gu shi bian* 古史辨 or *Debates on Ancient History* movement of the 1920's and 30's denied the antiquity of much of the classics' creation, and certainly denied their sagely pedigree.[2]

These trends have had their parallels in the West. The historicism of nineteenth-century German biblical scholars sowed the first doubts about the revealed nature of scripture. Then, in the early twentieth century the advent of the Radio Age coincided with an all-out assault on the literary origins of the entire classical canon. Again in biblical studies, form critics asserted that they could detect the oral roots of many of the stories in the Bible.[3] Similar approaches became evident with respect to the Greek classics. The celebrated work of Milman Parry on oral-formulaic poetry suggested that Homer, for instance, never set pen to paper;[4] later studies have indeed demonstrated that Greece was essentially nonliterate until about 700 B.C.[5]

Western sinology has drawn inspiration from these scholarly trends in both China and the West. Much of its effort to trace China's early literature has focused on the philosophical works of the Hundred Schools after the time of Confucius. Deserving as these works are of such close scrutiny, the relative inattention to the classics in which it has resulted may derive also in part from doubts expressed by numerous scholars about their historicity. Indeed, far from being the great source for the history of the period that the classics had always been for traditional historians, because of questions about their date and authorship it would seem that the *Zhouyi*, *Shangshu* and even the *Shijing* have actually retarded the study of "Three Dynasties" China (i.e., Xia, Shang, and Western Zhou) among Western sinologists, at least among those concerned with its literary creations. True, there has been a relative handful of scholars drawn to the paleographic record of the time—the oracle-bone inscriptions of the Shang dynasty and the bronze inscriptions of the Western Zhou dynasty, but they have tended to disregard, whether deliberately or not, the received literary tradition. Meanwhile, the few published attempts to study the creation of the classics—primarily the *Shijing* or *Classic of Poetry*—have either not gone beyond narrow linguistic interests,[6] or have been mechanical attempts to apply to the Chinese context methodologies developed in the West.[7] It would seem almost as if there has been an unstated assumption among many Western sinologists that if the Western canon were not originally written, then China's must not have been either.

My own past studies of the ancient Chinese paleographic record—principally Western Zhou bronze inscriptions—have convinced me that, despite the prejudices of the iconoclasts and the comparatists, ancient China was a supremely literate culture, at least at the royal court and among the social elite, and was fully capable of producing the literary works of the received canon usually attributed to it. While bronze vessels of all sorts were the premier status markers of the time, I would argue that their value was at least heightened by, and perhaps due in large measure to, the inscriptions in or on them.[8] Those bronze inscriptions now serve as our best primary sources for the history of the Western Zhou dynasty; after all, they are preserved for us today exactly as written by their composers three thousand years ago. Nevertheless, there is evidence that when they were written they were but secondary or even tertiary documents.

For instance, the virtually identical inscriptions on a set of vessels, of which at least ten still survive, cast for a man named Song 頌 on the occasion of his appointment to command various warehouses show that the inscription was based on a written command document presented to Song during an audience at the royal court.[9] Similar to literally hundreds of other examples, the inscription begins by specifying when and where the king received Song in audience (in this case, on a date that probably corresponds to 10 May 825 B.C., in the Great Chamber of the Kang Palace's Zhao Temple), and what other officials were on hand to assist the king (in this case, the Intendant Yin 宰引 and the Scribe Guo Sheng 史虢生). The narrative here continues somewhat more fully than do other inscriptions in that it also records how Intendant Yin received the prepared command document,[10] presumably written on wooden or bamboo strips. Then Scribe Guo Sheng was called upon to read out the text of the command.[11] After the command had been read out loud to Song, together with an enumeration of the gifts to be given to him,[12] the prepared strips were in turn handed to him.[13] Song accepted them, suspended them from the sash securing his robe, and exited from the court. When Song subsequently commissioned the casting of the vessels to commemorate this appointment, he must have copied the text of the prepared command document,[14] merely adding to it his dedication of the vessel to his deceased parents, and a prayer for various kinds of blessings for himself, the ability to serve the king, and descendants to continue his sacrifices for "tenthousand years." Since the inscription is perhaps the best description we have of this ubiquitous investiture ceremony, it deserves to be translated in full.

Song gui

It was the third year, fifth month, after the dying brightness, *jiaxu* (day 11); the king was at the Zhao (Temple) of the Kang

Palace. At dawn the king entered the Great Chamber and assumed position. Intendant (*zai*) Yin to the right of Song entered the gate and stood in the center of the court. Yinshi received the king's command document. The king called out to Scribe (*shi*) Guo Sheng to record the command to Song.

The king said: "Song, (I) command you to officiate over and supervise the Chengzhou warehouses, and to oversee and supervise the newly constructed warehouses, using palace attendants. (I) award you a black jacket with embroidered hem, red kneepads, a scarlet demi-circlet, a chime pennant, and a bridle with bit and cheek-pieces; use (them) to serve."

Song bowed and touched his head to the ground, received the command, and suspended the strips from his sash in order to go out. He returned and brought in a jade tablet. Song dares in response to extol the Son of Heaven's illustriously fine beneficence, herewith making (for) my august deceased-father Gongshu and august mother Gongsi (this) treasured offertory *gui*-tureen, to use to send back filial piety and to beseech vigor, pure aid, thorough riches, and an eternal mandate. May Song for ten-thousand years be long-lived, truly ministering to the Son of Heaven (until) a numinous end, and (have) sons' sons and grandsons' grandsons eternally to treasure and use (it).

There is also evidence in the bronze inscriptions suggesting that copies of these command documents were kept in the royal archives, and were consulted by the king and his scribes when reappointing an individual to a position. Many inscriptions quote the king as saying "formerly I commanded you . . ."; fortunately, two inscribed vessels cast at different times for a single individual named Captain Dui 師兌 show that this phrase introduces a direct quotation of the previous command document. The "First Year Shi Dui 師兌 *gui*" (Sh 31.187:751) inscription, probably cast in 857 B.C., records, in addition to all of the usual narrative of an investiture inscription, the specific command to Captain Dui "to assist Shi Hefu in supervising the Horse Runners (*zouma*) of the left and right and the Horse Runners of the five cities." The "Third Year Shi Dui *gui*" (Sh 31.188:758) which I believe was cast in the year 851 B.C., records the command to Shi Dui: "I have already commanded you 'to assist Shi Hefu in supervising the Horse Runners of the left and right.' Now I extend your command, commanding you to regulate and supervise the Horse Runners."

In addition to records of these appointments within the royal bureaucracy, bronze inscriptions suggest that the royal archives contained many other sorts of records as well. The inscription on the "Shi Qi 師旂 *ding*" (Sh 13.67:752) describes a hearing for a Captain Qi after troops under his command had mutinied. After the sentence had been pronounced, the inscription continues that Captain Qi's assistant "therewith reported to the Central Scribe to document it" (*yi gao Zhong Shi shu* 以告中史書). As might be expected, registries of agricultural lands were kept. For instance, the inscription on the "Ke 克 *xu*" records that "the king commanded Yinshi's assistant Scribe Nin to register Provisioner Ke's fields and men" (*dian Shanfu Ke tian ren* 典善夫克田人).[15] Other inscriptions explicitly mention the drawing of maps to establish the boundaries of fields;[16] presumably these maps were stored in a "Map Chamber" (*Tushi* 圖室) mentioned in at least two different inscriptions as being in the royal palace in Zhou.[17]

Similar references to written documents emananting from the royal court abound also in the classics traditionally assumed to date from Western Zhou times. Sometimes the references are in such a natural and off-hand manner as to leave little question about the ubiquity of such written documents. For instance, the *Shijing* poem "Chu che" 出車 (Mao 168), which recounts the hardships of an extended military campaign, relates that the troops "feared these strip documents" (*wei ci jian shu* 畏此簡書), presumably the documents containing the king's command to advance. In the "Shao gao" 召誥 chapter of the *Shangshu*, the mention of a speech given by the Duke of Zhou 周公 to the survivors of the Shang elite assembled at the new city of Chengzhou 成周 indicates that the Duke read from a prepared text: "The Duke of Zhou then in the morning used a document to command the many Yin" (*Zhougong nai zhao yong shu ming shu Yin* 周公乃朝用書命庶殷).

Several other chapters of the *Shangshu* indicate that written documents were also used extensively in ceremonies at court. In the "Luo gao" 洛誥 chapter, after the mention of a sacrifice to the past kings, the present king, King Cheng (r. 1042/35–1006 B.C.), is described as commanding Recorder Yi "to intone in prayer the record" (*zhu ce* 祝冊), presumably the prepared text of the prayer.[18] In the "Gu ming" 顧命 chapter, which describes in fascinating detail the death of King Cheng and the installation of his son as King Kang (r. 1005/03–978 B.C.), at the climactic point at which the deceased king's last will and testament is presented to the new king, on the altar of the ancestral temple, the Grand Scribe is described as "clutching the document" (*bing shu* 秉書) and reading the command out loud to the king. And in the famous story related in the "Jin teng" 金藤 chapter, the final version of which however was almost certainly produced long after the events described, the Duke of Zhou in performing a divination on behalf of the ailing King Wu (r. 1050/45–1043 B.C.) had the text of his prayer inscribed (*ce zhu* 冊祝) before making cracks in the turtle shells. After the divination was completed, the Duke had the strips stored in a metal-bound coffer, where they were eventually discovered by King Cheng. I think that the scope and nature of all of these references to writing during the Western Zhou period leave no doubt about the literary abilities and interests of the Zhou people. As Herrlee Creel said sixty years ago, "We simply have to accept the fact that the Chous [Zhous] were a people who liked to write books."[19]

The eight studies presented in this book all address, in one way or another, the books that the Zhou people wrote. Two studies each treat the *Zhouyi* or *Changes of Zhou*, the *Shangshu* or *Venerated Documents*, and the *Shijing* or *Classic of Poetry*; one treats a text currently found in the *Yi Zhou shu* 逸周書 or *Remainder of the Zhou Documents*, and another treats a later historical record, the *Zhushu jinian* 竹書紀年 or *Bamboo Annals*, as it relates to the reigns of the Zhou kings Wu and Cheng. In all of these studies, I have tried to consider first and foremost how and why the text was originally written, and what it meant in its original context. In some cases I have also followed the history of the text and its exegesis in later periods, sometimes being able to show how and why later philosophical beliefs required that the text's original meaning be changed or obscured. The studies were written over a period of fifteen years but, if I might paraphrase Confucius, I would like to think there is a single thread running through them.

   The first study, "Marriage, Divorce, and Revolution: Reading between the Lines of the *Book of Changes*," although published in 1992, derives from and represents the central thesis of my 1983 doctoral dissertation "The Composition of the *Zhouyi*." In this study, I examine one historical vignette mentioned in the line statements of the *Classic of Changes*, the marriage of King Wen of Zhou (r. 1099/57–1051 B.C.) to a daughter of the penultimate Shang king Di Yi (r. 1105–1087 B.C.). Using the modern historiography of the *Gu shi bian* movement, I argue that the text implies, especially when read in conjunction with the *Shijing*, that the marriage failed but that King Wen and a secondary wife subsequently produced an heir, the future King Wu, who would eventually overthrow the Shang and establish the Zhou dynasty. I go on to argue, in part using traditional views of the *Classic of Changes*, that the recognition of this notion of reversal, of the changeability of fortune, became the central organizing theme of the *Classic of Changes* when it achieved its final form late in the Western Zhou period. The use I make in this study of both modern and traditional exegeses is a paradigm of what I have tried to do in all of these studies—using new evidence to reconsider, while trying to remain faithful to, traditional understandings. This is why—apart from just the chronological priority of its subject matter—I have put this study at the head of the book.

The second study, "'New' Evidence on the Zhou Conquest," is the first article that I ever published, though it is here presented substantially revised. In it, I examine the "Shi fu" 世俘 chapter of the *Yi Zhou shu*, a text which provides an annalistic account of the Zhou conquest campaign against the Shang. Because the text describes the conquest as being extremely violent, a situation at variance with the Confucian expectation that rulers as virtuous as kings Wen and Wu of Zhou ought not to have encountered any resistance to their rule, since at least the fourth century B.C. it has often, perhaps usually, been regarded as a forgery, and thus removed from the *Shangshu* and preserved only in the less prestigious *Yi Zhou shu*. Nevertheless, by comparing the language of the text to that of Shang oracle-bone and Western Zhou bronze inscriptions, I have attempted to show that the "Shi fu" chapter could only have been written in the early Western Zhou dynasty, and that it must be the original version of the "Wu cheng" 武成 chapter of the *Shangshu*, the present "Wu cheng" ironically enough being the real forgery. Although I have revised the study in more or less important ways to reflect my present understanding of the text and the language of the early Western Zhou, I retain the youthfully hyperbolic conclusion:

> [M]odern scholars are justifiably excited whenever a bronze vessel bearing an inscription is unearthed. But earth is not the only thing that can bury authentic records. In the case of this "Shi fu" text, Confucian idealism has been nearly as obscurant. Let us not succumb to our own prejudices against "unattested" evidence, but instead examine this text just as we would a newly discovered bronze inscription.

It is the sentiment that has spurred me throughout these fifteen years to produce the other studies in this book.

The third study, "On the Authenticity of the *Bamboo Annals*," is the one really anomalous piece in the book since it does not treat a pre-Confucian classic, but rather focuses on an annalistic history compiled around 300 B.C.

However, I include it here for three reasons. First, the portion of the history that I examine concerns the death of King Wu of Zhou, which features so importantly in early Zhou history and in several of the other studies presented here. Second, the argument that I make in the study, that the text of the *Annals* was changed, albeit inadvertantly, in the third century A.D. in order to conform with contemporary historical understanding, but that it is possible to use new evidence to restore the original text, coincidentally demonstrating the authenticity of the text (or at least a portion of it), strikes me as similar to what I have attempted to do in many of the other studies included here. And third, while we do not have any similar annalistic histories written during the Western Zhou period, I would be very surprised if they did not exist, and in essentially the form we see in the *Bamboo Annals*.

This is followed by two complementary studies on the two nonroyal founding fathers of the Western Zhou dynasty, the Duke of Zhou and the Duke of Shao 召公. In "The Duke of Zhou's Retirement in the East and the Beginnings of the Minister-Monarch Debate in Chinese Political Philosophy," which was actually the latter of the two studies, I examine two chapters in the *Shangshu* purportedly written by these two figures, arguing that they reflect two radically different views of government, one based on royal prerogative and the other on ministerial control. I also argue against most, but not all, received wisdom that the Duke of Zhou, the proponent of ministerial control, was the loser of this debate and was forced out of the government because of this. This may explain why he was so little mentioned in other contemporary documents. The Duke of Shao, on the other hand, figures importantly in all of the different sources from the Western Zhou: the *Shangshu*, *Shijing*, and, perhaps most importantly, bronze inscriptions. In "The Role of Grand Protector Shi in the Consolidation of the Zhou Conquest," I examine those sources pertaining to the Duke of Shao, both before and especially after the time of his debate with the Duke of Zhou, concluding that perhaps more than any other figure he was responsible for the regular primogeniture succession policy that characterized the Zhou monarchy.

In "From Liturgy to Literature: The Western Zhou Ritual Reform and the Development of the *Classic of Poetry*," the most recently written of the studies included here, I begin by returning to one of the sources involving the Duke of Shao, the "Gu ming" chapter of the *Shangshu*, which describes the duke's role in the installation of King Kang after King Cheng's death. By comparing three poems found in the "Zhou *Song*" 周頌 section of the *Shijing* to wording in the "Gu ming" chapter, I suggest that these earliest poems were originally liturgical in nature, intended to be recited in the course of court ceremonies. Going on to examine poems centering on sacrifices to the ancestors, I find a significant difference between those that formal linguistic evidence suggest were created early in the Western Zhou and those that must have been created after the time of King Mu (r. 956–918 B.C.), a difference that is essentially that between performative and descriptive poetry. I suggest that this change in poetic form and function coincided with a major change in the Zhou performance of ritual that becomes evident in the archeological record beginning about the time of King Mu. While I draw on the archeological evidence of inscriptions in virtually each of the studies presented in this book, I am pleased that in this study I have been able to incorporate something of the material culture of the time, as seen in archeological remains.

The seventh study, "The Composition of 'Qian' and 'Kun' Hexagrams of the *Zhouyi*," features yet another methodology that has proved very important in recent years in the study of the Western Zhou: historical astronomy or, as it is becoming known, archeoastronomy. This study, heretofore published only in Chinese,[20] is presented here essentially unchanged from my doctoral dissertation. While working on that dissertation at Stanford University, I had many occasions to listen to my teacher David Nivison and my classmate David Pankenier discuss their researches on archeoastronomy and early Zhou history. As luck would have it, the reading that I did in the history of Chinese astronomy by way of educating myself sufficiently to follow their discussions led to an insight regarding the textual structure of "Qian" and "Kun" hexagrams, the first two, and most important hexagrams of the *Classic of Changes*. In large measure this insight influenced my entire understanding of the process by which the *Zhouyi* was created, as is evident also in the first paper here, "Marriage, Divorce, and Revolution."

The final paper in the book, "How the Poetess Came to Burn the Royal Chamber," is a close reading of the *Shijing* poem "Ru fen" 汝墳 (Mao 10). As in so many of the other studies, I argue that the original meaning of this poem, in this case an explicitly sexual meaning, was subsequently changed or obscured (in this case, I suspect, deliberately) by didactic Confucian editors. By combining the advances of modern scholarship on the *Shijing* with paleographic evidence—what the text of the poem must have looked like both in its original context and to the Han dynasty editors of the text, I suggest a reading for the critical third stanza that is consistent with the sexual imagery of the first two stanzas. The reading may be wrong (which may be why this is the only study in the book that has not previously been published), but it is one that makes the poem more enjoyable to me; I hope it will make it enjoyable to you as well.

Indeed, I hope that in reading these studies you the reader will experience some of the joy and fascination that I have had over the last decade and a half considering anew literary classics that have been supremely influential in one of the world's great civilizations for almost three thousand years. Now approaching the end of the twentieth century, the convergence of intellectual trends and archeological evidence places us in a unique position to see how these classics may have been created.

NOTES

1. This tendency culminated in the absurd claims of Kang Youwei 康有爲 (1858–1927) that Liu Xin 劉歆 (46 B.C.–A.D. 23) had forged all of the classic texts; for succinct surveys of Kang and his predecessors, who, it should be pointed out, were more reasonable, see Benjamin A. Elman, *From Philosophy to Philology: Intellectual and Social Aspects of Change in Late Imperial China* (Cambridge, MA: Council on East Asian Studies, Harvard University, 1984), 22–25; Benjamin A. Elman, *Classicism, Politics, and Kinship: The Ch'ang-chou School of New Text Confucianism in Late-Imperial China* (Berkeley: University of California Press, 1990), esp. 222–31.

2. *Gu shi bian*, ed. Gu Jiegang 顧頡剛 *et al.*, 7 vols. (1926–41; rpt. Shanghai: Shanghai Guji chubanshe, 1982). In another irony, the development of archeology in China, which at first was associated with the "scientific" spirit of the iconoclasts, has now, almost at the end of the twentieth century, served to restore much of the antiquity to the classical tradition, as I will attempt to show further in this Introduction and, indeed, throughout the studies in this book.

3. For a concise introduction to the history and nature of form criticism, see Gene M. Tucker, *Form Criticism of the Old Testament* (Philadelphia: Fortress Press, 1971).

4. For the classic statement of Parry's theory of oral-formulaic poetry, see Albert Lord, *A Singer of Tales* (Cambridge, MA: Harvard University Press, 1960).

5. See, for instance, Eric A. Havelock, *Preface to Plato* (Cambridge, MA: Harvard Belknap Press, 1963).

6. W. A. C. H. Dobson, *The Language of the* Book of Songs (Toronto: University of Toronto Press, 1968).

7. See C. H. Wang, *The Bell and the Drum* (Berkeley: University of California

Press, 1974), for an application of the Parry-Lord notion of oral-formulaic poetry to the *Shijing*.

8. There is some evidence that bronze vessels with the longest inscriptions were the most prized by the people of the time, those with long inscriptions tending to be preserved in family's ancestral altars, while those with shorter inscriptions were buried in tombs; for statistics demonstrating this tendency, see Edward L. Shaughnessy, *Sources of Western Zhou History: Inscribed Bronze Vessels* (Berkeley: University of California Press, 1991), 158–63, table 13 and the discussion on p. 157.

9. For the most complete presentation of the inscription, see Shirakawa Shizuka 白川靜, *Kinbun tsūshaku* 金文通釋, *Hakutsuru bijutsukanshi* 白鶴美術館誌 24 (1968), Entry 137, 153–73 (references to this work will hereafter be in the form Sh 24.137:153). There are at least two *hu* 壺 vases, three *ding* 鼎 caldrons, and five *gui* 簋 tureens, all with virtually identical inscriptions, differing primarily in linear scansion and also in reference to the type of vessel being cast. The inscription presented here is that of the "Song *gui*."

10. Other inscriptions that mention receipt of the written command document from the king include the "Mian 免 *gui*" (Sh 21.115:464), "Yuan 袁 *pan*" (Sh 29.177:590), and "Zou 趕 *gui*" (for which, see *Shang Zhou qingtongqi mingwen xuan*, ed. Shanghai Museum, 4 vols. to date (Beijing: Wenwu chubanshe, 1986–), no. 423.

11. The term used here, *ce ming* 冊命, literally "to record the command," is found in scores of Western Zhou investiture inscriptions. While there has been debate over the meaning of the term, it seems to me that the sense suggested sixty years ago by Herrlee Creel, "command by reading a document containing orders," is essentially correct; see Herrlee Glessner Creel, *Studies in Early Chinese Culture: First Series* (Baltimore: Waverly Press, 1937).

12. It would seem that a record of the gifts to be awarded had also been written in advance; for inscriptions that mention no command but only the award of gifts, the award being specified as being in writing (*ce xi* 冊錫), see "Xiu 休 *pan*" (Sh 25.146:296), "Xing 癲 *xu*" (Sh 50.*Ho*15:379) and "Thirteenth Year Xing *hu*" (Sh 50.*Ho*15:384), as well as the "Yuan *pan*," mentioned above (n. 10).

13. For a similar example, see the "Shanfu Shan 善夫山 *ding*" (Sh 26.154:357), and from the Eastern Zhou period, the "Huanzi Meng Jiang 洹子孟姜 *hu*" (Sh 38.217:388).

14. For an inscription that explicitly mentions that it records the king's commands, see the "Rong 榮 *gui*" (Sh 11.59:591).

15. There is also some suggestion that the inscription on the "Mai 麥 *zun*" (Sh 11.60:628) mentions the king's award to the Lord of Xing 邢 of the deeds (*ji* 齎 or 劑) to two-hundred families of retainers; for discussion of these deeds and household registries, see David N. Keightley, "Public Work in Ancient China: A Study of Forced Labor in the Shang and Western Chou" (Ph.D. diss.: Columbia University, 1969), 202–9.

16. The most famous and detailed of these is the "Sanshi 散氏 *pan*" (Sh 24.139:191); for another example, see the "Peng Sheng 倗生 *gui*" (Sh 20.112:423).

17. The Map Chamber is mentioned in the inscriptions on the "Shanfu Shan *ding*" and the "Wu Hui 無重 *ding*" (Sh 26.153:348).

18. The text of this prayer probably resembled those of the oracle-bone inscriptions, early Western Zhou examples of which have recently been discovered; see Edward L. Shaughnessy, "Western Zhou Oracle-Bone Inscriptions: Entering the Research Stage?" *Early China* 11–12 (1985–87), 146–94. There is evidence, however, that the better known Shang oracle-bone inscriptions were not written until after the divination rite had been completed; see David N. Keightley, *Sources of Shang History: The Oracle-Bone Inscriptions of Bronze Age China* (Berkeley: University of California Press, 1978), 45–46.

19. Herrlee G. Creel, *The Birth of China* (New York: Frederick Ungar, 1937), 255.

20. Xia Hanyi 夏含夷, "Zhouyi Qian gua liu long xinjie" 周易乾卦六龍 新解, *Wenshi* 文史 24 (1985), 9–14.

1

Marriage, Divorce and Revolution

Reading between the Lines of the *Book of Changes*

The enigmatic images contained in the *Book of Changes* (*Yijing* 易經 or *Zhouyi* 周易) have been interpreted, since shortly after the final redaction of the text, to refer to universal themes, transforming a text that was originally used in divination into a repository of wisdom for the ages.[1] While this tradition continues strong, more than 2,500 years after its first emergence, it has been challenged in the present century by a new historiographical tradition that has attempted to return ancient Chinese texts to the immediate historical contexts of their composition and to interpret their language within the strictures of that context.

Perhaps the first work of this new historiographical tradition to attract considerable notice was Gu Jiegang's 顧頡剛 (1893–1980) "*Zhouyi* guayaoci zhong de gushi" 周易卦爻辭中的故事 (Stories in the Hexagram and Line Statements of the *Book of Changes*), first published in 1929 and subsequently reprinted as the lead article in the volume of *Gushi bian* 古史辨 (Debates on Ancient History) devoted to the *Zhouyi*.[2] In this study, Gu rejected the notion that the *Zhouyi* was the product of inspired sages. By examining five historical vignettes that appear in the line statements of the *Zhouyi*, he argued that the text was compiled, over a long period of time, by a process of grouping together numerous individuated records of divination. These five vignettes span a period from before the Shang dynasty until the early Western Zhou dynasty. Briefly summarized, the five vignettes are: that Wang Hai 王亥, a predynastic leader of the Shang people, lost a herd of cattle ("Da zhuang" 大壯 34/5, "Lü" 履 56/6[3]); that Gaozong 高宗, temple name of the Shang king Wu Ding, well known from the numerous oracle-bone inscriptions deriving from

13

his reign, defeated an alien state known as Guifang 鬼方 or Devilland ("Jiji" 既濟 63/3, "Weiji" 未濟 64/4); that Di Yi, the penultimate king of the Shang dynasty, gave his daughter away in marriage, presumably to King Wen, leader of the Zhou people ("Tai" 泰 11/5, "Guimei" 歸妹 54/5); that Jizi 箕子, a Shang nobleman, feigned madness in order to escape the abuses of Di Xin, the last king of the dynasty ("Mingyi" 明夷 36/5); and that the Lord of Kang 康侯, younger brother of King Wu of Zhou, founder of the Zhou dynasty, received an award of investiture ("Jin" 晉 35).

Gu's study has been supremely influential in what has come to be known as the "new" *Zhouyi* studies, with both the selection of individual vignettes and his general conclusions informing much of the past half-century's scholarship regarding the text.[4] Since my own past work on the *Zhouyi* has put me within this tradition,[5] it is perhaps appropriate that I should also turn my attention to Gu's study. In this chapter I will examine one of the five vignettes— that involving the marriage between Di Yi's daughter and King Wen of Zhou— in the light of its historical context. Like Gu, I will also attempt to draw from this vignette more general conclusions regarding the nature of the *Zhouyi,* conclusions that I believe will show both advantages and disadvantages of the "new" tradition of *Zhouyi* exegesis.

The primary locus for this, the third of Gu Jiegang's five historical vignettes, is the fifth line of "Guimei" (The Marrying Maiden, 54) hexagram:

帝乙歸妹, 其君之袂不如其娣之袂良
Di Yi marries off his daughter; the primary bride's sleeves are not as fine as the secondary bride's.

Traditional commentators have preferred to see a universal moral principle inspiring the text of the *Zhouyi,* and interpretations of this line are not exceptions. Most of these commentators have viewed the text of the hexagram (i.e., the hexagram and line statements) and the hexagram picture (here, "Guimei" ䷵) as a single integral unit. Representative of this tradition with respect to this line of "Guimei" would be the Northern Song thinker Cheng Yi 程頤 (1033–1108). Cheng explains that the fifth line of "Guimei," being a broken or *yin* line, represents a female, the "daughter" referred to in the line statement, and that its position in the fifth place in the hexagram picture, regarded as the ruling position of a hexagram, indicates a woman who is in a position of respect, such as the daughter of a king. But, Cheng continues, the image in the line statement is intended to illustrate the sense of morality proper for a woman; just as the primary bride dresses in lesser finery than the secondary bride, so, too, should even the daughter of a king not have a haughty attitude or lose the way of compliance.[6]

We can let pass the question of just how universal this wisdom might be. As noted above, at least Gu Jiegang and his many recent followers have contended that the *Zhouyi* can be better understood by associating its images with particular historical references; in the case of this line in "Guimei," they see a reference to the wedding of Shang king Di Yi's daughter with King Wen of Zhou. Perhaps representative of scholars who have been influenced by Gu's historical interpretation of this line is Hellmut Wilhelm (1905–90), who explained the description of the bride's clothing in light of this historical context.

> We know from other sources that the cultural disparity between the Shang and Chou was large. [Original note: According to one tradition, King Wen would have been born in a pigsty. See Eduard Erkes, "Das Schwein im alten China," *Monumenta Serica* 7 (1942, 76).] The Shang princess, now dressed in Chou costumes, must have paled before her handmaidens, attired in the full splendor of Shang garments.[7]

We can also let pass the question of the relative cultural development of the Shang and Zhou peoples. A question that I would like to consider, however, is the use of images in the text of the *Zhouyi*. Wilhelm's reading strikes me as overliteral at the very least, denying to the author of the line any consciousness of the symbolic associations of images. What is more, despite the literalness Wilhelm brought to the interpretation of this line, he failed to consider the entirety of Gu Jiegang's own reconstruction of the marriage of the Shang princess and King Wen (a failing, I might add, in which he is joined by every other adherent of the "new" tradition known to me). It is true, of course, that Gu related this line to the wedding of Di Yi's daughter to King Wen, a wedding he found further described in the poem "Da ming" 大明 (Great Brightness; Mao 236) of the *Classic of Poetry* (*Shijing*).

大邦有子	The great state had a child;
俔天之妹	She was as if a daughter of heaven.
文定厥祥	[King] Wen determined their luck
親迎于渭	And personally met [her] on the [Wei River],
造舟爲梁	Building rafts into a bridge;
不顯其光	Illustrious was her radiance!

The "great state" (*da bang* 大邦) referred to in the first line of this stanza has generally been interpreted to be a predynastic Zhou euphemism for the state of Shang, an interpretation that Gu accepted. He also accepted the traditional interpretation that the remainder of the stanza describes King Wen's wedding with this "child" of Shang. But Gu did not stop with this. Instead, he continued his reading into the next stanza of "Da ming."

有命自天	There was a mandate from heaven
命此文王	Commanding this King Wen
于周于京	In Zhou, in the capital.
纘女維莘	The successor lady was [the one from] Shen,
長子維行	The elder child was [the one] to go,
篤生武王	And she faithfully bore King Wu.

Gu noted the curious description here of the mother of King Wen's son, King Wu, as being the "successor lady" (*zan nü* 纘女) from Shen, a small state traditionally said to have been ruled by descendants of the former Xia dynasty. Most commentaries to this poem explain that the mother of King Wu, known by tradition as Tai Si 太姒, is so characterized because she "succeeded" to the position of honor formerly held by Tai Ren 太妊, the mother of King Wen and the topic of an earlier stanza of this poem. However, as Gu argued, this raises the question of why a woman from the relatively insignficant and non-Shang state of Shen should have been referred to in the preceeding stanza as being from the "great state," elsewhere thought to refer exclusively to Shang. Because of this, Gu proposed that this "successor lady" from Shen succeeded the child of the "great state," assumed from the line statement of the *Zhouyi* to be the daughter of Shang king Di Yi, when this Shang princess failed to produce an heir to the Zhou kingship. This would then explain the symbolism of the *Zhouyi* line statement that "the primary bride's sleeves are not as fine as the secondary bride's," an image that seems to suggest that the secondary bride enjoyed greater favor or success than did the primary bride.

Perhaps because of his general argument that the text of the *Zhouyi* was compiled over a long period of time from records of more or less unrelated divinations, Gu focused his discussion of this vignette on just this one line statement, calling his interpretation little more than a "guess."[8] I believe that if he had also considered the other line statements of "Guimei" hexagram, he would have found further evidence regarding the failed marriage of Di Yi's daughter. The text reads in its entirety:[9]

54 *Guimei* ䷵: to campaign: inauspicious; nothing beneficial.

54/1 The marrying maiden with her younger sisters:
   The lame is able to walk;
     to campaign: auspicious.

54/2 The blind is able to see;
     beneficial for a dark person's divination.

54/3 The marrying maiden with the older sisters:
   Returns with the younger sisters.

54/4 The marrying maiden misses the time:
   She slowly returns to wait.

54/5 Di Yi marries off his daughter:
   The primary bride's sleeves are not as fine as the
   secondary bride's;
     the moon is nearly full:
      auspicious.

54/6 The woman holds the basket: no fruit;
   The man stabs the sheep: no blood.

For instance, the fourth line of the hexagram (54.4), that immediately preceeding the line with which we have been concerned to this point, consists of a rhymed couplet:

歸妹愆期, 遲歸有時
The marrying maiden misses her time [*gjə]
And slowly returns to wait [*djə].[10]

It does not seem overly impressionistic to take Gu's insight a step further and see in this line, also, an intimation that all was not well with the marriage. An even more compelling image of marital failure is to be found in the top line of the hexagram (54.6), immediately following the line noting the flaw in the primary bride's sleeve. This line consists of another rhymed couplet, this time of five-character lines, including the only clear example in the *Zhouyi* of conscious internal rhyme.

女承筐无實, 土刲羊无血
The lady holds the basket [*khwjaŋ]: no fruit [*djit];
The man stabs the sheep [*ljaŋ]: no blood [*hwit].

If the image of a fruitless basket were not obvious enough to evoke the notion of a barren woman, the term *cheng kuang* 承筐, here translated literally as "holds the basket," was by no later than the early Han dynasty a conventional euphemism for the vagina. The term appears, for instance, in a poem found at Mawangdui describing the movements of lovemaking, and has been translated by Donald Harper as "the receiving cannister."

> The recipe for whenever one will be conjoining Yin and Yang:
> Grip the hands, spit on the Yang side of the wrists.
> Stroke the elbow chambers.
> Go under the side of the armpits.
> Ascend the stove frame.
> Go under the neck zone.
> Stroke the receiving cannister.[11]

I have no way of knowing whether this vaginal sense was already current in the Western Zhou period or if (as I suspect) it was a literary flourish derived from this line of the *Zhouyi*. The parallel with the second line of the couplet, "the man stabs the sheep" (*shi kui yang* 士刲羊), the sexual symbolism of which strikes me as no less explicit, would seem to support the grammar I have used in rendering *cheng kuang* as "holds the basket." But there seems to be no mistaking the symbolism of this line: that the primary bride's basket held no fruit implies that she was barren and produced no offspring.

While the major insight here is drawn more or less directly from Gu's study, the consistent theme throughout these three line statements of "Guimei" hexagram, that there was some kind of problem in the marriage between Di Yi's daughter and King Wen of Zhou, seems to undermine his general thesis that the line statements of the *Zhouyi* derive from individuated records of divination and, therefore, do not share a consistent authorial perspective. Indeed, I think we can readily find other evidence of coherence within this single hexagram. For example, the role reversal between the primary bride and the secondary bride would seem to be intimated in the first two line statements of this same hexagram, "the lame is able to walk" (*bo neng lü* 跛能履) and "the blind is able to see" (*miao neng shi* 眇能視). (I will return to this notion of role reversal in the concluding section of this chapter.) But, and this is significant, I think we can find in other hexagram texts still more evidence of a consistent authorial perspective on the marriage of Di Yi's daughter.

Both traditional and modern scholars of the *Zhouyi* have noted that the sixty-four hexagrams of the text are arranged in thirty-two pairs, based either on an inversion of the hexagram picture (i.e., the bottom line becoming the top, the second the fifth, and so on; e.g., "Tun" [3] ䷂ is followed by "Meng"

[4] ䷁) or, in the eight cases where this would result in the same picture, the change of each line into its opposite (e.g., "Qian" [1] ䷀ is paired with "Kun" [2] ䷁). In numerous cases, the two hexagrams of a pair share common wording and images. Among the historical vignettes studied by Gu Jiegang, for instance, one might note that two lines seem to refer to Gaozong's attack on the Guifang or Devilland, and that these lines appear in the complementary hexagrams "Jiji" ䷾ (After Completion; 63) and "Weiji" ䷿ (Before Completion; 64).

> 63/3　商宗伐鬼方, 三年克之
> Gaozong attacked the Devilland,
>   in three years conquering it.

> 64/4　震用伐鬼方, 三年有賞于大國
> Zhen therewith attacked the Devilland,
>   in three years having an award from the great state.

Moreover, when we consider that "Jiji" and "Weiji" share the same basic hexagram picture, the latter simply being the inversion of the former, it will be seen that the third line of the one hexagram is none other than the fourth line of its complement.

Many similar examples exist elsewhere in the *Zhouyi*. Sometimes these interhexagrammatic relationships are formal and obvious, as in the following image found in both the fifth line of "Sun" ䷨ (Decrease; 41) and the second line of "Yi" ䷩ (Increase; 42).

> 41/5, 42/2　或益之十朋之龜, 弗克違
> Someone increases it with ten strands of turtles;
>   they cannot be disobeyed.

In other cases, hexagrams seem to be related only through repetition of a single word, which may even be used in two different senses, as in the case of the word *fou* 缶, "earthenware" or "drum," used in the fourth line of "Kan" ䷜ (29) and the third line of "Li" ䷝ (30).

> 29/4　樽酒簋貳, 用缶
> A beaker of wine and two tureens; use *earthenware*.

> 30/3　日昃之離 不鼓缶而歌, 則大耋之嗟
> The cleavage of the sun's obliquity:
>   if one does not beat the *drum* and sing,
>   then the old man this will sigh.

And, in still other cases, two complementary hexagrams might share just a general image, such as the dragon that appears throughout "Qian" (1) hexagram and again in the top line of "Kun" (2).

1/1	Submerged dragon.
1/2	See the dragon in the fields.
1/4	Now jumping in the depths.
1/5	Flying dragon in the sky.
1/6	The throated dragon.
1/7	See the flock of dragons without heads.
2/6	The dragon battles in the wilds; its blood is black and yellow.

As I believe I have demonstrated elsewhere,[12] the dragon here is an astronomical image, its motion through "Qian" hexagram corresponding to the motion of the constellation Green Dragon through the dusk skies from the middle of winter until the middle of autumn. The dragon's reappearance in "Kun," the other images of which seem to be related to the autumn harvest, signals its reunion beneath the dusk horizon at the beginning of winter with the constellation Bi 蠶 (Turtle), with which it is variously thought to do battle or to join in sexual union.

The complementary hexagram to "Guimei" ䷵, the fifty-fourth hexagram, is "Jian" ䷴ (53), the text of which reads as follows.

53	*Jian* ䷴: the woman returns: auspicious; benefical to divine.
53/1	The wild goose advances to the mountain stream: the little child has difficulties; danger; no harm.
53/2	The wild goose advances to the large rock: Drinking and eating merrily; auspicious.
53/3	The wild goose advances to the land: The husband is on campaign but does not return, The wife is pregnant but does not give birth.
53/4	The wild goose advances to the tree: And now gains its perch; no harm.
53/5	The wild goose advances to the hillock: The wife for three years is not pregnant; In the end nothing overcomes it.[13]

53/6   The wild goose advances to the hill:[14]
       Its feathers can be used as insignia;
       auspicious.

The only wording in this text obviously shared with "Guimei" is the hexagram statement, "the woman returns," which, due to the ambiguity of the word *gui* 歸, can either mean "the woman marries" or "the woman returns (to her own home)," an ambiguity that, as noted above (n. 10), seems to be deliberately employed in the fourth line of "Guimei." However, I would suggest that Gu Jiegang's insight that the marriage between Di Yi's daughter and King Wen ultimately failed allows more associations to be seen on a conceptual level. It is not difficult, for instance, to see an association between the third and fifth line statements of "Jian": "The husband is on campaign but does not return; The wife is pregnant but does not give birth" and "The wife for three years is not pregnant; In the end nothing overcomes it," and the poetic couplet that comprises the top line statement of "Guimei": "The woman holds the basket: no fruit; The man stabs the sheep; no blood."

More important, I think it is possible to perceive a formal literary association between the two hexagrams once we recognize the structure of the individual line statements within "Jian." Each of these statements is introduced by a four-character phrase containing the image of a wild goose's advances to higher and higher topographic points (an organizational structure evident in the line statements of several other hexagrams as well; see, for instance, "Xian" [31], "Ding" [50] and "Gen" [52]). These repeated descriptions of the goose's advance, similar to what has been termed "incremental repetition" in the *Shijing*, are followed by descriptions of the human condition, and are formally related with them through rhyme. As many modern scholars have noted, this is analogous to the use of nature imagery in the *Shijing* to evoke (*xing* 興) corresponding events in the human realm. Indeed, the wild goose itself appears frequently in the *xing*-evocations of the *Shijing*, where contrary to its later symbolism of marital union, it consistently evokes the theme of marital separation. For instance, the first stanza of the poem "Hong yan" 鴻鴈 (Wild Goose; Mao 181) reads:

鴻鴈于飛	The wild goose in flight,
肅肅其羽	Whoosh, whoosh, its wings:
之子于征	This man on campaign
劬勞于野	Toiling in the wilds;
爰及矜人	Coming to the pitiable man
哀此鰥寡	Sorrow for this solitary widow.

The image of the wild goose as a harbinger of marital separation (perhaps because it was seen flying in formation at the onset of winter, the time when military campaigns were launched) is by no means unique to this poem. Among further examples is a poem that juxtaposes the goose image with a different nature evocation, a fish, which Wen Yiduo 聞一多 (1899–1946) has shown persuasively to be a sexual image, generally representative of the male sexual member.[15] The poem "Jiu yu" 九罭 (The Many-Stringed Net; Mao 159) begins coquettishly with the first blush of romantic involvement between a young woman and her lover, but when, in the second stanza, a goose appears, in wording almost exactly the same as the lines of "Jian" hexagram, problems arise in the relationship.

九罭之魚	The many-stringed net's fishes:
鱒魴	Rudd and bream.
我覯之子	I meet this man:
袞衣繡裳	Fine-woven jacket and embroidered skirt.
鴻飛遵渚	The wild goose flies along the sandbar:
公歸无所	The duke has no place to which to return
於女信處	A spot to sleep with you.
鴻飛遵陸	The wild goose flies along the hill:
公歸不復	The duke returns but does not come back
於女信宿	To sleep the night with you.

Consider, too, the final stanza of the poem "Xin tai" 新臺 (New Terrace; Mao 43), a poem that has traditionally been viewed as a veiled criticism of Duke Xuan of Wei 衛宣公 (r. 718–700 B.C.) for carrying on an affair with the wife of his son.

魚綱之設	The fish net, this is set;
鴻則離之	A wild goose then is caught in it:
燕婉之求	A pretty one this he sought:
得此戚施	But got this ugly toad-buffoon.[16]

In all three of these cases, the wild goose evokes a theme of marital separation or romantic discord. I would suggest that the image of the wild goose in the individual line statements of "Jian" hexagram, which are, after all, closely contemporary with the *Shijing*, shares this same evocative value. Thus, the image of the wild goose advancing to the "land" in the third line (53/3) evokes the response in the human condition that "the husband is on campaign but does not return; the wife is pregnant but does not give birth," or, somewhat less directly, that its advance to the "hillock" in the fifth line evokes the response "the wife for three years is not pregnant; in the end nothing overcomes it."

I would like to go further than this to suggest that this evocation governs not only the individual line statements of "Jian," but that the entire hexagram with the wild goose as its primary image serves as a sort of *xing*-evocation for its complementary hexagram "Guimei." Just as the introductory image of the "wild goose advancing to the land" in the third line of "Jian" necessarily evokes the association in the human realm that "the husband is on campaign but does not return; the wife is pregnant but does not give birth," so, too, does the general image of the wild goose of "Jian" necessarily lead to the description of human events in "Guimei" in which the marriage of Di Yi's daughter went awry, presumably because of the daughter's barrenness.

If this suggestion has any merit at all, the *Zhouyi* would reflect considerably more than the random compilation of individuated divination records. While I would not want to go so far as to suggest that it is the product of sagely inspiration, it is not too much to say that considerable creative consciousness is apparent in the composition of the text. If the reader's interest in the *Zhouyi* were purely aesthetic, it would suffice to note the consistency with which images operate throughout the texts of these hexagrams. But throughout history, readers have perceived the *Zhouyi* to be something more, a book that not only comments on the human condition but that also provides insight into it. Without making any claims that the *Zhouyi* is, in fact, a storehouse of universal wisdom, I think it is possible to show that the author or authors of the text attempted to draw out some of the implications of these imagistic associations.

It is not difficult to imagine that a failed marriage between the king of the Zhou people and the daughter of the king of the then-reigning Shang dynasty, a dynasty that the Zhou would overthrow within about fifty years, would be regarded as a portent in its own right for the developing political relations between the two peoples. While it perhaps is surprising that these political implications do not seem to be noted in the texts of "Jian" and "Guimei," they do not go unremarked elsewhere in the *Zhouyi*. There is one other reference, in the fifth line of "Tai" 泰 (11) hexagram, to the marriage of Di Yi's daughter.

11/5 帝乙歸妹以祉; 元吉
  Di Yi marries off his daughter with happiness;
    primary auspiciousness.

While nothing else in the text of this hexagram appears to be explicitly related to this marriage,[17] it is not difficult to see associations with the more abstract theme of inversion present in the first two lines of "Guimei," in which the lame come to walk and the blind come to see. Indeed, inversion is such an integral part of the interpretation of "Tai" hexagram, the name of which seems to mean "Happiness,"[18] that it has invariably been read together with its hexagram complement "Pi" 否 (Negation; 12) as a conceptual pair. Since the two hexagrams are related in all of the ways noted above, formally, lexically, and conceptually, it is best to consider them together.

Tai

11   *Tai* ䷊: The small go, the great come;
         auspicious; receipt.

11/1   Pluck the madder with its stem;
         to campaign: auspicious.

11/2   Bundle the dried grass and use it to wade the river:
         Do not distance yourself from friends left behind;
         you will not gain favor in the central ranks.

11/3   There is no flat without a slope, no going without a return:
         Do not commiserate with the captive;
         In food there is good fortune;
         divining about difficulty: no harm.

11/4   Flit-flitting: not wealthy with his neighbors:
         Unguarded against capture.

11/5   Di Yi marries off his daughter with happiness:
         primary auspiciousness.

11/6   The city wall falls into the moat:
         Do not use troops;
         From the city announce the mandate;
         divining: trouble.

Pi

12   *Pi* ䷋: Not beneficial for the young lord to divine;
         The great go, the small come.

12/1   Pluck the madder with its stem;
         Divining: auspicious; receipt.

12/2   Bundle the offering:
         For the small man auspicious,
         For the great man not fortunate.

12/3 Bundle the meat.
12/4 There is a mandate:
      Fields separate happiness;
        no harm.
12/5 The beneficence is negated:
      They're lost, they're lost;
      Tied to the bushy mulberry;
        for the great man: auspicious.
12/6 Falling into naught:
      At first negative, later happy.

These two hexagrams contain at least three and perhaps four points of formal textual similarity. First, the hexagram statements, "The small go, the great come" and "The great go, the small come," are obvious reversals of each other (their wording doubtless also being significant). Second, the first lines, "Pluck the madder with its stem," are identical in both hexagrams; and third, the second and third lines of "Pi," "Bundle the offering" and "Bundle the meats," share the same structure as the second line of "Tai," "Bundle the dried grass." Finally, the repetition of the word "mandate" (*ming* 命) in the top line of "Tai," "from the city announce the mandate," and in the fourth line of "Pi," "There is a mandate," may be significant.

In a more general sense, it is clear too that these two hexagrams share a common theme. Whatever the original meaning of the words *tai* 泰 and *pi* 否, words which have come to be understood—because of their use here in the *Zhouyi*—as an antithetical pair symbolizing happiness and sadness, good and bad, the central theme of the two hexagrams is the inevitability of reversal. This is announced most clearly in the reversal of the hexagram statements, each of which by itself also reflects reversal ("The small go, the great come"). The line statements as well reflect this theme. Thus, the third line of "Tai" states "There is no flat without a slope; no going without a return," while the top line of "Pi" echos this with "At first negative, later happy." I suspect that some of the more concrete images in the two hexagrams also refer to this theme, such as "The city wall falls into the moat" in the top line of "Tai," and "The beneficence is negated" in the fifth line of "Pi."

I am confident this interpretation of the relationship between these two hexagrams is in line with traditional *Yijing* exegesis, and I suspect that even Gu Jiegang and his adherents, who consider the text to be but a random compilation, would be hard-pressed to deny either their formal or conceptual coherence. But Gu's historical insight has proven too important in the interpretation of "Guimei" to be dismissed out of hand. I think it is again possible to synthesize the two exegetical positions, tying the text to a particular historical referent but seeing a conscious attempt to draw general philosophical implications from it.

Assuming that the image of "Di Yi marrying off his daughter with happiness" is the governing image of "Tai" (Happiness), then knowing that this marriage proved to be unsuccessful (at least for Di Yi's daughter), it becomes a simple matter to see why this hexagram must be followed by "Pi" (Negation). Indeed, assuming an association between this fifth line of "Tai" and its structural complement, the second line of "Pi," it is probably also possible to see in the technical divination terminology of that line, "For the small man (woman?) auspicious, For the great man [woman?] not," a reference both to the primary bride's ("the great man") barrenness and also to the secondary bride's ("the small man") eventual "succession" to bear King Wu. This successful reversal may also be intimated in the final line of "Pi," which ends "At first negative, later happy."

While the failure of this particular marriage is the primary image informing this hexagram pair, I think this image came in turn to portend the failing relations between the Shang and Zhou peoples. With the eventual Zhou conquest of Shang (in 1045 B.C.), the more general notion of role reversal seen in "Guimei" hexagram's contrast between the primary bride and the secondary bride would naturally also have been associated with the Zhou replacement of Shang, the "great state." If so, then I think, too, that the image of "the city wall falling into the moat" (*huang* < *gwaŋ 隍) in the top line of "Tai," the line that follows immediately after the reference to the marriage of Di Yi's daughter, can readily be associated with the Zhou conquest, a sense made all the more explicit by the rhyming phrase "From the city announce the mandate" (*ming* < *mjiŋ 命). But by the time of the text's composition, probably toward the end of the Western Zhou (771 B.C.), at a time when the Zhou mandate had come in its own turn into peril, the Zhou conquest and mandate themselves must also have come to be viewed almost as portents, or at least as topics deserving of yet another level of generalization and abstraction.

I hope this brief analysis of four hexagrams of the *Zhouyi* has demonstrated that, while Gu Jiegang's vignette-based interpretation of the text has proven to be an exceptionally powerful exegetical insight into the meanings that individual lines had in their original context, by focusing exclusively on individual lines Gu, and particularly his followers, failed to see the meaning behind the meaning. Indeed, it seems to me that traditional interpreters such as Cheng

Yi and thousands of others, despite their often ahistorical impressionism, have come closer to perceiving why, if not how, the *Zhouyi* came to be composed. I use the word "composed" here deliberately. Certainly, the *Zhouyi* is not the product of divine inspiration; but, given the sorts of associations that tie these four hexagrams together,[19] both formally and conceptually, neither is it just a random compilation. Future studies of the *Zhouyi* would do well to combine the particularistic historicism of the "new" scholarship with the associative reasoning of traditional interpretations to divine anew the hand of human creativity.

NOTES

1. The *Book of Changes* developed within the mantic tradition of ancient China and was especially related to the type of divination using milfoil or yarrow stalks practiced by the Zhou people. The manipulation of the stalks produced a numerical result that came to be expressed as either a solid or broken line, which when grouped together in sixes produced a set of sixty-four different graphs or hexagrams. By perhaps the end of the Western Zhou dynasty (1045–771 B.C.), texts were associated with each of these hexagrams and also with each of the six lines of each hexagram. It is difficult today to know just how these hexagram and line statements, usually terse evocations of the human or natural world, were used to divine the future. By the late third century, several commentaries (usually enumerated as ten, and thus termed the "Ten Wings") came to be attached to the text. It was these commentaries, traditionally believed to have been written by Confucius (551–479 B.C.), that transformed the original divination manual into a wisdom text, a status formally recognized in 135 B.C. when the *Book of Changes* was ranked as the first of all classics.

   To differentiate between these two strata and functions of the *Book of Changes*, I use the title *Zhouyi* (Changes of Zhou) when referring to the hexagram and line statements of the text, especially as understood in the context of their original (Western) Zhou composition. On the other hand, I use the title *Yijing* (Classic of Changes) when referring to the text complete with its canonical commentaries (the so-called "Ten Wings") and especially when regarded as a classic.

2. Gu Jiegang 顧頡剛, "Zhouyi guayaoci zhong de gushi," *Yanjing xuebao* 燕京學報 6 (1929), 967–1006; rpt. in *Gushi bian*, ed. Gu Jiegang (1931; rpt. Shanghai: Shanghai guji chubanshe, 1982), vol. 3, 1–44.

3. Here and throughout this essay, I refer to hexagram and line statements

by the name of the respective hexagram, its number in the standard sequence of sixty-four, and, following a slash, the number of the line from one to six, starting from "one," representing the bottom line (*chu* 初), and ending with "six," representing the top line (*shang* 上).

4. See, e.g., Gao Heng 高亨, *Zhouyi gujing jinzhu* 周易古經今注 (Shanghai: Kaiming shudian, 1947); Li Jingchi 李鏡池, *Zhouyi tanyuan* 周易探源 (Beijing: Zhonghua shuju, 1978); Li Jingchi, *Zhouyi tongshi* 周易通釋 (Beijing: Zhonghua shuju, 1981); Gerhard Schmitt, *Sprüche der Wandlungen auf ihrem geistesgeschichlichen Hintergrund*, Deutsche Akademie der Wissenschaften zu Berlin, Institut für Orient-forschung Veröffentlichung, Nu. 76 (Berlin: Akademie-Verlag, 1970); Hellmut Wilhelm, *Heaven, Earth, and Man in the Book of Changes* (Seattle: University of Washington Press, 1977), 56–62; Richard Alan Kunst, "The Original 'Yijing': A Text, Phonetic Transcription, Translation, and Indexes, with Sample Glosses" (Ph.D. diss., University of California, Berkeley, 1985).

5. Edward L. Shaughnessy, "The Composition of the *Zhouyi*" (Ph.D. diss., Stanford University, 1983).

6. Cheng Yi, *Zhouyi Chengshi zhuan* 周易程氏傳 (Preface dated 1099; rpt. in *Wuqiubei zhai Yijing jicheng* 無求備齋易經集成, ed. Yan Lingfeng 嚴靈峰 [Taipei: Chengwen chubanshe, 1975], vol. 15), p. 265.

7. Wilhelm, *Heaven, Earth, and Man in the Book of Changes*, 62.

8. Gu Jiegang, "*Zhouyi* guayaoci zhong de gushi," 14.

9. For textual notes and substantiation of the translations offered here, see Shaughnessy, "The Composition of the *Zhouyi*," 239. Note that the presentation of the line statements in this translation is inverted from the positions of the lines in the hexagram picture; i.e., the bottom line of the hexagram (54.1) is given at the top of the English text. Note also that variations in the indentations of lines reflect what I perceive to be their different strata: Topic (no indentation); Injunction (single indentation); and Divination Terminology (double indentation). For discussion of this intralineal stratification, see ibid., 136–58.

10. Two uses of the word *gui* 歸 in this couplet seem to be consciously differentiated, the first referring to the maiden's "marriage" and the second to her "return" to her own home. Reconstructions of the Old Chinese pronunciations are those of Li Fanggui as given in Axel Schuessler, *A Dictionary of Early Zhou Chinese* (Honolulu: University of Hawaii Press, 1987).

11. Donald Harper, "The Sexual Arts of Ancient China as Described in a Manuscript of the Second Century B.C.," *Harvard Journal of Asiatic Studies* 47.2 (1987): 204.

12. Shaughnessy, "The Composition of the *Zhouyi*," 266–87; Xia Hanyi 夏含夷 (Edward L. Shaughnessy), "Zhouyi Qiangua liulong xinjie" 周易乾卦六龍新解, *Wenshi* 文史 24 (1985): 9–14.

13. There is some question here whether this phrase "In the end nothing overcomes it," forms a couplet with the preceding phrase, "The wife for three years is not pregnant," or if it is technical divination terminology that falls outside of the line's imagery. The rhyme between *ling* 陵 < *ljeŋ, "hillock," and *sheng* 勝 < *sthjenh, "overcome," perhaps supports the former interpretation, which informs the translation given here.

14. I here follow Li Jingchi, *Zhouyi tanyuan*, 126, and the Qing scholars that he cites in emending the *lu* 陸, "land," of the received text to *e* 阿, "hill."

15. Wen Yiduo 聞一多, *Wen Yiduo quanji* 聞一多全集 (1948; rpt. Beijing: Sanlian shudian, 1982), 117–38.

16. I here follow Bernhard Karlgren's wonderful translation of the last word, *cishi* 戚施, "toad-buffoon"; see Bernhard Karlgren, *The Book of Odes* (1944; rpt. Stockholm: Museum of Far Eastern Antiquities, 1974), 29.

17. Perhaps the image of "madder" in the first line does suggest some kind of romantic disruption, as it does for example in the *Shijing* poems "Dongmen zhi shan" 東門之墠 (The East Gate's Altar; Mao 89) and "Chu qi dongmen" 出其東門 (Exiting its East Gate; Mao 93). As I will show below, "Tai" is also very closely related to its hexagram complement, "Pi," so the image of a "bushy mulberry" in the fifth line of that hexagram may also be pertinent. For a *Shijing* poem where the mulberry serves as a *xing*-evocation for a divorce, see "Meng" 氓 (The People; Mao 58).

18. I say "seems" because, even though *tai* is consistently interpreted to mean "happiness" from the very beginning of the *Yijing* exegetical tradition, there is no etymological evidence to substantiate this meaning in the Western Zhou period.

19. I have been asked on several occasions, most recently by one of the anonymous referees of this paper, to comment on just how pervasive interhexagrammatic relationships are within the *Zhouyi*. Certainly, I think it is an easy matter to see relationships, both formal and conceptual, between such hexagram pairs as "Lin" ䷒ (Look Down Upon; 19) and "Guan" ䷓ (Look Up At; 20), "Sun" ䷨ (Decrease; 41) and "Yi" ䷩ (Increase; 42), and "Jiji" ䷾ (Already Across; 63) and "Weiji" ䷿ (Not Yet Across; 64). And, as mentioned above, I think there is also no question but that "Qian" ䷀ (1) and "Kun" ䷁ (2) are bound into a single conceptual unit, as must also be, for instance, "Ge" ䷰ (Revolution; 49) and "Ding" ䷱ (Caldron [with an extended meaning of Stabilization]; 50). Thus, the brief answer

is that such pairs govern about one-quarter of the entire text of the *Zhouyi*. However, this answer leaves me dissatisfied. I wish I could say to what extent the apparent lack of the feature among the other three-quarters of the sixty-four hexagrams is due to their differing compositional origins (the question of the textual stratification of the *Zhouyi* is one that both I [Shaughnessy, "The Composition of the *Zhouyi*," 326n82] and Richard Kunst ["The Original 'Yijing'," 33, 52, 123, etc.] have commented upon in various exploratory ways but one that requires much more study) or even to my inability to understand them (which I am not embarrassed to admit remains substantial).

2

"New" Evidence on the Zhou Conquest

The inscription on the "Li 利 *gui*" (Sh 50.Ho14:321), a vessel unearthed in 1976 in Qishan 岐山 county of Shaanxi province, by substantiating certain key assertions of traditional Chinese historiography, has once again focused attention on King Wu's (r. 1049/45-1043) conquest of the Shang and his consequent establishment of the Zhou dynasty. It is the expectation, and ever increasing reality, of discovering ancient records, usually in the form of bone or bronze inscriptions, that makes the study of early China so vibrant and open to new interpretations. Unfortunately, however, in the excitement over these new inscriptional discoveries, some scholars have rejected, or at least neglected, other written records of the period that have come to us by way of the more circuitous route of historical transmission. This is not exclusively due to the prejudices of the modern "scientific" historian. In the case of at least one document, the "Shi fu" 世俘 chapter of the *Yi Zhou shu* 逸周書, the fullest account of the Zhou conquest was rejected outright as early as 2,300 years ago by one of the first known historians of ancient China—Mencius (371–289 B.C.; the text was known to Mencius as the "Wu cheng" 武成; see below, pt. II.). And with the prestige accruing to his thought from other considerations, Mencius's rejection of the account of the conquest given by the "Shi fu" and the idealized history he proposed in its place have continued as more or less orthodox until the present. But the modern historian has a responsibility to consider objectively all of the evidence at hand. The "Shi fu" is, I believe, worthy of such careful consideration. Therefore, I offer here a translation of the text and a discussion of its authenticity, in the belief that ancient records are discoverable in places other than the soil of north China.

31

PART I: TRANSLATION AND CRITICAL TEXT

THE GREAT CAPTURE[1]

I It was the fourth month, day *yiwei* (day 32); King Wu achieved rule over the four directions and went through the countries that Yin had commanded.[2]

維四月乙未日, 武成辟四方, 通殷命有國.

II It was the first month, *renchen* day 29), the [day of] expanded dying brightness. On the next day, guisi [day 30],[3] the king then in the morning set out from Zhou and went on campaign to attack the Shang king Zhou. On *jiazi* (day 1), five days after [the day] after the dying brightness of the following second month, [they] arrived in the morning and defeated the Shang, thence entirely decapitating the Shang king Zhou and shackling [his] one hundred evil ministers.

維一月壬辰旁死霸, 若翌日癸巳, 王乃朝步自周, 于征伐(商王)紂, 越若來二月既死霸越五日甲子, 朝至于商, 則咸劉商王紂, 執夫惡臣百人.

III Grand Duke Wang was ordered to secure the area. On the coming day, *dingmao* (day 4), Wang arrived and reported about ears taken and captives. On *wuchen* (day 5), the king then performed a *yu*-exorcism and an inspection tour, and [then] made a commemorative sacrifice to King Wen.[4] [On] this day the king established [his] government.

太公望命禦方, 來丁卯, 望至告以馘俘. 戊辰, 王逐禦循, 祀文王, 時日, 王立政.

IV Lü Ta was ordered to attack Yue and Xifang. On *renshen* (day 9), Huang Xin arrived and reported about ears taken and captives. Hou

呂他命伐越戲方, 壬申, 荒新至告以馘俘, 侯來命伐靡集于陳, 辛巳, 至告以馘俘, 甲申百弇命以虎賁誓, 命伐衛俘.

Lai was ordered to attack Miji and/ at Chen. On *xinsi* (day 18), [he] arrived and reported about ears taken and captives. On *jiashen* (day 21), Bai Ta was ordered to address the Tiger Vanguard, being ordered to attack Wei. He reported about ears taken and captives.

V On *xinhai* (day 48), presentation of the captured caldrons of the Yin king. King Wu then reverently displayed the jade tablet and the codice, making an announcement to the heavenly ancestor Lord on High. Without changing his robes,[5] the king entered into the temple. Holding the yellow axe,[6] he spoke and regulated the many states. The flutists [played] nine refrains. The king's honored ancestors from Taiwang, Taibo, Wangji, Yugong, and King Wen to Yi Kao were arrayed and elevated, in order to report the crimes of Yin. The flutists entered. The king, holding the yellow axe, confirmed the elders of the countries.

辛亥薦俘殷王鼎, 武王乃翼矢琰矢憲, 告天宗上帝, 王不革服, 格于廟; 秉黃鉞, 語治庶國; 籥人九終, 王烈祖自太王、太伯、王季、虞公、文王、邑考以列升, 維告殷罪, 籥人造; 王秉黃鉞, 正國伯.

On *renzi* (day 49), the king, wearing the royal attire and displaying the jade tablet, entered the temple. The flutists entered. The king, holding the yellow axe, confirmed the rulers of the states.

壬子, 王服袞衣, 矢琰, 格廟, 籥人造; 王正秉黃鉞, 邦君.

On *guichou* (day 50), presentation of the 100 captured nobles of the Yin king. The flutists entered. The king was displaying the jade tablet, holding the yellow axe, and grasping a dagger-axe. The king entered; the

癸丑, 薦俘殷王士百人, 籥人造; 王矢琰, 秉黃鉞, 執戈: 王入; 奏庸: 「大享」, 一終, 王拜手稽首, 王定; 奏庸: 「大享」三終.

bell was struck:[8] the "Great Sacrifice," one refrain. The king folded his hands and touched his head to the floor. The king [lit. settled =] sat; the bell was struck: the "Great Sacrifice," three refrains.[9]

On *jiayin* (day 51), inspection of the military Yin at Muye.[10] The king suspended red and white pendants (from his sash). The flutists played "Wu."[11] The king entered and caused the "Ten-Thousand" (Wan) dance to be advanced, presenting "Brightly, Brightly," three refrains.

On *yimao* (day 52), the flutists played "Venerable Yu [i.e., Yu the Great] begat [Kai =] Qi," three refrains.[12] The king sat.

VI On *gengzi* (day 37), Chen Ben was ordered to attack Mo; Bai Wei[13] was ordered to attack Xuanfang; and Huang Xin[14] was ordered to attack Shu.[15]

On *yisi* (day 42), Chen Ben and Huang Xin arrived (from) Shu and Mo[16] and reported the netting of the Lord of Huo, the capture of the Lord of Ai, the Lord of Yi and 46 minor ministers, and the netting of 803 chariots,[17] reporting about ears taken and captives. Bai Wei arrived and reported about the netting of Xuanfang and the netting of 30 chariots, reporting about ears taken and captives. Bai Wei was ordered to attack Li: he reported about ears taken and captives.

甲寅, 謁戎殷于牧野, 王佩赤白旂, 籥人奏「武」, 王入進萬獻:「明明」, 三終

乙卯, 籥人奏「崇禹生啓」, 三終, 王定.

庚子, 陳本命伐磨, 百韋命伐宣方, 荒新命伐蜀.

乙巳, 陳本, 荒新, 蜀、磨至; 告禽霍侯, 俘艾侯、佚侯, 小臣四十有六, 禽禦八百有三十兩; 告以馘俘, 百韋至, 告以禽宣方, 禽禦三十兩, 告以馘俘, 百韋命伐厲; 告以馘俘.

VII King Wu hunted and netted 22 tigers, 2 panthers, 5,235 stags, 12 rhinoceri, 721 yaks, 151 bears, 118 yellow-bears, 353 boars, 18 badgers, 16 king-stags, 50 musk-deer, 30 tailed-deer, and 3,508 deer.

武王狩: 禽虎二十有二, 貓二, 麋五千二百三十五, 犀十有二, 氂七百二十有一, 熊百五十有一, 罷百一十有八, 豕三百五十有二, 貉十有八, 麈十有六, 麝三十, 鹿三千五百有八

VIII King Wu had pursued and campaigned in the four directions. In all, there were 99 recalcitrant countries, 177,779 ears taken registered,[18] and 310,230 captured men. In all, there were 652 countries that willingly submitted.

武王遂征四方: 凡憝國九十有九國. 馘磨億有七萬七千七百七十有九, 俘人三億萬有二百三十, 凡服國六百五十有二.

IX It was the fourth month, six days after [the day] after the expanded growing brightness, *gengxu* [day 47], King Wu arrived in the morning and performed a burnt-offering sacrifice in the Zhou temple, [stating] "It is I, the young son, who brings peace to the glorious ancestors."[19]

維四月既旁生霸越六日庚戌武王朝至燎于周廟, 維予沖子綏文考.

King Wu descended from [his] chariot and caused Scribe Yi to intone the document in the declaration to heaven. King Wu then shot the hundred evil ministers of (Shang king) Zhou.[20] He beheaded and offered their sixty minor princes and great captains of the caldrons, and beheaded their forty family heads and captains of the caldrons.[21] The supervisor of the infantry and the supervisor of the horse first [attended] to their declaration of the suburban sacrifice; then the southern gate was flanked with the captives to be sacrificed,[22] all of whom were given

武王降自車, 乃俾史佚繇書于天號, 武王乃發于紂夫惡臣百人, 伐右厥六十小子鼎大師, 伐厥四十夫家君鼎師, 司徒, 司馬 初厥于郊號乃夾于南門; 用俘皆施佩衣衣, 先馘入, 武王在祀, 大師負商王紂縣首白旂, 妻二首赤旗, 乃以先馘入燎于周廟.

sashes and clothes to wear. The ears taken were first brought in. King Wu attended to the sacrifice and the Great Master shouldered the white banner from which the head of Shang king Zhou was suspended and the red pennant with the heads of his two consorts. Then, with the first scalps, he entered and performed the burnt-offering sacrifice in the Zhou temple.

On the next day, *xinhai* (day 48), he performed a sacrifice in his position (as king), therewith making a *yue*-offering to heaven.

若翌日辛亥, 祀于位, 用籥于天位.

Five days later on *yimao* (day 52), King Wu then sacrificed in the Zhou temple the ears taken of the many countries,[23] declaring, "Reverently, I, the young son, slaughter six oxen and slaughter two sheep. The many states are now at an end." [He] reported in the Zhou temple, saying, "Of old I have heard that [my] glorious ancestors emulated the standards of the men of the Shang; with the dismembered body of [Shang king] Zhou, I report to heaven and to Ji [i.e., Hou Ji]." He [lit. used =] sacrificed the minor offerings—sheep, dogs and boar—to the hundred spirits, the water and the earth,[24] declaring to the altar of the earth, saying, "It is I, the young son, who brings peace to the glorious ancestors; may it reach to the young son." He sacrificed 504 oxen to heaven and to Ji, and sacrificed 2,701 sheep and boar,

越五日乙卯, 武王乃以庶國馘祀于周廟: "翼予沖子斷牛六, 斷羊二, 度國乃竟." 告于周廟曰: "古朕聞文考脩商人典; 以斬紂身告于天于稷." 用小牲羊. 犬、豕于百神、水、土; 誓于社曰: "惟予沖子綏文考至于沖子." 用牛于天于稷五百有四, 用小牲羊、豕于百神、水、土二千七百有一.

the minor offering, to the hundred spirits, the water and the earth.

X The Shang king Zhou was in the suburb of Shang on that *jiazi* (day 1) evening. Shang king Zhou took the Heavenly Wisdom jade and jewels and wrapping them thickly around his body, immolated himself. In all, 4,000 (pieces of) jade were reported to have been fired. On the fifth day, King Wu then caused 1,000 men to seek them. The 4,000 pieces of jade[25] were burnt [but] the Heavenly Wisdom jade and jewels[26] were unburnt in the fire. King Wu then treasured and shared all of the Heavenly Wisdom jade [pieces]. In all, King Wu captured 180,000 pieces of old Shang jade.

商王紂于商郊, 時甲子夕, 商王紂取「天智」玉琰, 環身厚以自焚, 凡厥有庶玉, 四千告焚, 五日武王乃俾千人求之, 四千庶玉則銷, 「天智」玉琰火在中不銷, 凡「天智」玉, 武王則寶與同, 凡武俘商舊玉億有八萬。

PART II: THE AUTHENTICITY OF THE TEXT

The significance of a text such as this would of course be enormous if it could be demonstrated to be a genuine product of the early Western Zhou period. In attempting to determine the authenticity of a transmitted document three factors must be considered: the history of the text's transmission, its linguistic usage, and whether the content is consistent with the purported historical context. In the following, each of these factors will be considered in turn and all three will, I believe, demonstrate beyond any doubt that the "Shi fu" is indeed a document contemporary with the events it describes.

1. Textual Transmission

The occurrence in the text of three full date notations (i.e., month, lunar phase, and cyclical day; see sections II and IX in the text), while constituting a source of confusion for later commentators (see below, part II.3), has proven to be a happy coincidence; the paucity of such dates has made each of them extremely valuable to scholars of ancient China's chronology. The first of these scholars, Liu Xin 劉歆 (c. 46 B.C.–A.D. 23), quoted these three dates verbatim and at rather considerable length in his *Shijing* 世經 (as quoted in the "Lüli zhi" 律曆志 chapter of the *Han shu* 漢書[27]), all the while identifying the source of the dates as the "Wu cheng" 武成 chapter of the *Shangshu* 尚書. The virtual identity of the two texts leaves no doubt that they derive from one and the same source. Except for two or three minor inversions of word order, the only difference of note lies in the first full date notation.[28] But the fact that the cyclical day specified in the "Shi fu" date ("It was the first month, bingchen [day 53], the [day of] expanded growing brightness") is incompatible with the date given for the battle at Muye 牧野, while the date given in the "Wu cheng" is both mathematically compatible and independently verifiable,[29] leads to the conclusion that the "Shi fu" text is here corrupt, and not a separate text, and should be emended in light of the "Wu cheng" text.

The coincidence of this quotation is by no means the only evidence that the present "Shi fu" text does in fact represent the original text of the "Wu cheng" chapter. The "Preface to the Documents" (*Shuxu* 書序) states with regard to the "Wu cheng":

武王伐殷; 往伐歸獸. 識其政事, 作武成
King Wu attacked Shang; he went out and attacked, returned and hunted. He made known the affairs of government and composed the "Wu cheng."[30]

While this description is inconsistent with the contents of the *guwen* 古文 "Wu cheng" text now extant, it corresponds perfectly with the "Shi fu" text. Especially noteworthy is the mention of hunting, which figures so prominently in the text of the "Shi fu" (section VII), but which in the *guwen* "Wu cheng" has been transposed into a pasturing of the war animals, symbolizing King Wu's pacifistic nature.[31]

Another early reference to the "Wu cheng" is also illustrative of the content of the "Shi fu," and not the "Wu cheng" now existing. Mencius, for whom ancient history was a vital philosophical topic, apparently was unable to reconcile his view of a moral imperative manifesting itself through the Zhou conquest with the narrative given in the "Wu cheng" text available to him. He voiced his opinion in a well-known passage.

Mencius said, "If one were to believe everything in the *Documents*, it would not be as good as not having the *Documents*. As for the

"Wu cheng" chapter, I accept only two or three strips and that is all. A humane man has no enemies in the world. With the most humane attacking the most inhumane, how could it be that the blood floated pestles?[32]

By the time of the Han dynasty, Mencius's view of history (and the attendant selection of historical sources) seems to have prevailed along with the Confucian school. Even the generally conscientious Sima Qian 司馬遷 (c. 145–86 B.C.) made no use of the "Wu cheng" *qua* "Shi fu" in his account of the Zhou victory, relying instead on the "Taishi" 泰誓 chapter of the *Shangshu* and especially the "Ke Yin" 克殷 chapter of the *Yi Zhou shu*, both of which contain linguistic features demonstrably anachronistic to the Shang-early Western Zhou period.[33] Apparently only the skeptical pragmatist Wang Chong 王充 (c. A.D. 27–97) was not seduced by the Mencian view of history. He said of this matter:

> Now there are those who say that, when King Wu defeated Zhou, the blades of his weapons were not stained with blood. When a man with such strength [as Shang king Zhou] that he could twist iron and straighten out hooks, with such supporters as Fei Lian and E Lai tried issues with the army of Zhou, King Wu, however virtuous he may have been, could not have deprived him of his natural abilities, and [Shang king] Zhou, wicked though he was, would not have lost the sympathy of his associates. . . .
>
> King Wu succeeded King Zhou, and Gao Zu took over the inheritance of Ershi Huangdi of the house of Qin, which was much worse than that of King Zhou. The whole empire rebelled against Qin, with much more violence than under the Yin dynasty. When Gao Zu had defeated the Qin, he still had to destroy Xiang Yu. The battle field was soaked with blood, and many thousands of dead bodies lay strewn about. The losses of the defeated army were enormous. People had, as it were, to die again and again, before the Empire was won. The insurgents were exterminated by force of arms with the utmost severity. Therefore it cannot be true that the troops of Zhou did not even stain their swords with blood. One may say that the conquest was easy, but to say that the blades were not stained with blood is an exaggeration.
>
> . . . According to the "Wu cheng," the battle in the plain of Mu was so sanguinary that the flow of blood floated pestles and

over a thousand *li* the earth was red. According to this account the overthrow of the Yin by the Zhou must have been very much like the war between the Han and Qin dynasties. The statement that the conquest of the Yin territory was so easy that the swords were not stained with blood is meant as a compliment to the virtue of King Wu, but it exaggerates the truth.[34]

In addition to its general approbation of the "Wu cheng" *qua* "Shi fu" text, Wang's statement also throws light on another feature of the identification problem; that is, Mencius's description of the "Wu cheng" as "the blood floated pestles" (*xue zhi liu chu* 血之流杵杵), which commentators of the *Mencius* have assumed to be taken verbatim from the "Wu cheng," and the absence of which in the "Shi fu" has led some scholars, Cheng Tingzuo 程廷祚 (1691–1767), for example, to dismiss the identification between the "Wu cheng" and the "Shi fu." But it is at least as likely that with this four-character phrase Mencius was simply using a euphemism for wide-scale bloodshed to describe the chapter—just as it would seem that Wang Chong was doing when he used the phrase "over a thousand *li* the earth was red" (*chi di qian li* 赤地千里) to describe the text. That the "Shi fu" does not contain these exact words should not imply that it was not the text consulted by Mencius—its record of 177,779 deaths, 310,230 captives taken, 99 countries defeated, and routine human sacrifice, fits better than anything else the description "the blood floated pestles."[36]

All of this suggests the following process for the identification of the "Wu cheng" with the "Shi fu." The text was originally an integral part of the early Western Zhou documents linked together as the *Documents* (*Shu* 書). But having been denounced by Mencius whose idealized view of history came to prevail, it was expunged from the *Documents*. By chance it was included in the collection of "left-over" texts, the *Yi Zhou shu*, which appears to have taken shape in the late fourth century B.C.[37] With the subsequent appearance of the forged *guwen* chapters of the *Shangshu*, including a spurious "Wu cheng" chapter consistent with the romantic notions of Mencius, even the title of the text was compromised.

Fittingly, this matter of title is the final piece of evidence linking the "Shi fu" with the "Wu cheng." Two methods of entitling ancient documents were current during the late Warring States-early Han period: a title could either characterize the general import or contents of the text, or it could be based on the first words or the most significant words of the first line. In the case of the "Shi fu" *qua* "Wu cheng" text, both of these methods seem to have been employed. "Shi fu," the "great capture,"[38] evokes the main theme of the text: the capture of the Shang domain, the capture of the Shang and their allies' subjects, the capture of the Shang treasures, and also the capture of the animals in the victory hunt; in all, an extremely appropriate title. But the germ of the title "Wu cheng" is also to be seen in the first line of the text, "Wu wang *cheng bi sifang* 武王成辟四方, "King Wu achieved rule of the four quarters." Taking the first words of the first two compounds, a common practice of the Warring States title-givers,[39] the result is, of course, "Wu cheng."[40]

In summary then, at least the following four points about the "Wu cheng"

- The *Hanshu*, "Lüli zhi" quotation, which accords, with the exception of one corruption, exactly with the "Shi fu" text;
- The *Shuxu* description, which is consistent with the contents of the "Shi fu";
- The characterizations of the text given by Mencius and Wang Chong;
- The possibility of deriving the title "Wu cheng" from the first line of the "Shi fu,"

leave little doubt that the "Shi fu" text in front of us now is in substance the "Wu cheng" text known to Mencius at the end of the fourth century B.C.

2. Linguistic Usage

While the identification of the "Shi fu" with the "Wu cheng," and especially its apparent existence as such as early as the time of Mencius, suggests the authenticity of the text, the most reliable criterion of its antiquity lies in its linguistic usage. Not only is the text free of the sort of tell-tale linguistic anachronisms that frequently mar forgeries, but language similar to that in the early Western Zhou chapters of the *Shangshu* has long attracted the attention of commentators.[41] More important, features of the text apparently anomalous within the context of the transmitted literature have appeared also in the inscriptions on oracle bones and bronze vessels.[42] In the following, I will discuss some of these idiomatic constructions that seem to me to verify the text's contemporaneity with the events it describes.

The significance of the full date notations is discussed elsewhere in this chapter with respect to other considerations (see Part II.1 and II.3), but let us again examine the date for the battle at Muye, this time from the standpoint of linguistic usage. The line reads:

越若來二月既死霸越五日甲子, 朝至于商, 則咸劉商王
紂

On *jiazi* (day 1), five days after [the day] after the dying brightness
of the following second month, [they] arrived in the morning and
defeated the Shang, thence entirely decapitating the Shang king
Zhou.

Compare this with a line in the "Shao gao" 召誥 chapter of the *Shangshu*:

越若來三月惟丙午朏, 越三日戊辰, 太保朝至于洛卜宅; 厥
既得卜, 則經營

In the following third month, on *bingwu* (day 43), the day of the
moon's appearance; three days later on *wushen* (day 45), the Grand
Protector arrived in the morning at Luo and divined about establishing residence; after he had obtained the divination, he thence
laid out the encampment.

Not only are the general structures of the two sentences similar, but such
idiomatic features as *yue ruo lai* 越若來, "at the following," *yue* 越 . . . *ri* 日,
" . . . days after," *zhao zhi yu* 朝至于, "arrived in the morning," and the
usage of *ze* 則, "thence," are identical. Moreover, in the "Junshi" 君奭 chapter
of the *Shangshu*, the construction *xian liu* 咸劉, "entirely decapitate," occurs
in a similar context: "*xian liu jue di*" 咸劉厥敵, "(King Wu) entirely decapitated his enemies." When it is considered that the date notation *jisipo* 既死
霸, "after the dying brightness," is standard in Western Zhou bronze inscriptions (but, significantly, never appears after that period), virtually every segment
of this "Shi fu" sentence represents attested early Western Zhou usage.[43]

Despite these parallels with the *Shangshu*, it is now recognized that a
more valid authenticating methodology is to compare usage with oracle-bone
and bronze inscriptions, materials presumably unavailable to the aspiring
forger. With this in mind, let us then consider the passage that follows immediately in the text. It reads "Taigong Wang *ming yu fang lai dingmao*" 太公望
命禦方來丁卯, and has been interpreted by several modern scholars as "The
Grand Duke Wang ordered the Yufang to come. On *dingmao* . . ."[44] Three
features demonstrate the fallacy of this interpretation.

The word *ming* 命 occurs throughout the "Shi fu" in a passive mode;
for example, "Chen Ben *ming fa* Mo" 陳本命伐磿, "Chen Ben was ordered
to attack Mo" (sec. VI). Although this usage has no parallels in the *Shangshu*
or *Shijing*, it does occur in the contemporary inscriptional literature. Consider, for example, the following pair of oracle-bone inscriptions:

甲申卜: 命啄宅正
Crack on *jiashen* (day 21): "Order Shi to make a residence at Zheng."
(*Yibian* 8898)

甲申卜: 啄命宅正
Crack on *jiashen* (day 21): "Shi is ordered to make a residence at Zheng." (*Yibian* 8893)

The subject-verb inversion in these two inscriptions clearly shows the possibility of *ming* being used in the passive voice. A perhaps more substantive example occurs in a later Western Zhou bronze inscription, that of the "Jing 競 *you*" (Sh 16.84:132). The first line of this inscription reads:

隹伯屖父以成㠯即東, 命伐南尸
It was when Bo Yifu took the Cheng troops and proceededto the east, being ordered to attack the Southern Yi.

In this line, *ming* must be construed as a passive.[45] It is also interesting to note that it occurs in the same construction as throughout the "Shi fu": *ming fa* 命伐, "ordered to attack."

Bringing this information to bear on the sentence under discussion, another oracle-bone inscriptional idiom, *yu fang* 禦方, appears. Although *yu* 禦 regularly means "to defend," because of its combination here with *fang* 方, "country," several renowned oracle-bone scholars have interpreted this idiom as a place name.[46] Analyzing the following examples, however, one notes that the compound never acts as the subject of a sentence nor precedes an active verb.

卜師: 乎禦方于商
Crack-making, Shi (divining); "Call to *yu fang* at Shang."
(*Houbian* 2.41.16)

壬午卜師貞: 玘命多視禦方于 . . .
Crack-making on *renwu*, Shi divining: "The king orders the many Shi (?) to *yu fang* at . . ." (*Houbian* 2.42.9)

. . 巳卜王貞: 于中商乎禦方
Crack-making on . . . -*si*, the king divining: "At Zhong Shang call to *yu fang*." (*Yicun* 348)

己卯卜: 王命禦方
Crack-making on *jimao*: "The king orders to *yu fang*."
(*Waibian* 30)

丙辰卜: 徦禦方
Crack-making on *bingchen*: "Proceed to *yu fang*."

(*Nanfang* 3.62)

乎勿乎禦方
I should not call to *yu fang*

(*Kufang* 595)

貞: 冓于入禦方
Divining: "Gou will at Ru *yu fang*."   (*Qianbian* 5.2.7)

辛亥卜中貞: 令冓以 . . 禦方于陟
Crack-making on *xinhai*, Zhong divining: "Order Gou to take . .
to *yu fang* at Zhi."   (*Jiabian* 3539)

The several examples here of *yu* following *hu* 乎, "to call out," are comparable
to such usages as *hu fa* 乎伐, "to call out to attack," *hu qu* 乎取, "to call out
to take," *hu bi* 乎比, "to call out to ally with," *hu lai* 乎來, "to call out to
come," and *hu chu* 乎出, "to call out to go out," where *hu* is always followed
by a verb.[47] This suggests that *yu fang* should also not be interpreted as a place
name, but rather is a verb-object compound.

An example of *yu* in a Western Zhou bronze inscription confirms this
verbal usage and also provides sufficient context to determine its meaning.
The inscription on the "Buqi 不嫢 *gui*" (Sh 32.193:814), which dates from
the reign of King Xuan (r. 827–782), reads:

> It was the ninth month, first auspiciousness, *wushen* (day 45); Bo
> *shi* said: "Buqi, secure the area (*yu fang* 駿方). The Xianyun widely
> attacked Western Yu. The king commanded us to follow up in the
> west. I came in return to present the catch. I ordered you to drive
> out and chase after (*yu zhui* 御追) at Luo. You took our war chariots
> and thoroughly attacked the Xianyun at Gaotao. You cut off many
> heads and shackled many captives to be interrogated. The
> belligerents greatly converged to counter-attack you, and you were
> endangered. The belligerents greatly pressed the attack but you were
> victorious, not taking our war chariots and sinking them in diffi-
> culty, but cutting off heads and shackling captives to be interro-
> gated." Bo *shi* said, "Buqi, you little child; you have begun adeptly
> in military merit. I present you one bow and a quiver of arrows,
> five families of servants, and ten fields of land, to be used in fulfilling
> your affairs." Buqi folded his hands and touched his head to the

ground, herewith making [for] my illustrious grandparents Gongbo and Mengji [this] sacrificial *gui*-tureen, and herewith entreating many blessings and long life without limit, eternal purity and a spiritual end. Would that my sons' sons and grandsons' grandsons eternally treasure and use it in sacrifice.

This inscription is related to that on the "Guoji Zibo 虢季子白 *pan*" (Sh 32.192:800), which provides the setting for the action described here. The "Guoji Zibo *pan*" has a full date placing it in the twelfth year of King Xuan's reign (816 B.C.) and narrates the court ritual marking a victory by Guoji Zibo. It appears that this victory, though conclusive, was not quite final, for while the "Buqi *gui*" inscription lacks a year notation, the otherwise complete date corresponds exactly with the thirteenth year of King Xuan's reign (815 B.C.). The content of the inscription shows this date to be correct. It begins with a reference to Boshi's (i.e., Guoji Zibo) recent victory, which is followed by an order to his lieutenant Buqi to complete the pacification of the area. This order, first mentioned in the opening prefatory paragraph, is further elaborated by the phrase "*yu zhui yu* Luo" 御追于𡟬, "to drive out and chase after at Luo," which is to say to conduct a sort of mopping-up operation.

This is also the meaning that the context of the "Shi fu" calls for. Significantly, it is also the meaning that Kong Zhao 孔晁 (c. A.D. 265), the earliest commentator of the text, apparently intended by his gloss: "*taigong shou ming zhui yu* Zhou *xun* Fanglai" 太公受命追御紂黨方來, "the Grand Duke received an order to chase after and *yu* (the Shang king) Zhou's ally, Fanglai." But because Kong, writing in the late third century A.D. was unfamiliar with the language of Shang Chinese, he was led to make one minor mistake in his comment.

Two words, *yi* 翌 and *lai* 來, are used in archaic Chinese to indicate future time. In Shang oracle-bone inscriptions, *yi* is used to indicate future days usually only one or two days distant but always within the same *xun* 旬 or ten-day week.

甲寅卜殻貞: 翌乙卯易日.
Crack-making on *jiayin* (day 51), Que divining: "On the next *yimao* (day 52), it will be a clear day."   (*Yibian* 6385)

癸卯卜殻: 翌甲辰酒大甲.
Crack-making on *guimao* (day 40), Que divining: "On the next *jiachen* (day 41), perform a wine libation to Da Dia."

(*Yibian* 7258)

乙酉卜賓貞: 翌丁亥不其易日.
Crack-making on *yiyou* (day 22), Bin divining: "On the next *dinghai* (day 24), it will not be a clear day."   (*Cuibian* 605)

In the "Shi fu" (sec. II), *yi* is used once to indicate the following day in a sequence, which is how it is also used in the "Shao gao" 召誥 and "Gu ming" 顧命 chapters of the *Shangshu*. *Lai* shows evidence of some change in usage between the Shang and Western Zhou periods.

In Shang oracle-bone inscriptions, *lai* indicates days in a subsequent *xun* from that of the time of reference.

戊辰卜爭貞: 來乙亥不雨
Crack-making on *wuchen* (day 5), Zheng divining: "On the coming *yihai* (day 12), it will not rain."   (*Qianbian* 7.27.2)

丁酉㱿貞: 來乙巳王入于勉.
Dingyou (day 34), Que divining: "On the coming *yisi* (day 42), the king will enter at Mian."   (*Xubian* 3.15.1)

自今辛至于來辛有大雨
From this *xin*-(day) all the way to the coming *xin*-(day), there will be a great rain.   (*Cuibian* 692)

癸丑貞: 來乙王彝于且 ...
Divining on *guichou* (day 50): "On the coming *yi* [day; i.e., *yimao* [day 52]], the king will perform an *yi*-ritual to Ancestor ... "
    (*Yicun* 714)

Western Zhou usage shows a subtle but important distinction. With the Zhou innovation of lunar phases as the preferred sublunar interval of time instead of the Shang *xun* or ten-day week, *lai* was no longer used to indicate a day in a future *xun*, but rather was used to indicate a day in a future month.[48] In the "Shi fu" case in question, "*lai dingmao*" 來丁卯, *dingmao* (day 4) is in the same *xun* as *jiazi* (day 1), the sentence's original time of reference, thus apparently contravening Shang usage. However, as the appended "Calendar of Events" (pp. 48–49) shows, this *jiazi* is the twenty-eighth day of the second month, requiring that *dingmao* be in the following month. Therefore, according to Zhou usage, which the "Shi fu" would of course follow, *dingmao* should be indicated by the time marker *lai*, as it is in this phrase. With *lai* thus separated from the previous phrase (serving neither as a verb meaning "to come" nor as part of a compound place name [such as Fanglai, as suggested by Kong Zhao 孔晁]), and given the other idiomatic usages discussed above (*ming* and *yu fang*), the entire sentence has to mean: "The Grand Duke Wang was ordered to secure the area. On the following *dingmao*, Wang arrived and reported about ears taken and captives."

The above two examples both demonstrate clusters of Shang–Western Zhou idioms. The text also abounds with individual vocabulary items with characteristics dating from that linguistic period. I will briefly illustrate just three or four of these.

The word *fu* 俘, "capture," of course occurs often in the text. Although in later usage *fu* is generally nominal, in this text it is used in threee distinct ways: as a noun meaning "captive" (*gao yi guo fu* 告以馘俘; secs. III, IV, VI), as a verb indicating the capture of humans (*fu* Aihou, Yihou 俘艾侯佚侯; sec. VI), and as a verb for the capture of inanimate objects (*fu* Yin *wang ding* 俘殷丑鼎; sec. V; Wuwang *fu* Shang *jiu yu* 武王俘商舊玉; sec. X). As the following examples demonstrate, the latter two uses were common in the language of the Shang and Western Zhou.

四日庚申亦出艱自北, 子矞告曰: 昔甲辰方征于蚁, 俘人
十又五人; 五日戊申方亦征, 俘人十又六人, 六月在 ...
Four days [later], on *gengsheng* (day 57), there again came trouble from the north. Prince Tuan reported saying: "Last *jiachen* (day 41), the *fang* were on campaign in You and captured fifteen men. Five days later, on *wushen* (day 45), the *fang* were again on campaign and captured sixteen men. Sixth month at . . .　　　(*Jinghua* 5)

執嘼二人, 隻聝四千八百□十二聝, 俘人萬三千八十一人,
俘馬□□匹, 俘車丗兩, 俘牛三百五十五牛, 羊丗八羊
I took prisoner 2 of their chiefs, obtained 4,8 . . 2 scalps, captured 13,081 men, captured . . . horses, 30 war chariots, 355 oxen, and 38 sheep.　　　　　　("Xiao Yu 小盂 ding"; Sh 12.62:682)[49]

毆俘士女羊牛, 俘吉金
We routed and captured men, women, sheep and oxen; we captured auspicious metal.　　　　　　("Shi Yuan 師寰 *gui*"; Sh 29.178:600)

As significant as the record of the captures is in the text, it is clear that for the Zhou composer of the narrative, the sacrifices, particularly the human offerings, that followed the captures held much greater symbolic significance. For instance, the parallel between the *liao* 燎 burnt-offering sacrifice here with that in the "Xiao Yu *ding*" inscription is striking (see above, n. 42). More subtle, perhaps, but equally characteristic of contemporary usage are the other terms used in the "Shi fu" for sacrifice. *Fa* 伐, which midway through the

CALENDAR OF EVENTS

Day 日	Month 12 建戌, 12 月	Month 1 建亥, 1 月	Month 2 建子, 2 月
1.		丁卯 4	丁酉 34
2.		戊辰 5	戊戌 35
3.		己巳 6	己亥 36
4.		庚午 7	庚子 37
5.		辛未 8	辛丑 38
6.		壬申 9	壬寅 39
7.		癸酉 10	癸卯 40
8.		甲戌 11	甲辰 41
9.		乙亥 12	乙巳 42
10.		丙子 13	丙午: King Wu reaches Zhou 43　army.
11.		丁丑 14	丁未 44
12.		戊寅 15	戊申 45
13.		己卯 16	己酉 46
14.		庚辰 17	庚戌 47
15.		辛巳 18	辛亥 48
16.		壬午 19	壬子 49
17.		癸未 20	癸丑 50
18.		甲申 21	甲寅 51
19.		乙酉 22	乙卯 52
20.		丙戌 23	丙辰 53
21.		丁亥 24	丁巳 54
22.		戊子 25	戊午: Army fords Yellow River 55　at Mengjin.
23.		己丑 26	己未 56
24.		庚寅 27	庚申 57
25.		辛卯 28	辛酉 58
26.		壬辰 29	壬戌 59
27.	甲子: Zhou army departs. 1	癸巳: King Wu departs from 30　Zhou.	癸亥 60
28.	乙丑 2	甲午 31	甲子: Zhou victory at Muye. 1　Grand Duke Wang
29.	丙寅 3	乙未 32	乙丑: ordered to secure capital. 2
30.		丙申 33	

CALENDAR OF EVENTS (2)

Day 日	Month 3 建丑, 3 月	Month 4 建寅, 4 月	Month 5 建卯, 5 月	Month 6 建辰, 6 月
1.	丙寅 3	丙申 33	乙丑 2	乙未 32
2.	丁卯 4: Wang reports success.	丁酉 34	丙寅 3	丙戌 33
3.	戊辰 5: King Wu performs rituals,	戊戌 35	丁卯 4	丁酉 34
4.	己巳 6: establishes government.	己亥 36	戊辰 5	戊戌 35
5.	庚午 7	庚子 37	己巳 6	己亥 36
6.	辛未 8: Ceremony at Jian; Jian; *Li gui*	辛丑 38	庚午 7	庚子 37: Attacks on Mo, Xuanfang, Shu.
7.	壬申 9: cast. Victory over Yue,	壬寅 39	辛未 8	辛丑 38
8.	癸酉 10: Xifang, attack on Chen.	癸卯 40	壬申 9	壬寅 39
9.	甲戌 11	甲辰 41	癸酉 10	癸卯 40
10.	乙亥 12	乙巳 42	甲戌 11	甲辰 41
11.	丙子 13	丙午 43	乙亥 12	乙巳 42: Victory reported.
12.	丁丑 14	丁未 44	丙子 13	丙午 43
13.	戊寅 15	戊申 45	丁丑 14	丁未 44
14.	己卯 16	己酉 46	戊寅 15	戊申 45
15.	庚辰 17	庚戌 47	己卯 16	己酉 46
16.	辛巳 18: Victory over Chen	辛亥 48: Presentation of Yin caldrons.	庚辰 17	庚戌 47: Liao-sacrifice in Zhou temple.
17.	壬午 19	壬子 49: Ritual ceremonies.	辛巳 18	辛亥 48: Sacrifice as king.
18.	癸未 20	癸丑 50: Presentation of Yin captives.	壬午 19	壬子 49
19.	甲申 21: Attack on Wei led by Bai Ta.	甲寅 51: Inspection of Yin army at Muye.	癸未 20	癸丑 50
20.	乙酉 22	乙卯 52: Musical ceremony.	甲申 21	甲寅 51
21.	丙戌 23	丙辰 53	乙酉 22	乙卯 52: Feudal lords come to court.
22.	丁亥 24	丁巳 54	丙戌 23	
23.	戊子 25	戊午 55	丁亥 24	
24.	己丑 26	己未 56	戊子 25	
25.	庚寅 27	庚申 57	己丑 26	
26.	辛卯 28	辛酉 58	庚寅 27	
27.	壬辰 29	壬戌 59	辛卯 28	
28.	癸巳 30	癸亥 60	壬辰 29	
29.	甲午 31	甲子 1	癸巳 30	
30.	乙未 32		甲午 31	

Western Zhou period came to be used exclusively to indicate military attacks, was the most commonly used specific human-sacrifice term in Shang oracle-bone inscriptions. The character graphically depicts the decapitation of a prisoner.[50] The use of *fa* in the "Shi fu," as, for example, "*fa jue sishi fu jia jun ding shi*" 伐厥四十夫家君鼎師, "(the king) beheaded their forty family heads and captains of the caldron," certainly indicates the same type of sacrifice.

In addition to specific sacrifice terms such as *liao* and *fu*, oracle-bone usage also included a pair of general sacrifice terms: *you* 㞢 or 又 (i.e., 侑) and *yong* 用.[51] Let us here consider just the case of *yong*.[52]

丁卯卜: 用夂于兄己
Crack-making on *dingmao*: "*Yong* captives to Xiong Ji."

(*Xubian* 1.44.1)

其用人牛十又五
[We] will *yong* men and oxen, fifteen.　　(*Nanbei*, "Ming" 525)

This sacrificial sense of *yong* is also evident in such early Western Zhou bronze inscriptions as that on the "Ling 令 *yi*" (Sh 6.25:276): "*yiyou yong sheng yu Kang gong*" 乙酉用牲于康宮, "On *yiyou*, *yong* offering in the Kang Palace." To these examples compare the sentence of the "Shi fu": "*yong niu yu tian yu Ji wubai you si*" 用牛于天于稷五百有四, "He [used =] sacrificed 504 oxen to heaven and to Ji," where *yong* is equally unmistakable as a sacrifice term.[53]

These Shang and Western Zhou linguistic features strongly suggest that the text was indeed composed at or about the time of the events it describes.

3. Content and Textual Integrity

The final criteria to be considered in judging the historical worth of any document are appropriate content and textual integrity. In the preceding discussion, specific points of linguistic usage have been shown to be appropriate to the Shang-Zhou transition era. In general flavor as well, it seems self-evident, as Wang Chong noted noted during the Han period (see above, p. 39), that the "Shi fu" is a realistic account of the events surrounding the conquest of one dynastic power and the investiture of a new people with that power. Granted, the observation of Wang Chong was based in large part on a commonsensical comparison with contemporary events, but such common sense generally makes for better historiography than the idealism characteristic of Mencius, for example.

It is within the sphere of textual integrity, however, that most scholars have presumed difficulties with the text. These difficulties revolve around the three full date notations. Disregarding for the moment the problems with the first of these dates (for which, see above, p. 38), the correlation between the second and third dates and the events that could have occurred within their interval is the crux of a perceived textual disorder. Based on the definition of lunar-phase terms identified with Wang Guowei 王國維 (1877–1927), the second date, that for the battle at Muye, corresponds to the twenty-eighth day of the second month, while the third date, that for the burnt-offering sacrifice in Zhou, corresponds to the sixteenth day of the fourth month.[54] The interval between these two dates is generally consistent, allowing one minor modification, with the interval of forty-seven days indicated by the cyclical days mentioned, *jiazi* (day 1) and *gengxu* (day 47).[55] If these two dates were the only evidence available, as they are in the *Han shu* quotation of the "Wu cheng," it would be a simple matter to make the minor calendrical modification required.[56] But the blessing, and to some the bane, of the "Shi fu" is that, to a great extent, it fills in the events that occurred during the interval (unfortunately not with full date notations, but always with cyclical days), and this chronicle demonstrates that such a simple forty-seven-day interval is impossible.

The impossibility of this simple calendrical sequence is shown most clearly by the dual occurrence of the cyclical date *xinhai* (day 48), the first time marking the presentation to King Wu of the captured Yin caldrons *in the Shang capital* (sec. IV), and the second time when King Wu ritually assumed his throne *in the Zhou capital* (sec. IX).[57] It is naturally inconceivable that a person 3,000 years ago could have performed actions in two places separated by some 550 kilometers *on the same day*. The inescapable conclusion is that these two *xinhai* day notations must refer to events separated by a full sixty-day cycle. This is consistent with both the sequence given in the text, and with the logistical requirements of moving an army from the environs of Anyang to Xi'an.[58]

Allowing for this extra sixty days between the battle at Muye and the victory ceremonies at Zhou, the interval is not 47 days but 107 days. When the cyclical days indicated for these events (i.e., *jiazi* and *gengxu* are inserted into a lunar calendar covering this 107-day interval (see the appended "Calendar of Events"), the lunar-phase notations for the two dates coincide exactly with their standard definitions. Such a calendar also brings to light another interesting feature: both the victory celebration at Zhou and the parallel ceremonies in the Shang capital began on the sixteenth day of their respective lunar months. This is not coincidental, for the sixteenth day of a lunation marks the day after the full moon, and evidence from Western Zhou bronze inscriptions confirms that it was during the pre-dawn hours of this day (i.e., still during the fifteenth night, when the moon is at its fullest) that this sort of victory celebration was commonly held.[59]

As appropriate as this correspondence between the lunar-phase notations and the cyclical days looks, there is one major problem: the sacrifice in the Zhou capital is stipulated as taking place in the *fourth* month, while this interval of 107 days beginning from the twenty-eighth day of a second month requires a *sixth* month. Stymied by this, Gu Jiegang 顧頡剛 (1893–1980), the most thorough modern commentator of the "Shi fu," despaired of being able to make sense of the text's calendrical system.[60] However, familiarity with the various scripts in which this text would have been transmitted may provide a solution to this conundrum. Recently, Zhou Fagao 周法高 has suggested that this confusion may have resulted from a mistranscription when the text, originally written in "archaic script" (*guwen* 古文), was transcribed into "seal script" (*zhuanwen* 篆文). The "seal script" form of *liu* 六, "six,"— 爪—is extremely similar to the "archaic script" form of *si* 四, "four"—爪, such that an original "sixth month" could easily have come to be read as "fourth month."[61] This simple emendation not only confirms the present arrangement of the text, but also shows the two full-date notations to be mutually corroborating, thus confirming the integrity of the text.

Finally, the calendrical reconstructions of Dong Zuobin 董作賓 (1895–1963) also offer a striking confirmation of this calendar of the "Shi fu." The calendar required by the "Shi fu," with lunar months beginning on cyclical days *dingmao* (day 4), *dingyou* (day 34), *bingyin* (day 3), *bingshen* (day 33), *yichou* (day 2), and *yiwei* (day 32), respectively (see the appended "Calendar of Events"), coincides precisely with that of the year 1045 B.C.,[62] the year which Professor David S. Nivison has, on the basis of several independent factors, determined to be the year of the Zhou conquest.[63] This firmly establishes that the "Shi fu" can be nothing other than an authentic account of the events immediately following that conquest.

PART III: THE CONQUEST CAMPAIGN

Being thus satisfied of the authenticity of the "Shi fu" text, it is possible to use it as the basis for the following chronicle of the Zhou conquest campaign.

Although the text of the "Shi fu" begins with King Wu's departure from Zhou on *guisi* (day 30), the twenty-seventh day of the first month (15 December

1046 B.C.), there is reason to believe that this did not mark the beginning of the campaign. The "Taishi" 泰誓 chapter of the *Shangshu* includes the curious statement, "It was on *bingwu* (day 43; correlated with the "Shi fu" calendar, the tenth day of the second month; 28 December 1046 B.C.) that the king reached the troops." Combined with the specificity of the "Shi fu" that King Wu, and presumably only King Wu (and his immediate retinue), departed on *guisi*, this shows that the Zhou army must have departed at an earlier date (as the logistics of the campaign would dictate; see n. 58). When did the army depart? A well-known tradition in the "Zhou yu" 周語 chapter of the *Guo yu* 國語 gives a precise astronomical date. The passage reads:

> 昔武王伐殷, 歲在鶉火, 月在天駟, 日在析木之津, 辰在斗
> 柄, 星在天黿
> Long ago, when King Wu attacked Yin, the Year Star was in Quail
> Fire, the moon was in the Heavenly Quadriga, the sun was in the
> Ford at Split Wood, the *chen* was in the Handle of the Dipper, and
> the Star was in the Heavenly Turtle.[64]

According to David Nivison, the combination of locations for Jupiter, the sun, moon, and the lunisolar conjunction given here, is satisfied by only one day during the years 1046–45 B.C.; that day is 16 November 1046.[65] Correlating this date with the dates required by the "Shi fu," it corresponds to the twenty-seventh day of the twelfth month. Computing then the cyclical day for this date, one finds that it is, certainly not by coincidence, a *jiazi* day. Deeply concerned with temporal portents, it is to be expected that the Zhou would select a particularly auspicious day on which to begin their conquest campaign. As the decisive battle at Muye, which the Zhou apparently timed to occur on a *jiazi* day, shows, there could be no day more appropriate for this than *jiazi*, the first of the cycle.

This concern for timely actions conceivably also dictated the departure date of King Wu. It is well known that the governmental custom during the late Shang (particularly period V) was for the king to divine on *gui* days, the last day of the ten-day week, as a means of ensuring good fortune in the coming ten days. It is plausible that the Zhou shared this divination tradition, in which case one might assume that on the morning of *guisi*, one month after the departure of the army, King Wu performed the final formal divination in the Zhou temple. Having thus ensured that future actions would be beneficial, he set out to join his troops. Whether in chariot or on horseback, there is no doubt that the king moved far more rapidly than the large Zhou army. That he overtook the troops on *bingwu* adds a practical verification of the date 16 November for the departure of the army, for this shows that King Wu in fourteen days covered the same distance that it took the army forty-three days to traverse, a ratio in speed of three to one that practical experience might indeed suggest.

The next mention of the conquest army's movements has them completing the crossing of the Yellow River at Mengjin 孟津 on *wuwu* (day 55; 9 January 1045 B.C.).[66] From there, a march of six days brought them on *guihai* (day 60; 14 January 1045 B.C.) to Muye, where they deployed in anticipation of the battle that would take place the next morning. Everyone now knows that the battle resulted in an overwhelming triumph for the Zhou army; but as the "Shi fu" shows, and as common sense should lead us to expect, it was by no means the end of all hostilities. Still to come would be a series of mopping-up operations before the Zhou could be secure in their victory. The first of these operations was initiated as soon as the victory at Muye had been won; the Grand Duke Wang, the commanding general of the Zhou forces, was ordered to secure the area of the Shang capital. Wang accomplished his mission in four days, and on the following day, *wuchen* (day 5; 19 January), King Wu formally declared the "establishment of government."

It is one thing to establish a government; it is quite another thing to ensure that it is a lasting one. The next section of the "Shi fu" mentions campaigns, beginning on *renshen* (day 9; 23 January), against a number of Shang vassal states located to the north and east of the former capital. But immediately before these campaigns began, King Wu presided over a sort of victory ceremony in an important cult center near the Shang capital. The "Li gui," the vessel discovered in 1976 which has excited so much interest because of its verification of the *jiazi* date for the battle of Muye, was cast after the presentation of metal to Youshi Li 有使利, its maker, by the king.[67] This presentation took place on *xinwei* (day 8; 22 January) at Jian 闟, which inscriptions on late Shang bronze vessels show to have been situated near the Shang capital and where a "great temple" (*taishi* 太室) was located.[68] When correlated with the narrative of the "Shi fu," this ceremony appears to have been intended to reward the soldiers after one great victory and to encourage them in the battles to come.

A mopping-up campaign against the states Yue 越, Xifang 戲方, Chen 陳, and Wei 衛 then lasted until *jiashen* (day 21; 4 February).[69] After the report of the successful conclusion of this campaign, the "Shi fu" record is blank for nearly a month. We can only conjecture that the time must have been filled attending to the routine duties of an occupation army. But on the first full moon after having thus put the former capital firmly under its control, the Zhou celebrated their victory in the Shang capital. The events of days *xinhai* (day 48; 2 March) to *yimao* (day 52; 6 March) are sufficiently well described in the text that they need no amplification here. Suffice it to make one general remark: these ceremonies display a certain diplomatic and psychological intuition on the part of King Wu. They seem to have been designed to invoke in the conquered Shang people awe and respect for the vigor of the Zhou conquerors, while at the same time attempting to minimize any feelings of enmity. It is undoubtedly for this reason that although King Wu was there presented with the captured Shang officials, he did not execute and sacrifice them immediately, but preferred instead to transport them back to the Zhou homeland.[70] Although section IX shows that he did indeed execute and sacrifice them there, this was exclusively a Zhou affair, well out of sight of the Shang people. It was perhaps in part because of this seeming policy of clemency that the Shang army was willing to submit to Zhou command, as the events of *jiayin* (day 51; 5 March) seem to suggest they did.

With the conquest now complete, not only in military terms but just as importantly politically (note the "confirmation" of the heads of states on days *xinhai* [day 48] and *renzi* [day 49]) and psychologically, King Wu and the Zhou army (or at least that portion of the army that was not to be garrisoned in the former Shang domain) were free to return to Zhou. Considering the logisitics of the march, the departure must have taken place very soon after the end of these ceremonies. But, even though the Zhou were now masters of the Shang and their subjects, that was no longer sufficient to content the people who considered themselves the recipients of Heaven's mandate to rule all of China. It was now incumbent upon King Wu to bring even those states in the west, hitherto enemies of both the Shang and the Zhou, under his control. This was effected by means of a final mopping-up operation, conducted against the states of Mo 磨, Xuanfang 宣方, Shu 蜀, and Li 厲, while the Zhou army was making its return to the Zhou homeland.[71]

With this western campaign successfully concluded (on *yisi* [day 42; 25 April]) and all recalcitrant states now submissive, King Wu, once again in the Zhou capital, was then free to celebrate his victory at home. The celebrations again began on the first full-moon after this occasion (*gengxu* [day 47; 30 April]), and this time were marked by a rather liberal shedding of human blood. Despite the protestations of later Confucians that the founding fathers of the Zhou were too virtuous to engage in such violence, the "Shi fu" leaves no doubt that they engaged in the practice with all the vigor for which the Shang, their more "civilized" predecessors, were noted. Whether or not the victims' blood propitiated the Zhou ancestors, it must certainly have demonstrated-to the Zhou people that they were indeed now the rulers of China.

In conclusion then, modern scholars are justifiably excited whenever a bronze vessel bearing an inscription is unearthed. But earth is not the only thing that can bury authentic records. In the case of this "Shi fu" text, Confucian idealism has been nearly as obscurant. Let us not succumb to our own prejudices against "unattested" evidence, but instead examine this text just as we would a newly discovered bronze inscription. Whether in terms of chronology, military affairs, or court ritual, it has much to tell us about the very early Zhou.

NOTES

1. The recension and these textual notes are based on the Sibu congkan text of *Yi Zhou shu* (the "Shi fu" comprises chapter 40, 4.9a–12a), which is a photo-reprint of a Ming Jiajing era edition (printed in 1543). In these notes it is this text that is intended when I refer to the "original text." I have also extensively consulted the critical recension by Gu Jiegang 顧頡剛 (*"Yi Zhou shu* Shi fu pian jiaozhu xieding yu pinglun" 逸周書世俘篇較注寫定與評論, *Wenshi* 文史 2 [1962], 1–42), which not only presents Gu's original research but also synthesizes the various Qing editions and scholarship. The original version of this article (*Early China* 6 [1980–81]: 57–79) provided lengthy notes substantiating the translations offered for many of the problematic passages in the text. Here I modify the translation slightly and reorganize the presentation of its substantiation, noting only readings that emend the original text, while moving some of the grammatical discussion to part II.2 below, and the geographical identifications and some of the historical discussion to parts II.3 and III.

2. It would seem that this summation is a later addition to the basic text, akin to the "Preface to the *Documents*" (*Shuxu* 書序). The record, however, does seem reliable when correlated with the remainder of the chapter. According to my chronological reconstruction of the events, *yiwei* (day 32) marks the first day of the fourth month, a time at which King Wu and the Zhou army were returning through former Shang territory to the Zhou homeland (see p. 55, and especially the appended "Calendar of Events.")

3. The original text reads 維一月丙辰旁生魄若翼日丁巳; the emendation is based on the quotation in *Hanshu* 漢書, "Lüli zhi" 律曆志

(21B.1015–16) of Liu Xin's 劉歆 *Shijing* 世經 , which in turn quotes the "Wu cheng" chapter of the *Shangshu*. The occurrence here of a full-date notation (i.e., month, lunar-phase, and cyclical day) makes it possible, when correlated with the two other full-date notations (Sec. II, Sec. IX), which are identical in the "Shi fu" and *Hanshu* texts, to determine the correctness of the "Wu cheng" date. For more discussion of these dates, see pp. 51–52.

4. Emending *zi si* 自祀 to *zhui si* 追祀, as given in Kong Zhao's 孔晁 (fl. A.D. 265) commentary. For further comments on this passage, see below, pp. 42–46.

5. Emending *ge* 格 to *ge* 革 on the basis of Kong Zhao's commentary: 不改祭天之服, "He did not change his clothes for sacrificing to heaven."

6. Following Zhu Youceng 朱右曾, *Yi Zhou shu jixun jiaoshi* 逸周書集訓校釋 and Gu Jiegang in adding *huang yue* 黃鉞 on the basis of parallel examples in the following text; see Gu Jiegang, "*Yi Zhou shu* Shi fu pian," 9n6.

7. The original text here reads *guiyou* 癸酉 (day 10), which, from the sequence of cyclical days, is obviously corrupt and should read *guichou* 癸丑.

8. Following Gu Jiegang in adding *ru* 入 after *wang* 王, as in similar constructions below; "*Yi Zhou shu* Shi fu pian," 11n20.

9. Following Lu Wenchao 盧文弨, *Yi Zhou shu* 逸周書, and Gu Jiegang, for both of which, see "*Yi Zhou shu* Shi fu pian," 11n23, in reading *yong* 庸 (i.e., *yong* 鏞) for *qi* 其.

10. Following Lu Wenchao in reading *rong* 戎 for *wo* 我.

11. *Zuo zhuan* 左傳 (Xuan 宣 12; see *Chunqiu Zuo zhuan zhengyi* 春秋左傳正義 [Shisan jing zhushu ed.], 23.180 [vol. 2, p. 1882]; see also, James Legge, *The Chinese Classics*, vol. 5: *The Ch'un Ts'ew with the Tso Chuen* [1872; rpt. Hong Kong: Hong Kong University Press, 1960], 320) states:

    武王克商 . . . 作武
    When King Wu had subdued Shang . . . he composed "Wu."

    "Wu" 武 is universally identified with the *Shijing* poem by that name (i.e., Mao 285). For a translation and discussion of this poem, see below, p. 167.

12. Deleting *zhong* 鍾. With the reign of Han Jingdi (i.e., Liu Qi 劉啓; r. 156–141 B.C.), the word *qi* 啓 became taboo and this line must have been changed to read *kai* 開 at that time. Qi was the son of Yu the Great, the progenitor of the Xia dynasty.

13. Bai Wei 百韋 should perhaps be identified with Bai Ta 百弇 in sec. IV above, the *wei* 韋 apparently-being a graphic garble for *ta* 弇. For further discussion of the possible identity of this figure, see below, n. 50.

14. The original text here reads *xin huang* 新荒. I reverse the order on the basis of the reading in sec. IV. It is of course possible that Xin Huang is the correct reading, in which case the first occurrence should be emended.

15. I here retain the original sequence of the text. Gu Jiegang, "*Yi Zhou shu* Shi fu pian," 14n13, rearranges the text, thinking with previous commentators that this campaign occurs in the same locale as that chronicled in sec. IV. However, the states here enumerated lie far to the west, in the vicinity of the Zhou capital, and on the basis of the cyclical dates given, this campaign would had to have taken place in the fourth month, just days before the victory celebration in the Zhou capital.

16. The original text is here corrupt, reading 陳本命新荒蜀磨至. I follow the emendation of Gu Jiegang, "*Yi Zhou shu* Shi fu pian," 13n7.

17. The number in the original text reads 八百有三百, an obvious corruption. The anomalous usage here of *yu* 禦 as "chariot" is dictated by the qualifier *liang* 兩. In later usage *yu* commonly indicates "charioteer," which might suggest "pairs of charioteers" here, especially in that this passage is otherwise an enumeration of human captives. However, there is no parallel for *liang* being used as a qualifier for humans, and I provisionally follow the commentators in reading "chariot."

18. In the original text this number begins 億有十萬; with *yi* 億 being defined in antiquity as *shi wan* 十萬 (100,000), the *shi wan* following is obviously corrupt. It should probably read *qi wan* 七萬, the archaic form of *qi*, 十, easily giving rise to this sort of confusion.

19. Adding *kao* 考 after *wen* 文 on the basis of the parallel text below.

20. I emend *fei* 廢, "to discard," to *fa* 發, "to shoot," as suggested by Qiu Xigui 裘錫圭, "Shi 'wu' 'fa'" 釋勿發, *Zhongguo yuwen yanjiu* 中國語文研究 2 (1981): 43–44, and *shi* 矢 to fu 夫 on the basis of the parallel usage in sec. II. The first of these emendations, as well as that noted in the following note, were not reflected in my original publication of this translation.

21. I follow Qiu Xigui ("Shi 'wu' 'fa,'" 45 in reading *jia* 甲, "armored," as a corruption of an original *hewen* 合文 *liushi* 六十, which in seal script would have been written 十.

22. Following Gu Jiegang in deleting *wu wang* 武王, "*Yi Zhou shu* Shi fu pian," 19n9.

23. The original text reads 武王乃以庶祀馘于國周朝; the emendation is based on the "Wu cheng" quotation in the *Hanshu* (21B.1015–16).

24. I here read *yu* 于 for the anomalous *yu* 於 in the original text.

25. I add *yu* 玉 after *shu* 庶, following Lu Wenchao, whose emendation is based on the *Taiping yulan* 太平御覽 text; see Gu Jiegang, "*Yi Zhou shu* Shi fu pian," 22n6.

26. I read *yan* 琰 for *wu* 玉, as in the parallel phrase above.

27. *Han shu*, 21B. 1015–16.

28. It is true that the "Wu cheng" date for the battle at Muye reads "third month" (*san yue* 三月) rather than "second month" (*er yue* 二月), but this is universally considered a textual corruption.

29. For a brief discussion of the dates to which these notations correspond and the lunar-phase definitions on which they are based, see below, n. 54. For a more detailed discussion, see Edward L. Shaughnessy, *Sources of Western Zhou History: Inscribed Bronze Vessels* (Berkeley: University of California Press, 1991), 134–55.

30. *Shangshu* (Sibu beiyao ed.), 6.8a; see, too, James Legge, *The Chinese Classics*, vol. III: *The Shoo King or The Book of Historical Documents* (1865; rpt. Hong Kong: Hong Kong University Press, 1960), 8.

31. The *guwen* "Wu cheng" (Legge, *The Shoo King*, 308) states:

    歸馬于華山之陽, 放牛予桃林之野, 示天下弗服
    He sent back his horses to the south of Mount Hua, and let loose his oxen in the open country of Taolin, showing the empire that he would not use them *again.*

    Qu Wanli 屈萬里, "Du *Zhou shu* Shi fu pian" 讀周書世俘篇, in *Qingzhu Li Ji xiansheng qishi sui lunwenji* 慶祝李濟先生七十歲論文集 (Taipei: Qinghua xuebaoshe, 1965), vol. 1, 317–32, cites the hunting record of the "Shi fu" as one of the reasons he considers the text to be authentic. He points out that not only does the grammar resemble that of hunting notations found on Shang oracle bones, but, what is more, the numbers of animals recorded as being caught are consistent, species by species, with the Shang records.

32. *Mencius*, 7B/3.

33. The "Taishi" is a *guwen* chapter of the *Shangshu*; for a discussion of the anachronisms in the "Ke Yin," see Huang Peirong 黃沛榮, "Zhou shu yanjiu" 周書研究 (Ph.D. diss., National Taiwan University, 1976), 289–97.

34. *Lunheng* 論衡 (Sibu beiyao ed.), 7.14b–16a; tr. Alfred Forke, *Lun-Heng: Wang Ch'ung's Essays*, 2 vols. (1907; rpt. New York: Paragon Book Gallery, 1962), 482–84 (romanization modified).

35. Cheng Tingzuo, *Wanshu dingyi* 晚書訂疑 (Huang Qing jingjie ed.), 26.4a.
36. It appears, however, that whoever composed the text masquerading under the title "Wu cheng" also interpreted Mencius's characterization as a quotation, and in an attempt to camouflage his forgery, incorporated the phrase into his text.
   This presentation of Warring States and Han reflections on the "Wu cheng" has been adapted substantially intact from the seminal study by Gu Jiegang, "*Yi Zhoushu* Shi fu pian," 24–27.
37. Huang Peirong, "Zhou shu yanjiu," 141–236.
38. Due to a loan possibility of *shi* 世 for *da* 大 in archaic Chinese, commentators of the text generally interpret the title to mean *da fu* 大俘, "the great capture"; see, for example, Gu Jiegang, "*Yi Zhoushu* Shifu pian, 2. In terms of modification, this reading seems preferable to "world's capture."
39. For a fuller discussion, see Huang Peirong, "Zhoushu yanjiu," 300–302.
40. This also demonstrates that the traditional interpretation of this title, i.e., "The Successful Completion of the War" (see, for example, Legge, *The Shoo King*, 306), is incorrect. The title should be translated "(King) Wu's Achievement (of Rule)."
41. See the discussions by such Qing dynasty scholars as Wei Yuan 魏源, *Shu guwei* 書古微 (Huang Qing jingjie ed.), 171.17a–b, and Cheng Tingzuo, *Wanshu dingyi*, 26.4a. Modern scholars who have made linguistic studies of the text include Guo Moruo 郭沫若, *Zhongguo gudai shehui yanjiu* 中國古代社會研究 (1930; rpt. Beijing: Renmin chubanshe, 1954), 269–71; Gu Jiegang, "*Yi Zhoushu* Shifu pian," esp. 28–29; and Qu Wanli, "Du *Zhou shu* Shifu pian," 327–31.
42. Parallels between the "Shi fu" and the inscription attributed to the "Xiao Yu 小盂 *ding*" (the vessel is no longer extant) have been noted by many scholars of bronze inscriptions. Although badly preserved, the "Xiao Yu *ding*" inscription also records a victory celebration of sorts, and the language is so consistent, both in general and in technical points, with that of the "Shi fu" that it merits extensive quotation (in the translation of W. A. C. H. Dobson [*Early Archaic Chinese* (Toronto: University of Toronto Press, 1962), 231–32]; I highlight parallels with the "Shi fu" text).

> At dawn, the King entered the Ancestral Temple of the Zhou House, ... The Receiver of Guests waited upon *the guests of the States* [the feudal lords from outside metropolitan Zhou]. They

laid aside their travelling clothes [for ceremonial robes] and stood facing east. I, Yu, *with all the belted and beflagged (prisoners) of the Guifang* . . . . . . *entered the South Gate.* I reported "The King commanded me, Yu, together with . . . . to attack the Guifang . . . . . . *I took prisoner two of their Chiefs, obtained 4,812 scalps, captured 13,081 men, seized* . . . . horses, 30 chariots of war, 355 oxen, and 38 sheep.

I, Yu, ... say . . . . called out "report our campaign." *I took prisoner one of their Chiefs, obtained 237 scalps, captured* . . . . *men,* seized 104 horses and *100 (plus . .) chariots of war."*

The king . . said "We are pleased."

I, Yu, bowed deeply and saluted and, *together with the captured Chiefs, came forward and took my place in the Great Court.*

The King commanded Rong (one of the Chiefs of the Guifang) ". . their . . . . . . Chiefs, to examine its cause." . . The Earl of Ge . . . . . ., followed Shang.

The Chiefs were beheaded in the . . The King called out " . . . . *order Yu, with his prisoners and scalps, to come in at the (South) Gate and to present them* at the West Walk. With . . *to enter and sacrifice them by fire in the Ancestral Temple of the Zhou House."*

43. This comparison is adopted substantially intact from Gu Jiegang, "*Yi Zhoushu* Shifu pian," 6n5.
44. See, for example, Chen Mengjia 陳夢家, *Yinxu buci zongshu* 殷虛卜辭綜述 (Beijing: Kexue chubanshe, 1956), 283; Guo Moruo, *Zhongguo gudai shehui yanjiu*, 270; and Xu Jinxiong 許進雄, "Shi yu" 釋御, *Zhongguo wenzi* 中國文字 12 (1965): 8a.
45. Shirakawa Shizuka interprets *ming* here as a noun, being modified by *dong* 東 and the object of the verb *ji* 即. He interprets this to mean, "to respond to the Eastern order." Despite the awkwardness of his reading, Shirakawa objects that *ming* is never used as a passive, hence it cannot be so used here. Guo Moruo, on the other hand, states flatly that this is a passive use of *ming; Liang Zhou jinwenci daxi*, study 36.
46. See above, n. 44. Other scholars identifying *yu fang* as a place-name include Wang Guowei, Yang Shuda 楊樹達, and Chen Banghuai 陳邦懷; see Shirakawa Shizuka 白川靜, *Kinbun tsūshaku* 金文通釋, 32.817–19, for a summary of their views.
47. Xu Jinxiong, "Shi yu," 8a.
48. Dobson, *Early Archaic Chinese*, 88.

49. This translation is from Dobson, *Early Archaic Chinese*, 231; for the context, see above, n. 42.

50. A significant percentage of the corpses found at Anyang had been thus decapitated; see Shi Zhangju 石章如, *Xiaotun: Yizhi de faxian yu fajue, yibian* 小屯遺址的發現與發掘乙編 (Nangang: Academia Sinica, 1959), 7–8, 297–99.

51. For a discussion of these two general sacrifices verbs, see Yao Xiaosui 姚孝遂, "Shangdai de fulu" 商代的俘虜, *Guwenzi yanjiu* 古文字研究 1 (1979): 381–82.

52. I suspect that this usage of *you* is also evident in sec. IX of the "Shi fu," in the phrase 伐右厥六十小子鼎大師 "He beheaded and offered their sixty minor princes and great captains of the caldrons," but the reading of *you* 侑 for *you* 右, while adopted in the translation, is too uncertain to serve as evidence of authenticity.

53. The use of *yu* 于 in this line, as well as above in 告于天于稷 "I report to Heaven and to Ji" is also worthy of note. Compare, for example, *Xubian* 1.42.5: 毋又于且辛于毋辛 "Do not make an offering to Grandfather Xin and to Mother Xin" and *Cuibian* 32: 既燎于河于岳 "After performing a burnt offering sacrifice to the River-(spirit) and to the Mountain-(spirit)." Whether the second *yu* of these lines be interpreted as a reduplicative preposition or as a conjunction, the parallel between the "Shi fu" and the oracle-bone usage remains striking.

54. In his "Shengpo sipo kao" 生霸死考, Wang Guowei 王國維 demonstrated on the basis of bronze inscriptional evidence that the definitions Liu Xin gave for the lunar phase notations (defining "*shengpo*" as the full-moon and "*sipo*" as the new moon) were incorrect. Wang, on the other hand, divides the month into four quarters, with *chuji* 初吉 representing days 1 to 7 or 8, *ji shengpo* 既生霸 days 8 or 9 to 14 or 15, *ji wang* 既望 15 or 16 to 22 or 23, and *ji sipo* 既死霸 days 23 to the end of the lunation; "Wang Guowei, "Shengpo sipo kao," in *Guantang jilin* 觀堂集林 (1923; rpt. Beijing: Zhonghua shuju, 1959), 1.1a–1.4b (19–26). In his essay Wang discusses the dates of the "Shi fu" (as given in the *Hanshu* quotation), concluding that the date given for the battle of Muye designates the twenty-seventh day of the second month, while that for the fourth month designates the fifteenth day of the month. While generally reliant on Wang's thesis, the calendrical reconstructions presented in this paper represent a slight modification in detail. Instead of interpreting *ji sipo* as designating the first day of the fourth quarter, as does Wang, I interpret it to be the following day, "*ji*" having a common meaning of

"after." This entails a one-day divergence in the day placements within the lunation, my calendar giving the date for the battle of Muye as the twenty-eighth day of the second month, while the date for the burnt-offering sacrifice corresponds to the sixteenth day of the month.

55. For this forty-seven-day interval to be compatible with the lunar-phase notations of the two full-date notations, one would have to assume either two consecutive short (i.e., twenty-nine day) months, or that *jipang shengpo* 既旁生霸, "after the expanded growing brightness," refers to the tenth day of the lunation instead of the eleventh, and that six days later would then be the fifteenth instead of the sixteenth.

56. This is what Wang Guowei, for example, did in his "Shengpo sipo kao," referring only to the *Hanshu* "Wu cheng" quotation. But it is interesting to note that Liu Xin himself, who after all was quoting the original "Wu cheng," did not subscribe to this 47-day interval calendar. Based on his definitions for the lunar-phase notations, he dated the battle at Muye to the 5th day of the second month, and the sacrifice at Zhou to the 22nd day of the fourth month (fifth lunation), which was preceded by an intercalary month. In other words, he interpreted the text to require a 107-day interval.

57. Kong Guangsen 孔廣森, among others, has argued that both the ceremonies of sec. V and those of sec. IX took place in the Zhou capital; *Jingxue zhiyan* 經學卮言 (Huangqing jingjie ed.), 11.8347; for a similar rearrangement of the original text, see Gu Jiegang, "*Yi Zhou shu* Shi fu pian," 22–23. There is a compelling reason why this re-arrangement cannot be correct. In sec. IX, the captured nobles of the Shang are executed—first being shot and then beheaded—on *gengxu* (day 47). In sec. V, they are presented to the king on *guichou* (day 50). If these two sections were indeed to be conflated, one would have to explain why four-day-old, dismembered corpses should be presented to the Zhou king.

58. In the original version of this study (*Early China* 6 [1980–1981]: 70n3), I included a lengthy note demonstrating that an army's rate of march in ancient China would have been about fifteen kilometers per day. I now regard this as so unproblematic as to require no demonstration (for an excellent discussion of logistics in antiquity, see Donald W. Engels, *Alexander the Great and the Logistics of the Macedonian Army* [Berkeley: University of California Press, 1978]). Sec. IV of the "Shi fu" clearly shows the Zhou army still to have been in the vicinity of the Shang capital on *jiashen* (day 21), when Bai Ta was ordered to attack Wei 衛, apparently the Zhou name for the Shang city at present day Anyang. Sec. IX describes

King Wu arriving at the "Zhou temple" in the Zhou capital on *gengxu* (day 47) near present day Xi'an. Since Anyang is at least a seven-hundred kilometer march from Xi'an, it would take an army nearly twice as long as the twenty-six-day interval between these two dates to march back to Zhou, even if it were not fighting further battles in between (which sec. VI of the "Shi fu" shows the Zhou army to have done, attacking Mo 磨, Xuanfang 宣方, Shu 蜀, and Li 厲; for the locations of these states, see below, n. 71). These logistic constraints demonstrate that the arrangement of the original text is correct in inserting an extra sixty-day cycle between the records of events in the environs of the Shang capital and those in the Zhou capital.

59. Note especially that the ceremonies recorded in the "Xiao Yu *ding*" inscription take place on *ji wang* 既望, the sixteenth day of a lunation. See above, n. 42, and also the discussion in Dobson, *Early Archaic Chinese*, 231–33. For further evidence of this practice, see the inscription on the "Duo You 多友 *ding*," and the discussion of it at Edward L. Shaughnessy, "The Date of the Duo You *Ding* and Its Significance," *Early China* 9–10 (1983–85): 63–64.

60. Gu Jiegang, "*Yi Zhou shu* Shi fu pian," 31. Gu does discuss at some length the very interesting solutions of Kong Guangsen and Chen Yiwang 陳目綱. Both of these proposals ultimately fail, however, because of their reliance on Liu Xin's definitions of the lunar-phase notations.

61. Chou Fa-kao [Zhou Fagao], "On the Date of the Chou Conquest of Shang," *Guoli Zhongyang tushuguan guankan* 國立中央圖書館館刊 19.2 (1986): 28. In this article, Zhou was responding to a suggestion of mine made in the original version of this paper—that after the victory in the battle of Muye (late in the second month of the year), King Wu would have established a new calendar such that the third month would have become the new "first" month, and so, too, what would have been the sixth month would become the fourth month. I am now happy to accept Zhou's explanation as simpler and more elegant.

62. See Dong Zuobin 董作賓, *Zhongguo nianli zongpu* 中國年曆總譜, 2 vols. (Hong Kong: University of Hong Kong Press, 1960), vol. 1, 124.

63. David S. Nivison, "The Dates of Western Chou," *Harvard Journal of Asiatic Studies* 43.2 (1983), 481–580. Nivison subsequently reconsidered his date of the conquest (David S. Nivison, "1040 as the Date of the Zhou Conquest," *Early China* 8 [1982–83]: 76–78). However, for a detailed substantiation of the date 1045 for the Zhou conquest of Shang, see Shaughnessy, *Sources of Western Zhou History*, 217–36.

64. *Guo yu* (Sibu congkan ed.), "Zhou yu xia" 3.22b–23a.

65. This date was given in a preliminary version of Nivison's "The Dates of Western Chou" (see n. 44), which was the basis for my original discussion. Although Nivison subsequently suggested in the published version of his paper that this *Guo yu* passage is a late fabrication (pp. 510–12 note), a conclusion that seems to me certainly to be plausible, since this point does not materially affect the chronology presented here, I have not altered the original text of the article.

66. See for example, the "Preface to the Documents" (Legge, *The Shoo King*, 6–7), and *Shiji*, 4.121.

67. For a detailed discussion of this inscription, see Shaughnessy, *Sources of Western Zhou History*, 87–105.

68. For a discussion of the relationship between Jian and Shang, see Akatsuka Kiyoshi 赤塚忠, *Chūgoku kodai no shūkyō to bunka: In ōchō no saishi* 中國古代の宗敎と文化: 殷王朝の祭祀 (Tokyo: Kadokawa, 1977), 665, and 138ff.

69. Qu Wanli, "Du Shi fu pian," 329–30, has identified these places with the following *Chunqiu* period locales: Yue 越, the southwestern part of the state of Wei 衛; Xi 戲, in northeastern Zheng 鄭; Chen 陳, the state by the same name to the west of Song 宋, and Wei 衛, the state of the same name to the northeast of the former Shang capital. While I have been unable to correlate these identifications with evidence from oracle-bone inscriptions, as would be preferable, they seem generally reliable. The case of Wei, however, calls for some elaboration.

    There are two traditions regarding the location of Wei. The *Han shu* "Dili zhi" 地理志 (28A.1554) identifies it with Zhaoge 朝哥, the site of the battle of Muye. On the other hand, both the *Zuo zhuan* (Ding 4) and the "Wei Kangshu shijia" 衛康叔世家 chapter of the *Shi ji* (37.1589) identify it with the "Waste of Yin" (*Yinxu*) at Anyang. The "Shi fu" substantiates this latter identification. Zhaoge having been captured immediately after the battle at Muye, it would be redundant twenty days later to make it the target of a campaign. However, seeing Wei as the (perhaps former) capital of the Shang dynasty and presumably still an important cult center, at Anyang, approximately one hundred kilometers to the north, explains why it was the "Tiger Vanguard" (*huben* 虎賁), the crack troops of the army, who were explicitly ordered to attack it. This consideration was probably also applicable in the choice of commanders for the mission. The general ordered to lead the attack was Bai Ta 百弇, probably the same man who led the attack on Xuanfang (sec. VI; see, above, n. 13).

Both phonetic and graphic considerations lead me to identify this figure with Tanbo Da 檀伯達, a deputy of King Wu who figures prominently in the post-conquest events narrated in the "Ke Yin" 克殷 chapter of the *Yi Zhou shu* (4.3b), and possibly the maker of the "Li gui"; for this identification, see Shaughnessy, *Sources of Western Zhou History*, 91. This is the only general mentioned in the "Shifu," with the exception of the Grand Duke Wang (for whom there is of course a rich tradition), who can be so identified in other texts, suggesting perhaps that he was of a higher stature than the other generals, and hence suitable for leading so important a campaign.

70. Inscriptional evidence suggests Shang precedents for this type of postconquest behavior. Consider, for example, the following period V bone inscriptions:

小臣牆比伐, 擒危柔 . . . 廾人四, 爾千五百七十, 敏伯 . . .
丙車二丙, 肬百八十三, 函五十矢 . . . 用又伯度于大乙, 用
帷伯 . . . 敏于祖乙, 用柔于祖丁

Minor Vassal Qiang participated in the attack, netting [. . number of men of] Wei, 24 men of X, 1,570 men of Er, 1 . . . . [men of] Fan, . . 2 chariots, 183 shields, 50 auxiliary shields [?], and [X number of] arrows. Earl Wen was sacrificed to Da Yi, Earl Pi was sacrificed . . . , [Earl] Fan [was sacrificed] to Ancestor Yi, Mei was sacrificed to Ancestor Ding. (*Zongtu* 16.2)

內丁卜在攸貞: 王其乎□征執胄人方□, 焚□□弗每. 在
正月, 隹來正人方.

Crack on *bingwu* (day 43), divining at You: "The king should perhaps call out to . . to bring the manacled leader of the Renfang . . , and make a burnt-offering of . . . . . captives." In the first month, when [we] are coming [from] the campaign against the Renfang. (*Zheyan* 315)

Although unfortunately incomplete, both of these pieces allow interesting insights into the behavior of victors in warfare at the time of the Zhou conquest. *Zongtu* 16.2 records the capture of 1,694+ prisoners in the course of a battle, but, significantly, only the leaders of the four enemy states were sacrificed after the battle. (For a full discussion of the development of this custom, see Yao Xiaosui, "Shang dai de fulu," 385–90.) Likewise, in *Zheyan* 315, it is apparently only the leader of the Renfang, an enemy of the Shang, who is brought forward to face execution. The place of execution, You 攸, is also noteworthy, for the corpus of inscriptions concerning the campaign against these Renfang (see Dong Zuobin 董作賓, *Yin li pu* 殷曆譜 (Nanqi, Sichuan: Academia Sinica, 1945), *Xia* 9. 48a–63b) shows that You was an ally of the Shang in the campaign and served as a sort of forward base for the Shang army. Thus, the return to You before executing the leader of the Renfang would be comparable to King Wu's return to Zhou with the Shang nobles before executing them.

71. I have been unable to identify Mo and Li. However, both Xuanfang and Shu are mentioned often in Shang oracle-bone inscriptions and were clearly located to the west of Shang, probably in the southern part of present day Shanxi province; for this geography, see Chen Mengjia 陳夢家, *Yinxu buci zongshu* 殷虛卜辭述 (Beijing: Kexue chubanshe, 1956), 275–76, 295–96. Qu Wanli ("Du Shi fu pian," 329–30) notes that the absence of the name Xuanfang in later literature makes its occurrence here strong evidence for the authenticity of the "Shi fu." Its record of a Zhou attack against Shu may be even more significant. Although traditional accounts of the Zhou conquest generally list Shu as one of the eight major allies of the Zhou army (the *locus classicus* for which is the "Mu shi" 牧誓 chapter of the *Shangshu*), Inscription H11:68 of the Western Zhou oracle bones discovered in 1977 at Qishan, Shaanxi province reads: 伐蜀 "Attack Shu"; see *Wenwu* 1979.10: 40; a photograph of the shell is on pl. 5, no. 4, and a drawing can be found on p. 43, diagram 11. Since these oracle bones were apparently inscribed by the Zhou during the time of kings Wen and Wu, this inscription demonstrates that at about the time of the Zhou conquest of Shang Shu was indeed an enemy of the Zhou, just as the "Shi fu" indicates.

3

On the Authenticity of the *Bamboo Annals*

Within a recent five-year period, two of America's leading authorities on the history and philology of ancient China published in the *Harvard Journal of Asiatic Studies* (*HJAS*) sharply contradictory appraisals of the authenticity of the *Zhushu jinian* 竹書紀年 or *Bamboo Annals,* a text reportedly recovered in 280 A.D. from the Warring States–period tomb of King Xiang 襄 of Wei 魏 (d. 296 B.C.). David N. Keightley first represented the conservative historiographical perspective, not only rejecting outright the "*Jinben*" 今本 or "Current" version of the text as "a post-Song fabrication," but arguing also that the "*Guben*" 古本 or "Ancient" version of the text, reconstituted by scholars such as Zhu Youzeng 朱右曾 and Wang Guowei 王國維 on the basis of quotations in various pre-Song works, is "probably" of little historiographical value for the Shang and Western Zhou periods.[1] He concluded that even if it were possible to reconstitute the text exactly as it was put into the tomb of King Xiang of Wei, this would still represent only what was known, or was thought to have been known, at the turn of the third century B.C. about a period that ended half a millennium before. Five years later, David S. Nivison, in his complex analysis of the chronology of the Western Zhou dynasty, argued not only that the *Bamboo Annals* is a generally valuable source for the history and chronology of ancient China, but that the "Current" *Bamboo Annals* itself is a more or less faithful recreation of the original tomb-text, which in turn contained a more or less faithful chronology of the Shang and especially the Western Zhou.[2] According to Nivison, the "Current" *Bamboo Annals* contains most of the raw data required to reconstruct Western Zhou chronology, but this data had been subject to an editorial process that included at least eight discrete stages, six before the text even entered the tomb in the early third century B.C. and two more after it was exhumed in the late third century A.D. He believed that by "undoing" the changes that had been made at each of

69

these putative stages, it would be possible finally to arrive at what must have been the original annals of the period.

It goes without saying that if a synthetic chronological account of the late Shang and Western Zhou period such as that contained in the "Current" *Bamboo Annals* could be accepted as authentic to at least some degree, it would be a historiographical source of almost unparalleled value. (Indeed, only the *Shiji* 史記 of Sima Qian 司馬遷 would be of comparable importance.) But do we know enough about the period in question even to evaluate critically the authenticity of this source? Certainly, Nivison's arguments for the authenticity of the data he has utilized in one fashion or another in his chronological reconstruction are open to suspicions of circularity. His chronology must be correct for his interpretation of a multi-stage editorial process in the making of the *Bamboo Annals* to be correct, and, the same is true, to some extent, in reverse. But, it is never acceptable methodology to prove one unknown with another unknown. Keightley, on the other hand, has suggested several features that he would look for in an authentic text of this sort. Among these, certainly the most important is "the appearance in the annals of events, persons or phrases, whose historical existence is confirmed, not by later Zhou accounts, but by contemporary. . . inscriptions."[3] Apparently, it was his failure to find "touchstones" of this sort in the "Ancient" *Bamboo Annals* that caused him to question the historicity of the text.

SOME AUTHENTICATING "TOUCHSTONES" IN THE TEXT

It is true in the case of the Shang period, with which Keightley was evidently most concerned, that no such touchstones are to be found in the text. This is due in part to the nature of the annals themselves, which, as Keightley has noted and as we might expect of any historical document, grow increasingly less detailed the further into antiquity they go. But it is due also in part to the nature of the Shang inscriptional evidence, which provides very few personal names, aside from recipients of sacrifice which we would not expect to find in an annalistic record of the dynasty, and, especially after the "New School" reforms of Zu Jia 祖甲, very few records of any individuated events. When we come down to the Western Zhou dynasty, however, the quantity and nature of the bronze inscriptional record provides far more comparative evidence, and we find that there are at least a pair of names in the "Ancient" *Bamboo Annals* that correspond with this evidence. For instance, it is by now well-known that the *Bamboo Annals* account of the Gong He 共和 interregnum during King Li's exile at Zhi 彘 as a period during which Elder He 和 of Gong 共 reigned in the king's absence, is preferable to the *Shiji* interpretation of the period as a "joint harmony" reign of Duke Mu 穆 of Shao 召 and Duke Ding 定 of Zhou 周.[4] While this has indeed been verified by Western Zhou bronze inscriptions, it could be objected that it is not an absolute touchstone because both the *Zhuangzi* 莊子 and the *Lüshi chunqiu* 呂氏春代 refer obliquely to an Elder of Gong.[5] The same objection could be raised against the mention of a battle during King Li's reign involving a Guo Zhong 虢仲 and the Huaiyi 淮夷. Although this battle is confirmed in the "Guo Zhong 虢仲盨 *xu*," a vessel typologically datable to King Li's reign, it is also noted in the "Dongyi zhuan" 東夷傳 chapter of the *Hou-Han shu* 後漢書 and does not in itself add to the historical record of the period.[6]

But it was in his failure even to consider the "Current" *Bamboo Annals* that Keightley overlooked what can only be considered unquestionable touchstones in the text. Not only does the "Current" *Bamboo Annals* also contain the same references to Gong He and Guo Zhong as the "Ancient" version of the text, but there are at least a pair of other references that are confirmed only in the bronze inscriptional record. The first of these touchstones is an entry in the "Current" *Bamboo Annals* for the reign of King Xuan 宣, in particular, for the fifth year of that reign, recording that "Commander Jifu 吉甫 led troops to attack the Xianyun 玁狁 as far as the Great Plain." This same campaign is commemorated by Jifu 吉父 in the inscription on the "Xi Jia 兮甲盤 *pan*," certainly a King Xuan-period vessel.[7] It could be objected that this Jifu was widely known to have been associated with a campaign against the Xianyun by virtue of his mention in the *Shijing* poem "Liu yue" 六月 (Mao 177). But what is notable is that the "Xi Jia *pan*" is dated, like the "Current" *Bamboo Annals* entry, to the *fifth year*.[8] Nothing in the traditional record could explain a coincidence such as this.

Even more striking, however, is a comparison of the "Ban *gui*" 班段, certainly a middle Western Zhou vessel, with the "Current" *Bamboo Annals* account of King Mu's 穆 reign.[9] The "Ban *gui*" contains a lengthy inscription recording both a command to attack the "eastern countries" and the record that the campaign had concluded successfully three years later.

> It was the eighth month, first auspiciousness, at Zongzhou, *jiaxu* (day 11); the king commanded the Lord of Mao to succeed Duke Cheng of Guo in protecting the king's position, being a model to the four borderlands, and governing Fan, Shu, and Chao; and commanded that he be awarded tinkle-bells and a bridle.

The king commanded the Duke of Mao to take the states'
leaders and the infantry and chariotry and halberd-men to attack
the eastern countries [and?] the Yan belligerents. The king commanded the Lord of Wu, saying: "Take your division and go along
to the left of Father Mao." The king commanded the Lord of Lü,
saying: "Take your division and go along to the right of Father
Mao." Qian commanded, saying: Take your kinsmen and follow
father on campaign; go out of the city and protect father's person."

In three years we pacified the eastern countries, there being
none who do not submit to Heaven's majesty. . . .

Ban bowed and touched his head to the ground, saying " . . .
May sons and grandsons eternally treasure [it]."

Two figures appear prominently in this inscription, Duke Ban 班 of Mao 毛,
the caster of this vessel, and his son Qian 趩, the apparent commander of the
campaign. It has often been noted in studies of this inscription that Mao Ban
can be identified with a Duke Ban of Mao mentioned both in the "Current"
Bamboo Annals account of King Mu's reign and also in the *Mu tianzi zhuan*
穆天子傳, another text said to have been recovered from the tomb of King
Xiang of Wei.[10]

Twelfth year, Duke Ban of Mao, Duke Li of Gong and Duke Gu of
Feng led troops following the king to attack the Quanrong.

Although this campaign by Duke Ban against the Quanrong 犬戎, a western
enemy of the Zhou, is clearly not the referent for the inscription's campaign
against the "eastern countries," just such an eastern campaign is recorded in
two separate entries of the *Bamboo Annals* for the thirty-fifth and thirty-seventh
years of King Mu.

Thirty-fifth year, the men of Jing entered Xu. Lord Qian of
Mao led the troops, defeating the men of Jing at Zi.

Thirty-seventh year, (they) greatly raised the nine armies and
proceeded east to the Nine Rivers. Stacking turtles and alligators
into a bridge, they then attacked Yue as far as Yu. The men of Jing
came to pay tribute.

Lord Qian 遷 of Mao, a figure not mentioned elsewhere in the historical
record, is identified by commentators as the son of Duke Ban of Mao,[11] and
is almost certainly identifiable with Qian 趩, the son of Ban in the "Ban *gui*"
inscription.[12] What is more, the indication here of a three-year duration for

this eastern campaign matches exactly the inscriptional evidence. This then would seem to be the touchstone for which Keightley sought, and it certainly suggests that the "Current" *Bamboo Annals* is not the shameless forgery it is usually claimed to be.

Even if it were possible to continue in this vein, discussing each name and every event mentioned in the "Current" *Bamboo Annals*, and due to the limitations of our information concerning either the Shang or Western Zhou dynasties it is not possible, it would be a task requiring more diligence than I possess and more space than the editors could reasonably grant.[13] Besides, a single well-chosen and thoroughly analyzed example can often be more enlightening than hundreds of undigested (and, for the reader, perhaps indigestible) examples. Therefore, I propose instead to examine in detail just the "Current" *Bamboo Annals* account of the death of King Wu 武 of Zhou, an event of no little significance for the history of both the Shang and Western Zhou dynasties and one for which there is reasonably abundant comparative information from the *Shiji* and even from occasional references in pre-Qin texts. Before examining the "Current" *Bamboo Annals* itself, however, it will be necessary to consider all of the evidence regarding the date of King Wu's death found in sources through the late third century A.D., when the bamboo strips of the text were discovered and arranged by some of the most renowned scholars of the age. When we finally do turn to the account of this event contained in the "Current" *Bamboo Annals*, I am confident that we will be able to resurrect an important textual source for the history of early China, not from the tomb whence it first came just over 1700 years ago but from a too rigid iconoclasm of the "modern" age.

KING WU'S DEATH TWO YEARS AFTER THE CONQUEST OF SHANG

One of the most important discrepancies among proposed chronologies of Shang-Zhou history concerns the date of King Wu's death. All pre-Qin and Western Han sources variously imply that after his conquest of Shang, King Wu reigned for only two years before dying. The *locus classicus* for this chronology is the "Jin teng" 金縢 chapter of the *Shangshu*, a *jinwen* 今文 text the pedigree of which has been questioned but which was almost certainly composed no later than the Spring and Autumn period. This text begins:

> Two years after having conquered Shang the king was sick and uncomfortable.

Then comes a detailed account of a divination performed by the Duke of Zhou on behalf of King Wu, followed by an extremely terse mention of the king's death.

> The king on the next day then improved. After King Wu had died . . .[14]

Two problems appear in this account. First, despite the implication that King Wu's sickness and death were causally related, the text does not explicitly state that his death occurred in the same "second" year after the conquest as his sickness. Second, the phrase "*ji ke Shang er nian*" 既克商二年 is somewhat ambiguous, susceptible of being interpreted either cardinally, "two years after having conquered Shang" or ordinally, "the second year after having conquered Shang" (i.e., one year after the conquest).

The first of these problems, whether King Wu's death occurred in this second year, is addressed positively in the "Fengshan shu" 封禪書 chapter of Sima Qian's *Shiji*.

> King Wu had conquered Shang for two years; the realm was not yet pacified and he died.[15]

Although this record is also ambiguous as to the interpretation of *er nian* 二年, in a passage in the "Zhou benji" 周本紀 that is abstracted directly from the "Jin teng" chapter of the *Shangshu*, Sima Qian provides a prepositional "after" confirming that it should be read cardinally.

> Two years after already having conquered Yin . . . King Wu became sick. The realm had not yet been [gathered:] pacified and the host of dukes feared and reverently performed divination. The duke of Zhou then exorcised and purified [himself], made of himself a hostage and wished to substitute for King Wu. King Wu recovered, later, however, dying.[16]

This date of King Wu's death two years after his conquest of Shang, which is to say in the third year of the conquest regime, is confirmed in various ways in other early sources. The "Yao lüe" 要略 chapter of the *Huainanzi* 淮南子, a work completed about a generation before the *Shiji*, contains the following account of these years.

> King Wen developed it but did not complete it. King Wu succeeded to King Wen's development, and using the strategy of the Grand Duke drew in light taxes from all and personally took up his weapons

and armor, by way of attacking those without the Way and punishing the unrighteous, and addressed the troops at Muye by way of stepping [up] to the position of Son of Heaven. The realm was not yet settled and the territory within the seas was not yet ordered when King Wu wished to summon King Wen's commanding virtue to cause the Yi and Di each to come and present their wealth. The distant were not yet able to arrive; therefore he instituted three years of mourning, paying audience to King Wen between the two pillars by way of waiting for the distant borderlands. *King Wu reigned three years and then died.*[17]

Still another way of dating this same year is offered in the "Xiao wen" 小文 chapter of the *Guanzi* 管子, a work probably deriving from the late Warring States period.

King Wu attacked Yin, conquering it. In the seventh year [he] died.[18]

Although the dating notation "*qi nian*" 七年, "seventh year," is no less ambiguous than the "*er nian*" of the "Jin teng" account, and seems also to imply a postconquest reign for King Wu longer than the three years of the other sources, that it is actually consistent with them can be deduced by comparison with the immediate pre-conquest "Mandate" chronology of the *Shiji*. This chronology assumes that after his father King Wen had died, King Wu continued to enumerate the years of his own reign according to the year of King Wen's receipt of the "Mandate," and not according to his own year of succession.

Table 3.1
Shiji "Mandate" Chronology

Mandate Year	Event	Year of King Wu
1	King Wen's Declaration of Mandate	
7	Death of King Wen	
9	King Wu's Campaign to Mengjin	2
11	Beginning of Conquest Campaign	4
12	Conquest of Shang	5
	Death of King Wu	7

Since King Wu's reign began four years before the conquest of Shang, his death in the third year after this event would indeed have been in the seventh year of his personal reign.

One other Warring States text, the "Zuo Luo" 作雒 chapter of the *Yi Zhou shu* 逸周書, contains evidence supporting this chronology.

> King Wu conquered Yin and then set up the king's (i.e., Di Xin's) son Lü fu to maintain the Shang sacrifices. He established Guan shu in the east, established Cai shu and Huo shu at Yin to oversee the Yin ministers. After King Wu had returned, in the twelfth month of the next year he died at Hao and was buried at Mount Qi.[19]

This passage too is susceptible of various interpretations, the most common being that King Wu died in the year immediately following the conquest, or even in the year of the conquest itself.[20] This interpretation is contingent on the reference to the year of King Wu's death being directly related to the year of the conquest. But such an interpretation neglects the mention here of King Wu's appointment of Guan shu 管叔, Cai shu 蔡叔, and Huo shu 霍叔, three royal siblings, to oversee the former Shang domain. Two other chapters from the same stratum of the *Yi Zhou shu* explicitly date this appointment to the "thirteenth year."[21] The "Da kuang" 大匡 chapter begins:

> It was the thirteenth year. The king was at Guan. Guan shu himself became the Yin overseer. All of the archer-lords of the eastern domain received awards from the king. The king then visited them in the upper eastern domain.[22]

The "Wen zheng" 文政 chapter begins similarly:

> It was the thirteenth year. The king was at Guan. Guan and Cai opened the altar processional.[23]

Recognizing this thirteenth-year event as the immediate referent of the "Zuo Luo" phrase "after King Wu had returned, in the twelfth month of the next year," it is possible to see that this passage in fact dates King Wu's death to the twelfth month of the fourteenth year. Since, as we have seen above, the *Shiji* dates the conquest to the twelfth year, the "Zuo Luo" is therefore consistent with all of the other early sources in placing King Wu's death two years after the conquest.

KING WU'S DEATH
SIX YEARS AFTER THE CONQUEST

Despite the consensus found in these works of generally accepted historical value, all traditional chronological studies after the Han dynasty portray King

Wu as having reigned for six years after the conquest. The source generally considered the *locus classicus* for this chronology is the "Ming tang" 明堂 chapter of the *Yi Zhou shu*.

> The Duke of Zhou assisted King Wu in attacking [Shang king] Zhou and pacifying the world. Six years after having conquered Zhou, King Wu died.[24]

Although there can be no question as to how this passage is to be interpreted, there is however considerable question as to the date of the text in which it occurs. Above it was stated that the "Zuo Luo" chapter of the same book was written in the mid–Warring States period, which is indeed the period from which the original recension of the *Yi Zhou shu* dates.[25] It had traditionally been thought that the association of the *Yi Zhou shu* with the same discovery of bamboo books from King Xiang of Wei's tomb as produced the *Bamboo Annals*, an association attested in bibliographical sources as early as the "Jingji zhi" 經籍志 chapter of the *Sui shu* 隋書,[26] confirmed this early dating of the text. But more recent research on the nature and textual transmission of the *Yi Zhou shu* has demonstrated conclusively that the present text could not have been recovered from this tomb.

In the first place, the *Yi Zhou shu* was extant as an integral text, known as the *Zhou shu* 周書, throughout the nearly six centuries from King Xiang's burial in 296 B.C. through the opening of the tomb in A.D. 280. Not only is it listed in the "Yiwen zhi" 藝文志 chapter of the *Han shu* 漢書, but it is also quoted by name in such third century B.C. works as the *Han Fei zi* 韓非子, *Zhanguo ce* 戰國策 and *Lüshi chunqiu*, and by such Han dynasty works as the *Shiji*, *Shuo wen jie zi* 說文解字, and Zheng Xuan's 鄭玄 (A.D. 200–127) commentaries on the *Yili* 儀禮 and *Zhouli* 周禮.[27] More important still, a commentary by Kong Zhao 孔晁 (fl. A.D. 266) was added to the text sometime in the middle of the third century A.D., but certainly before the 280 opening of King Xiang's tomb.[28] Of the fifty-nine chapters of the *Yi Zhou shu* still extant, forty-two of them are commented upon by Kong Zhao, and it is significant that all of the Han and pre-Han citations of the text come from this corpus.

In the second place, the "*Zhoushu*" mentioned in the contemporary inventories of the seventy-five *pian* 篇 of texts recovered from the Ji Tomb is one of just four titles listed as constituting nineteen *pian* of "miscellaneous texts" (*zashu* 雜書).[29] Moreover, this text can probably be identified with a *Guwen Zhoushu* 古文周書 twice quoted in Li Shan's 李善 (d. 689) commentary on the *Wenxuan* 文選.[30] These two lengthy quotations are both mythologized narratives about King Mu of the Western Zhou, very similar in both style and content to the *Mu tianzi zhuan* but having no possible parallel in the received version of the *Yi Zhou shu*.

Despite these indications that no part of the now extant *Yi Zhou shu* was recovered from the tomb of King Xiang of Wei, a consideration of its transmission as recorded in the bibliographical treatises of early dynastic histories does confirm an early and persistent association of the text with this burial. After the earliest bibliographic notice of the text in the the *Han shu* "Yiwen zhi," which cites Liu Xiang 劉向 (79–8 B.C.) as having seen a *Zhou shu* in seventy-one *pian*, the *Sui shu* "Jingji zhi" is the first to list a *Zhou shu* in ten *juan* 卷 with a note describing the text as deriving from Jizhong, that is, the tomb in Ji County of present-day Henan in which King Xiang of Wei was buried. The "Jingji zhi" of the *Jiu Tang shu* 舊唐書, on the other hand, lists a *Zhou shu* in eight *juan* with a note describing this text as that of Kong Zhao's commentary.[31] These entries are followed by the "Yiwen zhi" of the *Xin Tang shu* 新唐書 with listings of both a *Jizhong Zhou shu* 汲冢周書 in ten *juan* and a *Kong Zhao zhu Zhou shu* 孔晁注周書 in eight *juan*.[32] Finally, from the "Yiwen zhi" of the *Song shi* 宋史 on,[33] there is only a single entry for a *Jizhong Zhou shu* in ten *juan*. In addition to these bibliographic entries, comments by two early Tang scholars also shed light on the textual history of the *Yi Zhou shu*. Yan Shigu 顏師古 (581–645), commenting on the *Han shu* "Yiwen zhi" listing, noted that at his time only forty-five *pian* of the original seventy-one were still extant.[34] At roughly the same time, however, Liu Zhiji 劉知幾 (661–721) explicitly mentioned in his *Shitong* 史通 that all seventy-one *pian* were still extant.[35] This, combined with the contradictory listings in the bibliographies (and especially in the *Xin Tang shu*), demonstrates that through the Tang there must have existed two separate texts, one in eight *juan* associated with Kong Zhao and one in ten *juan* thought to have come from the Ji County tomb of *Bamboo Annals* renown. The assimilation of the two texts must then have taken place sometime during the Northern Song dynasty. It is safe to assume that of the now extant fifty-nine chapters, the forty-two chapters for which Kong Zhao's commentary exists derive from the Kong Zhao textual tradition. Likewise, it would seem reasonable that those chapters for which there is no commentary must derive from the other textual tradition, that associated with Jizhong.

Turning now to the case of the "Ming tang" chapter in particular, I believe we can gain some indication of the origin of this "Jizhong" textual tradition of the *Yi Zhou shu*. It is significant first that this chapter belongs to the group of seventeen extant chapters not commented upon by Kong Zhao, suggesting that it was not yet extant by the middle of the third century A.D., and ought therefore to derive from the "Jizhong" textual tradition. It is, however, equally significant that the text blatantly imitates the "Ming tang wei" 明堂位 chapter of the *Liji* 禮記, a fact that suggests that it could date no earlier than the Eastern Han,[36] and certainly not as early as the 296 B.C. interment of King Xiang of Wei. If we are correct, on the one hand, in associating this chapter with the "Jizhong" textual tradition and also, on the other hand, in rejecting the archaeological provenance of a Warring States tomb text for it, then I think we are forced to conclude that this "Ming tang" chapter, and perhaps the entire "Jizhong" textual tradition, must have originated at about the time of the tomb's discovery and perhaps within the circle of scholars engaged to work on the *Bamboo Annals* and other unearthed texts.

While the "Ming tang" statement that King Wu died "six years" after his conquest of Shang thus undoubtedly derives from a late "forgery," it is not entirely without precedent. Indeed, it represents well the consensus of the scholarly world as of the late third century A.D. This consensus had its origins in the chronological studies of Liu Xin 劉歆 (46 B.C.–A.D. 23), studies which are now almost unanimously considered to have been mistaken but which were generally accepted by most traditional historians. With regard to the date of King Wu's death, in particular, Liu correlated a tradition recorded in the *Da Dai Liji* 大戴禮記 that King Wu was born when King Wen was only fifteen years old, with another tradition recorded in the *Xiao Dai Liji* 小戴禮記 that King Wen died at the age of ninety-seven and King Wu died at the age of ninety-three.[37] From this, and correlating also what he knew about the chronology of the immediate conquest period, Liu concluded that King Wu must have died seven years after the conquest.

> King Wen was fifteen when King Wu was born, and died nine years after receiving the mandate. Four years after he died, King Wu conquered Shang, his age at the time of the conquest being eighty-six. Seven years later he died. Therefore, the "Wen Wang shizi" chapter of the *Liji* says, "King Wen was ninety-seven when he died, and King Wu was ninety-three when he died." In all, King Wu reigned for eleven years.[38]

This chronological reconstruction has been roundly and properly criticized by modern scholars. Not only is the *Liji* tradition regarding the ages of kings Wen and Wu at their deaths of dubious historicity,[39] but even if it were to be accepted, Liu's own analysis is internally inconsistent. If King Wen were indeed fifteen at the time of King Wu's birth, then he would have been the elder by fourteen years. When he died at the age of ninety-seven, King Wu would have been eighty-three. And when King Wu conquered Shang four years later, he would have been eighty-seven, not eighty-six as stated by Liu. This in turn means that the length of his reign after the conquest would had to have been six years, not seven. Recent critics of Liu such as Gu Jiegang 顧頡剛 (1983–1980) and David Nivison have given various explanations for this internal contradiction,[40] but it was probably due simply to an attempt on Liu's part to reconcile this tradition with at least one of the early sources containing a record of King Wu's death. In this case, he undoubtedly selected the *Guanzi*, which, as noted above, seems to state that King Wu died seven years after the conquest.

Gu and Nivison were by no means the first to notice the internal contradiction in Liu Xin's chronology for the death of King Wu. By the middle of the third century, Wang Su 王肅 (189–256) had corrected Liu's calculations, becoming the first scholar of record to state, albeit rather circuitously, that King Wu died six years after the conquest.

> King Wen was fifteen when King Wu was born. He was ninety-seven when he died, nine years after receiving the mandate. King Wu was then eighty-three. In the thirteenth year he attacked (Shang king) Zhou. In the next year, at the age of eighty-eight, he became ill. He was ninety-three when he died.[41]

Not long after Wang Su contributed this note to the confusion of Western Zhou chronology, Huangfu Mi 皇甫謐 (215–282), another great synthesizer of China's early history, also subscribed to this reconstruction placing King Wu's death six years after the conquest.

> In his second year, King Wu reviewed the troops as far as Mengjin. In the fourth year, he first attacked Yin, becoming the Son of Heaven. . . . In the winter of the tenth year, the king died at Hao.[42]

In short then, slightly more than two centuries after its dubious origin in the chronological reconstruction of Liu Xin, this tradition that King Wu died six years after his conquest of Shang had been accepted by two of the greatest scholars of the third century, Wang Su and Huangfu Mi, and must have been regarded by their successors as an established fact. It is thus no coincidence that the "Ming tang" chapter of the *Yi Zhou shu*, which we have suggested must have been composed at about the time of Huangfu Mi's death (i.e., 282) or shortly thereafter, should state explicitly that "six years after having conquered Zhou, King Wu died." It is also no coincidence that this same tradition is also evident in the *Bamboo Annals*, which was discovered and arranged at precisely this time. It is the story of this arrangement to which we now turn, and which will demonstrate beyond doubt that the text of the "Current" *Bamboo Annals*, at least insofar as its account of the death of King Wu is concerned, has been transmitted from the late third century A.D. to the present with absolute fidelity.

THE "CURRENT" *BAMBOO ANNALS* ACCOUNT OF KING WU'S DEATH

It will come as no surprise to scholars who suspect the authenticity of the "Current" *Bamboo Annals* that its present arrangement indicates that King Wu died in the sixth year after the conquest. The annalistic entry for the conquest comes in the twelfth year of King Wu's reign, generally consistent with the *Shiji* and most historically reliable sources,[43] and the entry recording his death is found in the seventeenth year. Not only is this latter record inconsistent with the authentic tradition that King Wu died two years after the conquest, but it is important to note that it also differs slightly from the third century A.D. tradition putting King Wu's death six years after, which is to say, in the seventh year after, the conquest. The anomaly of this inconsistency should cause us to examine more carefully the text of these annals. When we do, we find that the inconsistency has been caused by the transposition of a single bamboo strip from the reign of King Cheng 成, the second king of the dynasty, to the reign of King Wu.

The strip in question contains entries for fifteenth and sixteenth years and the opening year-notation for a seventeenth year, a passage forty graphs (inclusive of two separation spaces) long. This is precisely the number of graphs on a single bamboo strip of the original *Bamboo Annals* as they are described by Xun Xu 荀勗 (d. A.D. 289), one of the scholars responsible for the deciphering of these texts.

> They were all bamboo strips bound with silk cords. On the basis of my personal examination, the strips were two feet, four inches long of the "old" measure, were written in ink and had *forty graphs per strip*.[44]

Including the immediately preceding and succeeding entries, the passage reads (and see fig. 3.1 for a reconstruction of how the passage must have looked on the bamboo strips):

ANNALS OF KING WU, FOURTEENTH YEAR

Original King Wu Entry　　　　　　　　Transposed Strip

Fourteenth year, the king was sick.
The accomplished Duke of Zhou
prayed (for him) at the suburban
altar, made the "Jin teng,"

Fifteenth year, Sushen shi came to
audience. (The king) first hunted
in the borderland mountains. He
made an announcement at the city
of Mei. In the winter, the nine caul-
drons were moved to Luo.
Sixteenth year, Jizi came to court.
In the autumn, the royal troops
destroyed Pugu.
Seventeenth year,

and commanded the crown-prince
Song in the eastern palace. In the
winter, twelfth month, the king
died. He was fifty-four years old.

It will be noted that the sickness of King Wu and the Duke of Zhou's consequent writing of the "Jin teng," said in that text to have occurred two years
after the conquest, are here attributed to the fourteenth year, precisely two
years after the entry for the conquest in the twelfth year. This offers one more
confirmation for the cardinal interpretation of "*er nian*" suggested above. But,
as we have already noted, it is implied in the "Jin teng" chapter of the *Shangshu*
and explicitly stated in the "Fengshan shu" chapter of the *Shiji* that King Wu
died in the same year. This suggests that the record of King Wu's death, here
separated by exactly one bamboo strip, should follow immediately after the
mention of the Duke of Zhou's intercession on behalf of King Wu. When
this forty-graph passage with its entries for fifteenth, sixteenth, and seventeenth years is removed, then the record of King Wu's death becomes just one
part of the long annal for the fourteenth year. Not only does this restore the
death to the same year as the illness, but more important, it also accords with
the reliable pre-Qin tradition that King Wu's death came just two years after
the conquest.

　　Suggestive as this is, it is when we turn to the annals of King Cheng's
reign that the mistaken transposition of this strip becomes irrefutably evident.

It cannot be mere coincidence that through the first eighteen years of the reign of King Cheng, each year is provided with an annalistic entry, with the notable exception of the fifteenth, sixteenth and seventeenth years—precisely those years recorded on the strip we have suggested was transposed. Still more important than this negative evidence, however, there are at least two points of decisive positive evidence tying the contents of the transposed strip to this lacuna.

First, within the forty-graph passage itself, the mention of an "announcement at the city of Mei" in the fifteenth year has been interpreted by all commentators as an oblique reference to the "Jiu gao" 酒誥 chapter of the *Shangshu*, which is explicitly set in this city.[45] It is well-known that since the Song dynasty there has been considerable debate over whether this text, like the "Kang gao" 康誥 chapter of the same book, should be ascribed to King Wu or to the Duke of Zhou speaking on behalf of King Cheng. This is not the place to review this debate in detail, but in the absence of any persuasive historical argument to the contrary (as opposed to the philosophical arguments of the Song neo-Confucian adherents of a King Wu dating for the text), the ascription of the text to King Cheng in the *Zuo zhuan* 左傳 (Ding 定 4), the "Preface to the *Shu*" (*Shu xu* 書序), and throughout the *Shiji*, indeed in all pre-Song sources, seems to me sufficient evidence to accept the King Cheng dating.[46] And if this "announcement at the city of Mei" does indeed refer to the "Jiu gao," then it goes without saying that at least this phrase of the passage in question does not belong in the annals of King Wu.

Second, the next phrase of the forty-graph passage, "in the winter, the nine caldrons were moved to Luo," is entirely anachronistic for the reign of King Wu. From the "Shao gao" 召誥 and "Luo gao" 洛誥 chapters of the *Shangshu* it is apparent that the site of the city at Luo had not even been selected until the seventh year of the Duke of Zhou's regency, an event also noted in the *Bamboo Annals* for that year. Certainly, King Wu would not have moved the caldrons to a city that did not yet exist. But when we examine this record in the context of events transpiring in the eighteenth year of King Cheng, it can be seen to be closely related. There it is recorded that "in the first month, the king went to Luo, settling (*ding* 定) the caldrons." The use of the word "*ding*," which is part of a word-family including such words as *ding* 鼎, "caldron," *zheng* 正, "upright, correct," and *zhen* 貞, "to divine," indicates a ritual emplacement of the caldrons.[47] Based on the present ascription of the moving of the caldrons to King Wu's reign, more than twenty years would have elapsed before this ritual was performed. By correctly appropriating this phrase to the winter of King Cheng's fifteenth year, however, only slightly more than two years would have elapsed, a far more likely sequence of events.

Fig. 3.1. Reconstruction of annals of King Wu, 14th year

Fig. 3.2. Reconstruction of annals of King Cheng, years 13 to 18

Fig. 3.1

Strip 2:

命王世子誦于東宮冬十有二月王陟年五十四

Transposed Strip:

十五年肅慎氏來賓初狩方岳誥于沫邑冬遷九鼎于洛　十六年箕子來朝秋王師滅蒲姑　十七年

Strip 1:

十四年王有疾周文公禱于壇墠作金縢

Fig. 3.2

Strip 2:

多洛邑告成　十八年春正月王如洛邑定鼎鳳凰見遂有事于河

Transposed Strip:

十五年肅慎氏來賓初狩方岳誥于沫邑冬遷九鼎于洛　十六年箕子來朝秋王師滅蒲姑　十七年

Strip 1:

十三年王師會齊侯魯侯伐戎夏六月魯大禘于周公廟　十四年齊師圍曲城克之

RECONSTRUCTION OF ANNALS OF KING CHENG, YEARS THIRTEEN–EIGHTEEN

Strip One

Thirteenth year, the royal troops joined with the Archer-lord of Qi and the Archer-Lord of Lu to attack the belligerents. In the summer, sixth month, Lu grandly performed the Di-ritual at the temple of the Duke of Zhou.

Fourteenth year, the troops of Qi surrounded the citadel of Qu, conquering it.

Transposed Strip

Fifteenth year, Sushen shi came to audience. [The king] first hunted in the borderland mountains. He made an announcement at the city of Mei. In the winter, the nine caldrons were moved to Luo.

Sixteenth year, Jizi came to court. In the autumn, the royal troops destroyed Pugu.

Seventeenth year,

Strip Two

in the winter, the city Luo was announced to be completed.

Eighteenth year, in the spring, first month, the king went to the city Luo, settling the caldrons. Phoenixes appeared and thereupon there was a sacrifice to the river.

The record of King Cheng's ritual "settling" of the caldrons at Luo in the first month of his eighteenth year also suggests further evidence that the annals of his reign for these years are incomplete. As these annals are presently constituted, the last entry of King Cheng's fourteenth year reads, "in the winter, the city of Luo was announced to be completed." It is not impossible that the Zhou would have waited a full year after the completion of the city to move the caldrons there, and then more than two more years to perform a ritual "settling" of them, but it does not seem very likely. I would suggest instead that this phrase now attributed to the winter of King Cheng's fourteenth year must originally have been located at the top of the bamboo strip containing the entry for the ritual activity in King Cheng's eighteenth year. In this way, it would continue the entry introduced by the thirty-eighth, thirty-ninth and fortieth graphs, "*shiqi nian*" 十七年, "seventeenth year," of the transposed bamboo strip (see the reconstruction of the bamboo strips in question, figs. 3.1–2).[48] This further clarifies the sequence of events relating to the completion

Fig. 3.3. Reconstruction of annals of King Cheng, years 1 to 14

元年春正月王即位命冢宰周文公總百官庚午周公誥諸侯于皇門夏六月葬武王于畢秋王加元服

武庚以殷叛周文公出居于東　二年奄人徐人及淮夷入于邶以叛秋大雷電以風王逆周文公于郊

遂伐殷　三年王師滅殷殺武庚祿父遷殷民于衛遂伐奄滅蒲姑　四年春正月初朝于廟夏四月初

嘗麥王師伐淮夷遂入奄　五年春正月王在奄遷其君于蒲姑夏五月王至自奄遷殷民于洛邑遂營

成周　六年大蒐于岐陽　七年周公復政于王春二月王如豐三月召康公如洛度邑甲子周文公誥

多士于成周遂城東都王如東都諸侯來朝冬王歸自東都立高圉廟　八年春正月王初莅阼親政命

魯侯禽父齊侯伋遷庶殷于魯作象舞冬十月王師滅唐遷其民于杜　九年春正月有事于太廟初用

勾蕭慎氏來朝王使榮伯錫蕭慎氏命　十年王命唐叔虞為侯越裳氏來朝周文公出居于豐　十一

年春正月王如豐唐叔虞嘉禾王命唐叔歸禾于周文公王命周平公治東都　十二年王師燕師城韓

王錫韓侯命　十三年王師會齊侯魯侯伐戎夏六月魯大禘于周公廟　十四年齊師圍曲城克之

of the city Luo. Earlier, in the eleventh year of King Cheng's reign, Bo Qin 伯禽, the son of the Duke of Zhou, had been commanded to "govern" (*zhi* 治), i.e., to bring to completion, the "eastern capital." With completion imminent, in the winter of the fifteenth year the caldrons were re-located there. After two final seasons of work, in the winter of the seventeenth year the city was announced to be completed. A month or so later, King Cheng himself came east to consecrate the new city. Closely tying the completion of the city and King Cheng's consecration of it, as this emendation does, seems more reasonable than the more than three-year interval required by the present arrangement.

The two points raised above seem to me to be incontrovertible evidence tying a substantial portion of the passage in question to King Cheng's reign. It may be asked if the other portions can also be related to that reign. Although the relations are not as absolute, a consideration of each of the phrases in turn will show them to be more appropriate in King Cheng's reign than in King Wu's.

The first phrase of the passage in question reports that "Sushen shi came to audience." In the annals for the ninth year of King Cheng, there is a similar entry.

> Ninth year, Sushen shi came to court. The king caused the Elder of Rong to award Sushen shi a command.

Although the fifteenth year court visit could conceivably have taken place in King Wu's reign, the twelve-year interval between visits thereby indicated being well within the activity span of an individual, I would contend that the difference in the wording of the entries indicates that the visit in the ninth year of King Cheng must have come first. By this I do not refer to the subtle difference between the terms "coming to court" (*lai chao* 來朝) and "coming to audience" (*lai bin* 來賓), which I am sure must also be significant but the significance of which I have no means of interpreting. Instead, I believe that the record in the ninth year entry that Sushen shi was "awarded a command" is the type of response we should expect out of a monarch when an independent state first pledges itself to an alliance. The unelaborated record in the fifteenth year, on the other hand, where it is simply recorded that Sushen shi came to "audience," seems to bespeak a prior relationship.

With regard to the second phrase, "[the king] first hunted in the borderland mountains," there are at least two reasons why it is more appropriate to King Cheng's reign than to King Wu's. First, in the entry for King Wu's twelfth year, after recounting events of the conquest campaign, the "Current" *Bamboo Annals* records that in the fourth month King Wu returned to Feng, performed a sacrifice in the great temple, arranged for the supervision of the former Shang territory, and "then hunted in Guan." While it may be objected that the adverbial "first" of the phrase in question refers only to hunting in the "borderland mountains," there can be no doubt that this was not King Wu's first hunting trip. In contrast, however, if we examine the remarkably complete annals for the first fourteen years of King Cheng's reign, we find that there is no entry recording a hunting expedition before this fifteenth year. It is not until the nineteenth year that such a record is found, and it is significant that that record is not qualified as being the king's "first" hunt. Second, and perhaps even more persuasive, this record was traditionally interpreted, and may indeed have been intended in the mind of the Warring States annalist responsible for the final redaction of the *Bamboo Annals*, to refer to the king's performance of the *feng* 封 and *shan* 禪 sacrifices atop Mount Tai, with the word *shou* 狩 interpreted as "an inspection tour."[49] It is significant that in the "Fengshan shu" chapter of the *Shiji*, Sima Qian explicitly notes that King Wu died before having had a chance to perform these sacrifices. He also notes, on the other hand, that the sacrifices did indeed begin with King Cheng.[50] Thus, whether the word *shou* of this phrase be interpreted in the archaic Chinese sense of "to hunt" or as "an inspection tour," as in classical Chinese, there is no reason to associate it with King Wu's reign while there is reason to associate it with King Cheng's reign.

After the entries recording the announcement at Mei and the moving of the caldrons to Luo, the next entry is dated to the sixteenth year and states that "Jizi came to court." It is well known from the "Hong fan" 洪範 chapter of the *Shangshu* that Jizi did have an audience with King Wu, after which time he is said to have gone into voluntary exile in what is now Korea. This must have confirmed the belief of the late third-century A.D. philologists charged with arranging the bamboo strips of the text that the strip containing this entry belonged in King Wu's reign. After all, if Jizi had gone to Korea after his audience with King Wu, how could he have had a similar audience with King Cheng? But, the audience between Jizi and King Wu is explicitly dated in the "Hong fan" to the thirteenth year of King Wu, a date confirmed in the "Zhou benji" chapter of the *Shiji* and elsewhere.[51] If we are to place any stock in these ancient traditions, it is hard to imagine that Jizi could have traveled to Korea and back within three years for a second audience with King Wu. Whether he would have returned seventeen years later for an audience with King Cheng, we can only conjecture. But, if we are to give any credence to the year notations of these entries, this record of a sixteenth year court audience by Jizi is at least as appropriate in the reign of King Cheng as in that of King Wu.

The last phrase of the passage in question, the record in the autumn of the sixteenth year that the "royal troops destroyed Pugu," also seems more appropriate to King Cheng's reign. As in the case of Sushen shi's court reception, there is a similar entry elsewhere in the annals of King Cheng's reign recording a battle against Pugu. In the third year of that reign (actually the third year of the Duke of Zhou's regency), in addition to suppressing the rebellion of the Shang scion Wu Geng, the "royal troops" also "attacked Yan and destroyed Pugu." Although the word "*mie*" 滅 used in both of these accounts suggests the utter destruction, indeed the extermination, of this state, its occurrence in two separate entries logically requires a less severe interpretation. This is true regardless of the sequence of these entries. Granting this, I would point out, however, that according to the present arrangement of the text, Pugu was "destroyed" twice within five years. This is not impossible, but it is implausible. Moreover, the record in the thirteenth year of King Cheng that "the royal troops joined with the Archer-lord of Qi and the Archer-lord of Lu to attack the belligerents" would seem to be related to this sixteenth year destruction of Pugu, which was a state within the territory of Qi.

THE REASON FOR
THE "CURRENT" *BAMBOO ANNALS* ARRANGEMENT

One might reasonably ask why, given all of these associations of the passage in question with King Cheng's reign, and given the obvious lack of one strip as the annals of that reign are now arranged, this strip was mislocated. Certainly the distinguished group of scholars charged with reconstructing the text, possibly including Du Yu 杜預 (222–284), the renowned commentator of the *Zuo zhuan*, understood the oblique reference to the creation of the "Jiu gao," which they most certainly would have attributed to King Cheng.[52] Of course, the mention of Jizi's court reception probably confirmed them in their belief that this strip belonged in the annals of King Wu. But the real cause of their mistake in arranging the bamboo strips lay in two separate traditions regarding the chronology of the early Western Zhou dynasty. The first of these held that King Wu died six years after his conquest of Shang. As discussed in some detail above, by the last quarter of the third century A.D., this tradition had already been accepted as an established fact. The philologists and historians charged with arranging the text of the *Bamboo Annals* would surely have sought any means of interpreting this new source so as to accord with the accepted chronology. By coincidence, the annal for the fourteenth year of King Wu, recording first his illness and then his death, was written on two separate bamboo strips, each of which could be read independently. By still more coincidence, a third bamboo strip recorded annals for a fifteenth and sixteenth year and the year notation for a seventeenth year, and mentioned figures and events plausibly related with King Wu's reign. When this strip was inserted between the two strips recording King Wu's illness and death, the year of his death was changed from the fourteenth year to the seventeenth year, *the sixth year after* the twelfth year conquest. Although even this arrangement of the text was somewhat inconsistent with the tradition that King Wu died *six years after* the conquest, due to the ambiguity of the Chinese language in which numbers can be interpreted either cardinally or ordinally, this must have been close enough to satisfy the editors of the *Bamboo Annals*.

The force of this single third-century chronological tradition was undoubtedly reason enough for the editors of the text to transpose this bamboo strip from the annals of King Cheng to those of King Wu. They must have been absolutely convinced of the accuracy of their arrangement when they noticed that it also substantiated a second popular tradition regarding the chronology of the Western Zhou, that the reign of King Mu, the fifth king of the dynasty, began exactly one hundred years after the beginning of the dynasty. This tradition is first implied in the "Lü xing" 呂刑 chapter of the *Shangshu*, a late *jinwen* text probably composed in the Warring States period, and is also mentioned in the *Lunheng* 論衡 of Wang Chong 王充 (c. A.D. 27–97).[53] By the middle of the third century A.D., the implications of this tradition for the reign-by-reign chronology of the Western Zhou must already have been noticed and considered quite important.

At the beginning of the Eastern Han, Liu Xin had explicitly noted that beginning with King Zhao 昭, the fourth king of the dynasty, there were no records for the lengths of reign of the various Western Zhou kings.[54] Despite this, in the third quarter of the third century, Huangfu Mi cited a tradition that King Zhao had reigned for fifty-one years.[55] Although it is not possible to specify the person or source responsible for this tradition, and although Huangfu Mi was certainly unaware of how it had originated, it is however possible to demonstrate how it was derived. A combination of three different chronological records in the *Shiji*, that King Wu died two years after the conquest, that the Duke of Zhou ruled as regent for seven years after King Wu's death, and that during the rule of kings Cheng and Kang 康, the third king of the dynasty, there was forty years of peace, which must have been interpreted as the sum total of these two reigns,[56] suggested that forty-nine years had elapsed from the time of the conquest, which could naturally be considered as the beginning of the dynasty, until the beginning of King Zhao's reign. Then, in order to substantiate the tradition that King Mu's reign began exactly one hundred years after the beginning of the dynasty, a simple subtraction of this original forty-nine year-period from the total of one hundred years indicated that King Zhao reigned for fifty-one years.

Table 3.2
Derivation of Tradition that King Zhao Reigned 51 Years

Reign	Length
Beginning of dynasty through Mu	100
Post-conquest King Wu	-2
Regency of Duke of Zhou	-7
Cheng and Kang period of peace	-40
King Zhao	51

Despite Huangfu Mi's acceptance of this fifty-one-year reign length for King Zhao, since he did not accept the *Shiji* evidence regarding the year of King Wu's death, in his own *Diwang shiji* 帝王世紀 it was necessary to offer a radically different chronology of this period. To the fifty-one-year reign of King Zhao and the six (or seven, if the conquest year itself is included) years he believed King Wu reigned after the conquest, Huangfu added the twenty-six years that had traditionally been ascribed to King Kang's reign, accounting for eighty-three or eighty-four years between the beginning of the dynasty and the beginning of King Mu's reign. Also attempting to substantiate the hundred-year tradition, he was then forced to shorten the reign of King Cheng to just sixteen years, including also the seven years of the Duke of Zhou's regency.

Table 3.2
Huangfu Mi's One Hundred Year Chronology

Reign	Length
Post-Conquest King Wu	6/7
King Cheng (including 7-year regency)	16
King Kang	26
King Zhao	51
From conquest to beginning of King Mu	99/100

The numerological contortions perpetrated in these chronologies demonstrate better than anything else just how strong this tradition regarding the first year of King Mu's reign must have been in the third century A.D.

When the *Bamboo Annals* were discovered shortly after the writing of Huangfu Mi's *Diwang shiji*, however, an entry recording the death of King Zhao during a campaign against the southern state of Chu 楚 in his nineteenth year, which, parenthetically, is almost certainly confirmed by bronze inscriptions of this reign,[57] made it immediately apparent that the fifty-one year figure for his reign had no basis in fact. Despite this, the editors of the text were not willing to reject the hundred year tradition that was also regarded as an established fact in their intellectual milieu. In addition to indicating a nineteen-year reign for King Zhao, this newly unearthed source also verified the long-standing traditions that King Cheng had reigned for thirty-seven years (including the seven years of the Duke of Zhou's regency) and that King Kang had indeed reigned for twenty-six years. Adding these figures together, eighty-two of the one hundred years preceding King Mu's reign were thought to be accounted for. The tradition therefore required that the beginning of the dynasty, in some sense, had to have been seventeen (counting inclusively) or eighteen (counting exclusively) years before King Cheng's succession. For King Wu to have died in the fourteenth year of his reign, the tradition would have been invalidated.[58] But since, having rearranged the bamboo strips for the reigns of kings Wu and Cheng, they believed that these *Bamboo Annals* indicated that King Wu died in the seventeenth year, by reinterpreting the beginning of the dynasty to refer to the beginning of King Wu's reign, and by counting the years from that point to the beginning of King Mu's reign inclusively, they were also able to substantiate exactly this one-hundred-year tradition.

Table 3.4
The "Current" *Bamboo Annals* One-Hundred Year Chronology

Reign	Years
King Wu's entire reign	17
King Cheng (including 7-year regency)	37
King Kang	26
King Zhao	19
From beginning of Wu to beginning of Mu	99/100

Although the combined reigns of kings Wu, Cheng, Kang, and Zhao thus total only ninety-nine years, once again the ambiguity of the Chinese language with regard to the cardinal and ordinal use of numbers (as well as inclusive and exclusive counting) renders this effectively equivalent to one hundred years. That this is in fact what was in the minds of the arrangers of the text is confirmed by a comment in the "Current" *Bamboo Annals* for the first year of King Mu, stating that "from King Wu through King Mu was one hundred years."[59]

CONCLUSIONS

In conclusion then, from this discussion regarding the year of King Wu's death and particularly the account given in the "Current" *Bamboo Annals*, we have seen two things. We have seen first that King Wu died two years after his conquest of Shang. This is the year agreed upon by all pre-Qin and Western Han sources (i.e., the "Jin teng" chapter of the *Shangshu*, the "Zuo Luo" chapter of the *Yi Zhou shu*, the *Guanzi*, *Huainanzi*, and *Shiji*), and there can be no doubt that it is also the year indicated by the original tomb-text of the *Bamboo Annals*. But we have also seen that the bamboo strips comprising the *Bamboo Annals* were rearranged upon their exhumation in A.D. 280 so as to indicate that King Wu died in the sixth year after the conquest, consistent with a tradition that had begun in the Eastern Han and had become dominant by the time this text was discovered. Does this re-arrangement of the text confirm what most scholars have long believed, that the "Current" *Bamboo Annals* is hopelessly distorted and of little historical value? I think not. In fact, I think this shows quite the opposite to be true. A simple emendation based on proven philological principles has allowed us to reconstitute the original arrangement of the annals. More important still, we have seen that the single misplaced passage is comprised of forty graphs, exactly the number of graphs reported to have been on a single bamboo strip of the text. This demonstrates beyond doubt that at least this one passage is exactly as it came out of the ground in A.D. 280, indeed, exactly as it went into the ground in 296 B.C., with not even a single graph having been added or deleted in the ensuing seventeen centuries of traditional textual transmission. And if even one passage of the text can be proven in this way to be not a "post-Song fabrication," then I would suggest that we must be open to the possibility that the entirety of the "Current" *Bamboo Annals* has been transmitted with similar fidelity. This certainly does not mean that scholars are now free to accept the text uncritically. Indeed, in the case discussed in this paper, it was only after a detailed critical examination that its historical reliability could be recovered. But it does mean that in the future, no serious student of early China will be able to disregard the testimony of the *Bamboo Annals*, even, and perhaps especially, as found in the "Current" version of the text.

NOTES

1. David N. Keightley, "The *Bamboo Annals* and Shang-Chou Chronology," *HJAS* 38.2 (December 1978), 423–38. See pp. 423–24 for references to the works of Zhu Youzeng and Wang Guowei.

2. David S. Nivison, "The Dates of Western Chou," *HJAS* 43.2 (December 1983), 481–580.

3. Keightley, "The *Bamboo Annals* and Shang-Chou Chronology," 437–38.

4. For this entry in the "Ancient" *Bamboo Annals*, see Fan Xiangyong 范祥雍, *Guben Zhushu jinian jijiao dingbu* 古本竹書紀年輯校訂補 (Shanghai: Renmin chubanshe, 1962), 30; for the *Shiji*, see *Shiji* (Beijing: Zhonghua shuju, 1959), 4.144. All subsequent references to the dynastic histories will be to the Zhonghua shuju editions.

5. The "Shi Hui 師zz毀 *gui*" (Shirakawa Shizuka 白川靜, *Kimbun tsūshaku* 金文通釋 [Kobe: *Hakutsuru bijutsukan shi*, 1962–], Vol. 31, inscription 186, p. 740ff; hereafter cited in the form Sh 31.186:740) records Elder He acting in the place of the king; *Zhuangzi* (Sibu beiyao ed.), 9.15b; *Lüshi chunqiu* (Sibu beiyao ed.), 14.16b.

6. Fan Xiangyong, *Guben Zhushu jinian jijiao dingbu*, 30; Guo Zhong *xu*, Sh 25.144:275; *Hou-Han shu*, 85.2808.

7. "Xi Jia *pan*," Sh 32.191:785. The graph *fu* 甫 of literary texts is commonly written as *fu* 父 in bronze inscriptions.

8. Although the date of the campaign is given in the "Current" *Bamboo Annals* as "sixth month" and in the "Xi Jia *pan*" as "third month," the third month date of the inscription refers to the command to begin the campaign. It is apparent from the context of the inscription, however, that the campaign had concluded just at the end of summmer; see the remarks of Wang Guowei quoted at Sh 32.191:789. Thus, the date given in the *Bamboo Annals*, which must refer to the end of the campaign, is consistent with the inscriptional record even to the month.

9. "Ban *gui*" (Sh 15.79:34); see too W.A.C.H. Dobson, *Early Archaic Chinese* (Toronto: University of Toronto Press, 1962), 179–84. This vessel, the inscription of which has been known since the Qing dynasty even though the vessel itself had been lost, was rediscovered in 1972 in a bronze scrapheap in back of the Palace Museum in Peking; see Guo Moruo 郭沫若, "'Ban *gui*' de zai faxian" 班殷的再發現, *Wenwu* 文物 1972.9, 2. Several early studies of the inscription had dated it to the reign of King Cheng (see Guo Moruo, *LiangZhou jinwenci daxi kaoshi* 兩周金文辭大系考釋, [1935; Rev. ed. Beijing: Kexue chubanshe, 1956], 20; Chen

Mengjia 陳夢家, "Xi-Zhou tongqi duandai" 西周銅器斷代, Part 2, *Kaogu xuebao* 考古學報 1955.10, 70), but since Tang Lan's 唐蘭 discussion of the inscription in 1962 ("Xi-Zhou tongqi duandai zhong de 'Kang gong' wenti" 西周銅器斷代中的康宮問題, *Kaogu xuebao* 1962.1, 38), and especially since the rediscovery of the vessel in 1972, there is now a general consensus (even though Guo refused to change his original opinion) that it dates instead to King Mu.

10. *Mu tianzi zhuan* (Sibu beiyao ed.), 4.4a. For the "Current" *Bamboo Annals*, a convenient text with English translation is found in James Legge, *The Chinese Classics: The Shoo King, or the Book of Historical Documents* (1883; rpt. Hong Kong: Hong Kong University Press, 1960, prolegomena, 112–76 (the present entry is found on p. 150). All translations in this paper, however, will be my own.

11. The father-son relationship between Mao Ban and Mao Qian has been noted by commentators of the "Current" *Bamboo Annals*; see, e.g., Lei Xueqi 雷學淇, *Zhushu jinian yizheng* 竹書紀年義證 (rpt. Taipei: Yiwen yinshuguan, 1977), 334 (22.166b).

12. Although this identification has not previously been noticed, there can be no doubt that the graphs *qian*/*ts'ian 遷, "to go, to move," and *qian*/*k'ian 趯/遣, "to send, to move," are cognate. The Qian of the "Ban *gui*" inscription appears also in the inscription on the "Meng *gui*" 孟段 (Sh 15.79:30), where he is called Duke Qian Zhong of Mao 毛公趯仲; see Sh 15.79:30.

13. It has long been known that the chronology of the Eastern Zhou, especially of the states of Liang 梁 (i.e., Wei) and Qi 齊, contained in the *Bamboo Annals* (both "Current" and "Ancient" texts) is preferable to that of the *Shiji*; for a thorough discussion of the value of the *Bamboo Annals* in this regard, see Yang Kuan 楊寬, *Zhanguo shi* 戰國史 (Shanghai: Renmin chubanshe, 1983), 585–92; see too, D.C. Lau, *Mencius* (Harmondsworth: Penguin Books, 1970), 205–13; Jeffrey K. Riegel, "Ju-tzu Hsi 孺子瘨 and the Genealogy of the House of Wei 魏," *Early China* 3 (1977): 46–51. Due to the inability of Sima Qian to present any absolute chronology before 842 B.C., a similar comparison is not possible for the Western Zhou or earlier. It is possible, however, to give a brief statistical description of that portion of the "Current" *Bamboo Annals* concerned with the Western Zhou dynasty. Cataloging the discrete entries under six broad categories, "Royal Appointments, Audiences, and Ritual Activity," "Royal Travels," "Military Affairs," "Notices of Deaths," "Harvest and Meterology" and "Supernatural Portents," the following distribution is obtained.

Reign	Court Activity	Royal Travel	Military Affairs	Death Notices	Harvest Meterol.	Portents
Wu (12–17)	5	2	2	1	1	0
Cheng	21	11	9	2	2	2
Kang	5	2	0	5	0	1
Zhao	1	0	2	1	4	1
Mu	10	7	7	4	0	0
Gong	1	0	1	1	0	0
Yih	0	1	3	1	2	0
Xiao	1	1	1	1	1	0
Yi	1	1	2	2	1	0
Li	2	1	3	11	5	0
Xuan	9	1	11	22	1	3
You	3	0	5	3	7	0
Total	59	27	46	54	24	6

I would suggest that this distribution among royal court activity, royal travels, and military affairs is generally consistent with the picture of the Western Zhou state obtained from contemporary bronze inscriptions, and when all six categories are considered the overall distribution is consistent with such other examples of the annalistic genre as the *Spring and Autumn Annals*.

14. Legge, *The Chinese Classics*, vol. 3, 351.
15. *Shiji*, 28.1364.
16. *Shiji*, 4.131.
17. *Huainanzi* (Sibu beiyao ed.), 21.6a–b.
18. *Guanzi* (Sibu beiyao ed.), 16.10b.
19. *Yi Zhou shu* (Congshu jicheng ed.), 5.134–35.
20. The standard commentary of Kong Zhao 孔晁 (fl. 266 A.D.) specifically interprets this as referring to the next year. Both Gu Jiegang 顧頡剛, "Wuwang de si ji qi niansui he jiyuan" 武王的死及其年歲和紀元, *Wenshi* 文史 18 (July 1983), 2, and Nivison, "The Dates of Western Chou," 534, argue instead that it refers to the year of the conquest.
21. For a discussion of the redaction history of the *Yi Zhou shu*, see pp. 77–8. All three of these chapters belong to the "Kong Zhao" tradition.
22. *Yi Zhou shu*, 4.95.
23. *Yi Zhou shu*, 4.99.
24. *Yi Zhou shu*, 6.215.

25. For a study of the date and nature of the original redaction of the *Yi Zhou shu*, see Huang Peirong 黃沛榮, "*Zhoushu* yanjiu" 周書研究 (Ph.D. diss., National Taiwan Univ., 1976), 141–236.

26. *Suishu*, 33.959.

27. *Hanshu*, 30.1705; *Han Fei zi* (Sibu beiyao ed.), 17.1b–2a; *Zhanguo ce* (Sibu beiyao ed.), 3.11a, 22.1a; *Lüshi chunqiu* (Sibu beiyao ed.), 19.14a; *Shiji*, 112.2956; *Shuo wen jie zi Duan-zhu* 段注 (Sibu beiyao ed.), 1A.11b, 4A.13b, etc. (cited as "*Yi Zhou shu*"); *Yili Zheng-zhu* 鄭書 (Sibu beiyao ed.), 5.50a; *Zhouli Zheng-zhu* 鄭注 (Sibu beiyao ed.), 37.10b; see too, Huang Peirong, "*Zhoushu* yanjiu," 46–47.

28. Although the exact dates of Kong Zhao are not known, he is described as a close contemporary of Wang Su 王肅, who died in A.D. 256 at the age of sixty-eight, and the last mention of Kong Zhao as being still alive comes in an imperial invitation of 266. That he must have been deceased by the time of the Jizhong discovery some fifteen years later is confirmed by the absence of his name in the detailed lists of scholars said to have worked on deciphering the bamboo strips; see Huang Peirong, "*Zhoushu* yanjiu," 59–62.

29. The detailed inventory of this discovery is found in the *Jinshu* 晉書 biography of Shu Xi 束哲 (51.1432–33), where the miscellaneous texts are said to be a "Zhou shi tian fa" 周食田法, "Zhou shu" 周書, "Lun Chu shi" 論楚事, and a "Zhou Muwang meiren Sheng Ji sishi" 周穆王美人盛姬死事.

30. *Wenxuan* (Sibu beiyao ed.), 14.4b and 15.4a. As an example of the nature of this text, the first of these quotations reads: "When King Mu was hunting there was a black bird like a pigeon which fluttered about and then perched on the yoke [of his chariot]. The driver lashed at it with the reigns, whereupon the horses ran out of control and could not be stopped, tipping the chariot and injuring the king's left thigh."

31. *Jiu Tang shu*, 46.1993.

32. *Xin Tang shu*, 58.1463.

33. *Song shi*, 203.5094.

34. *Han shu* 30.1706, n. 3.

35. Liu Zhiji, *Shitong tongshi* 通釋 (Sibu beiyao ed.), "Liu jia," 1.2a (quoted by Huang Peirong, "*Zhoushu* yanjiu," 35).

36. For a study of the date of redaction of the *Liji*, see Jeffrey K. Riegel, "The Four 'Tzu Ssu' Chapters of the *Li Chi*: An Analysis and Translation of the *Fang Chi, Chung Yung, Piao Chi,* and *Tzu I*" (Ph.D. diss., Stanford University, 1978), especially pp. 2–43. With such filiation between two texts, it

would normally be possible for either to be the model for the other. In this case, however, since the "Jizhong" tradition of the *Yi Zhou shu* appears not to have been current at all during the Han dynasty, it is highly unlikely that the editor of the *Liji*'s "Ming tang wei" chapter could have consulted this "Ming tang" chapter.

37. *Da Dai Liji* quoted at *Shangshu zhengyi* 正義 (Sibu beiyao ed.), 11.1a; *Liji zhengyi*, 20.2a; see too Gu Jiegang, "Wuwang de si ji qi niansui he jiyuan," 3–4.

38. *Han shu*, 21B.1016.

39. It is physically improbable that King Wen would have sired his first child (Bo Yi Kao 伯邑考) at the age of thirteen *sui* 歲 and that King Wu would still be siring children well into his eighties (recall that King Cheng, King Wu's eldest son, was still too young at the time of Wu's death to assume his royal duties, and that after Cheng there was at least one other royal offspring, Tangshu Yu 唐叔虞). In addition, the "Du yi" 度邑 chapter of the *Yi Zhou shu* (which, however, is of the "Jizhong" textual tradition) records King Wu stating just after his conquest of Shang, "heaven's displeasure with Yin began sixty years ago, before I was even born." This accords well with the record in the *Bamboo Annals* (both the "Current" and "Ancient" versions) that King Wu was fifty-four when he died.

40. Gu Jiegang, "Wuwang de si ji qi niansui he jiyuan," 15; Nivison, "The Dates of Western Chou," 545–46.

41. Quoted at *Shangshu zhengyi*, 15.8b; see too Gu Jiegang, "Wuwang de si ji qi niansui he jiyuan" 6.

42. Huangfu Mi, *Diwang shiji* 帝王世紀 (Congshu jicheng ed.), 31.

43. It is important to note that in the "Current" *Bamboo Annals* this twelfth year is considered to be in King Wu's personal regnal calendar, while the *Shiji* and most other early sources consider it to be in a joint kings Wen-Wu calendar beginning with King Wen's "receipt of the mandate." For an initial discussion of the significance of this difference, see below, n. 59.

44. "*Mu tianzi zhuan* xu" 序, 1a.

45. Legge, *The Chinese Classics*, vol. 3, 141; Lei Xueqi, *Zhushu jinian yizheng*, 244 (17.121a–b).

46. There is a succinct and well-balanced review in Legge, *The Chinese Classics*, vol. 3, 381–83.

47. For a discussion of this word-family, see K. Takashima, "Some Philological Notes to *Sources of Shang History*," *Early China* 5 (1979–80), 55.

48. Even more remarkable than the exact fidelity in transmission represented in this one forty-graph passage, if the record of King Cheng's reign in the

"Current" *Bamboo Annals* is arranged into strips of forty graphs each, but deleting the *ganzhi* 干支 year-notation as a later insertion (see fig. 3.3, p. 86), then the tenth strip ends with the phrase "fourteenth year, the troops of Qi surrounded the citadel of Qu, conquering it," exactly as predicted from the requirements of the transposed strip (compare strip 1 of King Cheng's reign in fig. 3.2). I am grateful to David Nivison for calling this to my attention.

49. Legge, *The Chinese Classics*, vol. 3, 144; Lei Xueqi, *Zhushu jinian yizheng*, 243–44 (17.121b).
50. *Shiji*, 28.1364. An even more explicit statement that the inspection sacrifices were first performed by King Cheng can be found in the *Baihu tong* 白虎通 (Congshu jicheng ed.), 3A.153.
51. Legge, *The Chinese Classics*, vol. 3, 320; *Shiji*, 4.131.
52. In his *Zuo zhuan* houxu" 後序, Du Yu describes the then recently discovered *Bamboo Annals*. Recall that the *Zuo zhuan* explicitly dates the command to the Archer-lord of Kang, which was the occasion of the "Kang gao" and "Jiu gao" chapters of the *Shangshu*, to the reign of King Cheng; see above, p. 83 and notes 45–46.
53. Legge, *The Chinese Classics*, vol. 3, 588; *Lunheng* (Sibu beiyao ed.), 1.12b.
54. *Han shu*, 21B.1017.
55. Huangfu Mi, *Diwang shiji*, 32.
56. *Shiji*, 4.134.
57. There are a number of inscriptions dating to the reign of King Zhao and related in their mention of an attack on Chu. One of these, the "Zuoce Huan 作冊睘卣 *you*" (Sh 5.22.236, but note that Shirakawa mistakenly dates the vessel to King Cheng), carries a partial date of "nineteenth year," confirming at least that King Zhao was on campaign against Chu in this year.
58. Note that this holds true even if the fourteenth year were interpreted to be in the "mandate" calendar of the *Shiji* and other early sources; for the implications of this, see n. 59.
59. It is necessary to add one important qualifying note regarding the role played by this hundred year tradition for the reign of King Mu in the editing of the *Bamboo Annals*. The description of the *Bamboo Annals* in the *Jinshu* 晉書 biography of Shu Xi 束晳 (261–303) also mentions this tradition (*Jinshu*, 51.1432), but rather than dating the beginning of the hundred year period from the beginning of King Wu's reign, as does the "Current" *Bamboo Annals*, it states that it began from the Zhou "receipt of the mandate" (*zi Zhou shou ming zhi Muwang bai nian* 自周受命至

穆王百年). On the one hand, this proves that the "Current" *Bamboo Annals* arrangement placing King Wu's death in a seventeenth year must have been fixed already in the fourth century. But on the other hand, it also suggests that there were two separate textual arrangements current, one regarding this seventeenth year as being in King Wu's personal reign (the "Current" arrangement), and one regarding it as being in a dual-regnal calendar running consecutively from King Wen's receipt of the mandate through his death seven years later and then through ten years (four preconquest years, the conquest year itself, and five postconquest years) of King Wu's personal reign (the so-called "Ancient" arrangement). I see no way to determine whether this second "Ancient" version represents the "original" arrangement of the late third century A.D. editors of the *Bamboo Annals* or is simply a variant interpretation of the evidence contained in the original tomb text. But, that such an interpretation was possible at all suggests that the entries for eleven preconquest years of rule for King Wu found in the "Current" version could not have been present in the tomb text and must instead have been created out of whole cloth by the editors of the "Current" *Bamboo Annals*. Although this fabrication does not affect in any way the arrangement of the postconquest annals, with which we have been concerned in this paper, it does however seriously affect the annals of the last Shang king Di Xin 帝辛. This, in turn, has important implications for the absolute date of the Zhou conquest, a question too involved for brief discussion here. For a detailed discussion of this question and its implications, see my "The 'Current' *Bamboo Annals* and the Date of the Zhou Conquest of the Shang," *Early China* 11 (1985–87), 33–60.

4

The Duke of Zhou's Retirement in the East and the Beginnings of the Minister-Monarch Debate in Chinese Political Philosophy

Zhougong Dan 周公旦, the Duke of Zhou, is, after Confucius, probably the most honored figure in Chinese tradition. Indeed, as the crucial link between the sage kings of high antiquity and the philosopher sages of later times, the Duke of Zhou's stature has often been said to surpass even that of Confucius. The legend of the Duke's role in the founding of the Western Zhou dynasty, and especially of his service as regent for his young nephew, King Cheng of Zhou, is well known. Although the Duke was but a minister, he proved able to rule in place of the king and to bring order to the world. Yet, according to this legend, the Duke of Zhou was no usurper; instead, he was modest and public-spirited enough to yield authority when the king became capable of ruling in his own right. It was doubtless in recognition of the Duke's political achievement that Confucius is said to have exclaimed:

> 甚矣吾衰也. 久矣吾不復夢見周公.
> Extreme indeed is my decline; long indeed have I not again in my dreams seen the Duke of Zhou![1]

But Confucius recognized as well that whether the Duke of Zhou would appear or not owed more to Confucius's own virtues—and his own political status—than to those of the Duke.

Since the time of Confucius, the Duke of Zhou's appearances in the political discourse of China have generally served as a measure of the relative strengths of rulers and ministers. By the middle of the Warring States period when royal authority existed in name only, the cult of the Duke of Zhou for the first time reached a high tide, as manifested not only by his being elevated to moral equality with kings Wen (d. 1050 B.C.[2]) and Wu (r. 1049/45–1043 B.C.),[3] but also by the spreading of a notion of royal abdication in favor of virtuous ministers.[4] With the subsequent Qin unification, however, the authority of the ruler became absolute, and references to the Duke of Zhou virtually disappeared from political discourse.[5] Not until the end of Western Han, after the regencies of Huo Guang 霍光 (d. 69 B.C.) and especially Wang Mang 王莽 (33 B.C.–A.D. 23), did the Duke of Zhou reappear.[6]

When the Duke of Zhou did reappear on the political stage, he did so with authority. In Wang Mang's proclamation establishing the Xin dynasty, Wang appropriated the "Da gao" 大誥 chapter of the *Shangshu* 尚書 or *Book of Documents*, a text traditionally attributed to the Duke of Zhou, and consciously drew a parallel between himself and the duke.[7] This then gave rise, apparently for the first time, to the notion that the Duke of Zhou had not only served as regent for the young King Cheng (r. 1042/35–1006 B.C.), but had in fact ruled as "king."[8] From this time forth, regard for the Duke of Zhou revolved in large part around his "kingship." For instance, early in the Tang dynasty, the Duke, now viewed more as a member of the royal Zhou family than as a minister, was removed from the Confucian temple.[9] On the other hand, politically conservative *kaozheng* 考證 (evidential) scholars of the Qing dynasty elevated him once again to the highest status in the pantheon of historical heroes, a man who combined the ability to act in politics with profound philosophical wisdom.[10]

It is not my intention to continue this survey of the Duke of Zhou's appearances in later history. Instead, I will try to gain some glimpse of him during his own lifetime. To do this, I will review first what little is generally agreed upon regarding the historical-political background of the Duke of Zhou's life and his role in it. I will then take up in more detail three related sets of questions: whether the Duke of Zhou was called king during the time that he served as regent, the nature of his regency and especially why he returned power to King Cheng, and why and how he "retired." Of these questions, the second set will be my central focus. In my discussion, I will examine carefully two chapters of the *Book of Documents:* the "Jun Shi" 君奭 or "Lord Shi" and the "Shao gao" 召誥 or "Announcement of the Duke of Shao," which I will argue represent two sides in a debate over whether the Duke of Zhou should continue in power. Because I use these texts to show that the Duke's legitimacy was challenged—and even overturned—in his own day, I suspect that readers may view me as trying to debunk the legend of the Duke of Zhou. On the contrary, I would like to think that the sort of close contextual reading that I engage in here may serve to demonstrate why the Duke of Zhou—and the texts themselves—can still be meaningful today.

THE HISTORICAL CONTEXT OF THE DUKE OF ZHOU

For such an imposing figure, we know surprisingly little about the historical Duke of Zhou. Most sources agree that he was the fourth of ten primary sons of King Wen,[11] and that he became a principal lieutenant of King Wu in the Zhou conquest of Shang (in 1045 B.C.).[12] After the conquest, he continued to assist King Wu in the Zhou capital, while other royal siblings—including his other elder brother Guanshu Xian 管叔鮮—were deputed to oversee the former Shang territory near present-day Anyang 安陽. When King Wu died just two years later (in 1043 B.C.), leaving a son, King Cheng, who was probably still a minor, the Duke of Zhou assumed control of the government. There are indications that his brothers serving in the east viewed this action as a usurpation;[13] in any event, they soon joined together with Wu Geng 武庚, the scion of the last Shang king, and other former subjects of the Shang located still further east to rebel against the western Zhou rule. Over the course of the next two years, the Duke of Zhou, apparently in concert with the young King Cheng and yet another royal sibling, his elder half-brother Shi 奭, the Grand Protector (*taibao* 大保), suppressed the rebellion, extending and consolidating Zhou control throughout all of eastern China.

For the next four years, the Duke of Zhou maintained his status as regent (though he obviously shared authority within a triumvirate with King Cheng and Grand Protector Shi). It is during this period that most of the Announcement (*gao* 誥) chapters of the *Book of Documents* are supposed to have been made, documents in which the Duke of Zhou figures especially prominently. Unfortunately (at least for the purposes of narrative history), these documents consist primarily of political argumentation, and therefore have been studied more for their timeless philosophical content than for the light they shed on their immediate historical context. In the next sections, I will try to show how other sources might shed light on their historical context, and how that can help us better to understand their content.

THE QUESTION OF THE DUKE OF ZHOU'S "KINGSHIP"

The notion that the Duke of Zhou reigned as "king," apparently first enunciated in the Latter Han in the wake of Wang Mang's imperium and then resuscitated by Qing scholars after a long hiatus, is now most identified with two of the greatest twentieth-century historians of ancient China: Wang Guowei 王國維 (1877–1927) and Gu Jiegang 顧頡剛 (1893–1980). Both of these scholars introduced new sources to the discussion of this question. Wang Guowei, one of the first historians to study Shang oracle-bone inscriptions, argued that after the Zhou conquest of Shang, the Zhou maintained—at least initially—many of the Shang royal institutions, including especially the Shang royal succession policy of younger brother succeeding elder brother. Thus, according to Wang, when King Wu died just two years after the conquest, he was naturally succeeded, *as king*, by his younger brother Dan, the Duke of Zhou. When the Duke of Zhou then stepped down seven years later in favor of King Wu's eldest son, Song 誦 (i.e., King Cheng), this represented not an isolated act but a conscious reform of royal succession policy; that Zhou would thenceforth follow a policy of primogeniture demonstrates, again according to Wang Guowei, the central role the Duke of Zhou played in establishing Zhou institutions.[14]

Gu Jiegang developed this view still further. Though he alluded to it in many of his studies of the *Book of Documents*,[15] Gu's final and most complete argument for the kingship of the Duke of Zhou came in a posthumous essay entitled "Zhougong zhi zheng cheng wang" 周公執政稱王 (That the Duke of Zhou held the government and was called king).[16] In this article, Gu discussed in exhaustive detail much of the traditional textual evidence bearing on this question.[17] More importantly, he also cited new evidence, two Western Zhou bronze inscriptions, that he claimed show beyond doubt that the Duke of Zhou was referred to as "king." The first of these inscriptions is that on the "Mei *Situ* Yi 渃嗣土送 *gui*" (better known as the "Kanghou 康 侯 *gui*").[18]

Mei Situ Yi 渃嗣土殷 Gui

王來伐商邑征
The king came from attacking the Shang city, and went on
令康侯啚于衛
to command the Lord of Kang to be enfeoffed at Wei.
渃嗣土送眔啚
Yi, Supervisor of Lands at Mei, was conjointly enfeoffed,
作厥考障彝朙
and makes [for] his deceased father [this] sacrificial vessel. Family Emblem

As do virtually all commentators on this inscription, Gu identified the "Lord of Kang" (Kanghou 康侯) in the second line of the inscription with Kanghou Feng 康侯封, a younger brother of the Duke of Zhou. He also regarded this as a record of Kanghou Feng's enfeoffment at Wei 衛, the former Shang capital area, an interpretation that most scholars would also find unexceptionable.[19] Gu diverged from other scholars, however, when he went on to argue that since traditional sources affirm this enfeoffment took place during the Duke of Zhou's regency (and, in particular, immediately after the suppression of the Wu Geng rebellion, which seems to be alluded to in the first line of the inscription), King Cheng would have been too young at that time to participate personally in a military campaign,[20] and thus that the reference in the first line to the king attacking the Shang city could only refer to the Duke of Zhou.[21]

In a like manner, Gu Jiegang also cites a "Wang zai Lu 王在魯 *zun*" (more properly referred to as the "Cai 蔡 *zun*"), a rubbing of the inscription of which is in the Beijing Library (but has not previously been published):

CAI 蔡 ZUN

王在魯, 蔡錫貝十朋, 對揚王休, 用作障彝.

The king was at Lu. Cai, being awarded ten strands of cowries, in response extolls the king's beneficence, herewith making [this] sacrificial vessel.

Again without citing any explicit textual evidence, Gu stated that no Zhou king, whether of the Western or Eastern Zhou, was ever in Lu 魯.[22] However, since the Duke of Zhou would have been there in the course of his suppression of the Wu Geng rebellion, Gu concludes that the "king" mentioned in this inscription as being in Lu could refer only to him.

While I respect the initiative of Wang Guowei and Gu Jiegang in using contemporary sources to determine whether the Duke of Zhou was indeed called king during the time that he ruled the Zhou government, their arguments strike me as circular. For Wang, the Duke of Zhou had to establish a new succession policy in order to have been king under a putative old policy, and had to have been king in order to need to establish a succession policy. For Gu, an unnamed king in two inscriptions has to be the Duke of Zhou, so that the Duke of Zhou had to be called king. Rather than responding to these arguments in detail, I would prefer to adduce other Western Zhou bronze inscriptions that I believe show conclusively that King Cheng was recognized as king already during the suppression campaign against Wu Geng, which is to say, during the Duke of Zhou's regency.

The first inscription to consider is that on the "Qin 禽 *gui*" (Sh 3.10:103).

QIN 禽 GUI

王伐𣏂侯周公
The king attacked the Lord of Gai. The Duke of Zhou
某禽祁禽又
planned with Qin to make entreaty. Qin offered
𣪊祁王錫金百守
??[23] entreaty. The king awarded [Qin] one hundred measures of bronze,
禽用作寶彝
and Qin herewith makes [this] treasured vessel.

Most scholars use the mention of the Duke of Zhou in the inscription's first line to date this vessel to the opening years of the Western Zhou dynasty, a periodization consistent with the vessel style and calligraphy of the inscription. While a "Zhougong" 周公 could certainly also refer to a descendant of Zhougong Dan, the Duke of Zhou in whom we are presently interested, the further mention in lines two and four of a Qin 禽, the name of Dan's eldest son who was enfeoffed with the state of Lu at present-day Qufu 曲阜, Shandong, strongly suggests that the "Zhougong" here is Dan.

Further proof of this identification comes with the reference to an attack on the "Lord of Gai" 𣏂侯 mentioned in the first line. The graph 𣏂 should almost certainly be transcribed as *gai* 蓋, assuming the two "tree" elements of the inscriptional graph to be interchangeable with the "grass" signific of the *kaishu* 楷書 graph (a common substitution in early epigraphic sources[24]), and the bottom 皿 element of the *kaishu* graph to be a later accretion. Gai is the name of a state said by the *Han Feizi* 韓非子 to have been attacked by the Duke of Zhou in the course of suppressing the Wu Geng rebellion.[25] The name of this state seems also to have been written in other early Chinese texts as Yan 奄 (the difference between *gai* and *yan*, which were phonetically close in archaic Chinese, perhaps owing to dialectic differences),[26] which the *Shuo wen* 說文 says was located near present-day Qufu.[27] Finally, the *Shu xu* 書序 (Preface to the *Documents*) says that King Cheng attacked Yan *in the course of suppressing the Wu Geng rebellion*.[28] This is presumably the same royal attack mentioned in the first line of this inscription. Thus, since the inscription explicitly mentions both a "king" and the "Duke of Zhou," it would seem to be *prima facie* evidence that the two were differentiated. The king must have been King Cheng, and he must have been recognized as such even during the time that tradition holds the Duke of Zhou to have been serving as his regent.

Two other Western Zhou bronze inscriptions, both on vessels dating somewhat later than the time of King Cheng and the Duke of Zhou, also bear on this question. The inscription on the "Yihou Ze 宜侯夨 *gui*" (Sh 10.52:529), a vessel that almost certainly dates to the reign of King Kang (r. 1005/03–978 B.C.), begins with a notation that "[the king] inspected the map of King Wu's and King Cheng's attacks on Shang" ([*wang*] *sheng Wu wang Cheng wang fa Shang tu* [王] 省武王成王伐商圖). Traditional texts record only two Zhou attacks against Shang: one led by King Wu that resulted in the conquest, and one in the course of suppressing the Wu Geng rebellion (indeed, after this rebellion the Shang state was effectively dismantled, being replaced by the state of Wei 衛 ruled by Kanghou Feng). Thus, this mention on the "Yihou Ze *gui*" of an attack on Shang led by King Cheng must refer to the suppression of the Wu Geng rebellion. This again directly contradicts Gu Jiegang's assertion that King Cheng was too young to participate in this campaign.

Also worthy of consideration is the inscription on the "Shi Qiang 史牆 *pan*" (Sh 50.*Ho*15:335), the important King Gong (r. 917/15–900 B.C.) period vessel which is well known for its sketch history of the first seven generations of the dynasty. The inscription begins by describing King Wen as being "accordant with antiquity" (*yue gu* 曰古),[29] continues by saying that King Wu was "capturing and controlling" (*suo yu* 緐圉), and then goes on directly to say that King Cheng was "model and sagely" (*xian sheng* 憲聖). Although the Duke of Zhou is mentioned later in the inscription (as a minister of King Wu), he is not ranked here among the Zhou rulers; it is thus clear that the court scribes of the mid Western Zhou did not recognize him as having served as "king." It seems to me that these inscriptions are the best evidence we are ever likely to have regarding this question, and that they leave no doubt that the Duke of Zhou was never recognized as king during his lifetime.

THE QUESTION OF THE DUKE OF ZHOU'S REGENCY

If we were to rely on bronze inscriptions alone to study the history of the opening years of the Western Zhou dynasty, not only would we conclude that the Duke of Zhou was never recognized as king, but we might even conclude that he played little substantive role at all. Indeed, Herrlee G. Creel, unable to find much contemporary basis for the Duke's legend was prompted to ask,

"Why was the Duke of Chou so little mentioned and so seldom praised in Western Chou times?"[30] Aside from the above-mentioned "Qin *gui*" inscription, actions of the Duke of Zhou are commemorated in only two other contemporary inscriptions—those on the "*Xiaochen* Dan 小臣單 *zhi*" (Sh 3.9:89) and on the "Ran 斁 *fangding*" (Sh 3.10:115).[31] Both of these vessels appear to derive from accomplishments achieved during the suppression of the Wu Geng rebellion: the "Ran *fangding*" explicitly mentions attacks on the Dong Yi 東夷, Fengbo 豐伯, and Pugu 蒲姑,[32] while the "*Xiaochen* Dan *zhi*" records a "later digging out and conquest of Shang" (*hou ku ke Shang* 後 戕克商).[33] There is no reason to doubt this evidence that the Duke of Zhou was instrumental in this campaign and, thus, in the consolidation of Zhou rule.[34] But since two of these three inscriptions mention the king—King Cheng—in addition to and prior to the Duke of Zhou, they certainly do not support later views of the Duke of Zhou as having achieved the consolidation almost single-handedly.

Of course, bronze inscriptions are not the only evidence we have for the early Western Zhou dynasty. There are also several chapters from the *Shangshu* or *Book of Documents* that derive from the opening years of the dynasty. Although the date and authenticity of these chapters remain important topics for discussion, no serious study of the period can afford to ignore them.[35] In the following section, I will examine in some detail two of the chapters that bear directly on the Duke of Zhou's regency: the "Shao gao" 召誥 or "Announcement of the Duke of Shao" and the "Jun Shi" 君奭 or "Lord Shi." I believe that these chapters offer important clues as to the nature of the Duke of Zhou's regency—and particularly why it ended and how it was viewed thereafter during the Western Zhou. I hope, too, that this explication may also suggest new interpretive approaches to the study of the *Book of Documents*.

These two chapters of the *Book of Documents* concern, in addition to the Duke of Zhou, the other most important minister at the beginning of the Western Zhou: Duke Shi of Shao, the Grand Protector. Unlike the Duke of Zhou, Grand Protector Shi figures frequently in early Western Zhou bronze inscriptions. Vessels dating probably from the first years of King Cheng's reign show that the Grand Protector also played an instrumental military role in suppressing the Wu Geng rebellion.[36] Later vessels (dating well into the reign of King Kang) seem to portray him as a sort of *eminence grise*, the inscription on the "*Zuoce* Da 作冊大 *fangding*" in particular referring to him as "august heaven's helper" (*huang tian yin* 皇天尹).[37] The importance of the Grand Protector's roles in these bronze inscriptions is paralleled by references to him elsewhere in the *Book of Documents* as well as in the *Shijing* 詩經 or

Book of Poetry. For instance, in the "Gu ming" 顧命 or "Retrospective Command" chapter of the *Book of Documents*, which describes the installation ceremonies surrounding the succession of King Kang, it is Grand Protector Shi who presides over all of the ceremonies and who delivers the formal command of succession to the new king. In the *Book of Poetry*, whereas the Duke of Zhou is barely mentioned at all—and never in the Western Zhou portions of the text,[38] Grand Protector Shi (referred to as the "Duke of Shao") is described as one of the dynastic founders in two poems from the Daya 大雅 or Greater Traces section, poems that do date from the Western Zhou.

> 文武受命 (Kings) Wen and Wu received the mandate,
> 召公維翰 The Duke of Shao was the support.
> —"Jiang Han" 江漢 (Mao 262)

> 昔先王受命 In the past when the prior kings received the mandate,
> 有如召公 There was such as the Duke of Shao,
> 日辟國百里 Daily serving the state for one-hundred *li*.
> —"Shao min" 召旻 (Mao 265)

I believe that Grand Protector Shi's role in the consolidation of Western Zhou rule has not heretofore received adequate recognition from historians of the Western Zhou,[39] and that one consequence of this has been a failure to interpret properly the interactions between him and the Duke of Zhou as seen in the "Jun Shi" and "Shao gao" chapters of the *Book of Documents*.

The "Jun Shi": The Duke of Zhou Makes His Case

The "Jun Shi" purports to record an address made by the Duke of Zhou to Grand Protector Shi, encouraging him—even entreating him—to continue to cooperate in the governance of the state.[40] Part of the problem involved in the interpretation of the text concerns the date of this address. In the present arrangement of the *Book of Documents*, the "Jun Shi" comes after not only the "Shao gao" and "Luo gao" 洛誥 chapters, texts that can be dated on the basis of internal dates to the seventh year of the Duke of Zhou's regency, but also after the "Duo shi" 多士 and "Wu yi" 無逸, speeches apparently made in this same year or just after it. By implication, then, the address of the "Jun Shi" should date after this time.[41] This placement doubtless informs the now dominant commentarial tradition regarding the background of the address: that the Duke of Zhou was attempting to dissuade an aged Grand Protector

Shi from his wish to retire.[42] However, this explanation fails to take into account that, as shown by the inscriptions adduced above (n. 37), Shi continued to serve as the power behind the throne for at least another thirty or forty years. It also fails to account for the earliest explanations of the chapter's background.

According to the "Preface to the *Documents*," the Duke of Zhou's address in the "Jun Shi" was an attempt to ameliorate some dissatisfaction on the part of Grand Protector Shi.

召公爲保, 周公爲師, 相成王爲左右. 召公不悅. 周公作君奭.

The Duke of Shao served as Protector and the Duke of Zhou served as Instructor, advising King Cheng to the left and the right. The Duke of Shao was unhappy, (so) the Duke of Zhou made the "Jun Shi."[43]

The *Shiji* 史記 or *Historical Records* of Sima Qian 司馬遷 (145–c. 86 B.C.) amplifies this in important ways.

成王既幼, 周公攝政當國踐祚. 召公疑之, 作君奭. 君奭不悅周公.

King Cheng being young, the Duke of Zhou controlled the government, acting in the state as ruler. The Duke of Shao was suspicious of him, (and so he [i.e., the Duke of Zhou]) made the "Jun Shi." Lord Shi was unhappy with the Duke of Zhou.[44]

Sima Qian, thus, dates the address of the "Jun Shi" to the period of the Duke of Zhou's regency. This suggests that if Grand Protector Shi did indeed wish to retire from the government, it could not have been because of old age on his part but rather must have been occasioned by a disagreement he had with the Duke of Zhou.

This disagreement is also reflected in the text of the "Jun Shi" itself, which I will describe in some detail below. The "Jun Shi" begins with the Duke of Zhou noting that Heaven had sent down destruction on Yin, and that "we Zhou" (*wo you* Zhou 我有周) had received their mandate.

弗弔天降喪于殷. 殷既墜厥命, 我有周既受.

Unpitying Heaven sent down harm on Yin. Yin having dropped its mandate, we Zhou have received it.

After claiming that the Mandate of Heaven is not a matter of fate (and thus implying that it depends on good leadership), the Duke of Zhou continues, apparently quoting the Grand Protector himself, by reminding the Grand Protector that he (the Grand Protector) had already "approved of me."

嗚呼, 君已曰時我.
Wuhu! You lord have already said, "[You] approve of me."

Although this line is quite enigmatic, the Pseudo-Kong commentary's explanation that the Duke of Zhou was arguing to be allowed to continue in power is probably correct, at least in tone.[45] This seems to imply that Grand Protector Shi had indeed initially approved of the Duke of Zhou's exercising power, but now that the various crises (of the Wu Geng rebellion, the young king, etc.) had passed he must have withdrawn that approval and urged the Duke to step down. But, the Duke of Zhou cautions against being content with their present situation. He urges that they take the long view: can they be sure that the next generation, not knowing that the Mandate is not easy, will not lose it (*zai wo hou si zi sun . . . bu zhi tian ming bu yi . . . nai qi zhui ming* 在我後嗣子孫 . . . 不知天命不易 . . . 乃其墜命)?

The Duke of Zhou then seems to admit his own illegitimacy to govern (*zai jin yu xiaozi* Dan *fei ke you zheng* 在今予小子旦非克有正), but makes the apology that he is just ensuring that the "young man" (*chongzi* 沖子, presumably King Cheng) can benefit from his predecessors' merit. In this regard, he again quotes the Grand Protector, the sense of the quotation apparently being that the dynasty would be secure in the regular succession.

天不可信. 我道惟寧王德延, 天不庸釋于文王受命.
Heaven cannot[46] be trusted. [But] our way being the prolongation of King Wen's[47] virtue, Heaven will not therewith dispose of the mandate that King Wen received.

The Duke of Zhou qualifies this by a lengthy argument from history. All of the successful kings of the past relied on "virtuous" ministers: Cheng Tang 成湯 of Shang had Yi Yin 伊尹; Tai Jia 太甲 had Bao Heng 保衡; Tai Wu 太戊 had Yi Zhi 伊陟, Chen Hu 陳扈, and Wu Xian 巫咸; Zu Yi 祖乙 had Wu Xian 巫賢; and Wu Ding 武丁 had Gan Pan 甘盤.

公曰: "君奭! 我聞在昔, 成湯既受命, 時則有若伊尹, 格于皇天. 在太甲, 時則有若保衡. 在太戊, 時則有若伊陟、臣扈, 格于上帝; 巫咸, 乂王家. 在祖乙, 時則有若巫賢. 在武丁, 時則有若甘盤. 率惟茲有陳, 保乂有殷; 故殷禮陟配天, 多歷年所. 天惟純佑命, 則商實百姓王人."

The Duke said, "Lord Shi, I have heard that in antiquity, Cheng Tang having received the mandate, there was then such as Yi Yin to approach august Heaven; with Tai Jia, there was then such as Bao Heng; with Tai Wu, there were then such as Yi Zhi and Chen Hu to approach the Lord on High, and Wu Xian to regulate the royal family; with Zu Yi, there was then such as Wu Xian; and with Wu Ding, there was then such as Gan Pan. The leaders were this array, protecting and regulating the Yin. Therefore, the Yin rites rose to match Heaven, greatly passing through the years and places. Heaven being pure in its mandate, then it rewarded the nobility."

The Duke continues to claim that even King Wen of Zhou owed all of his success to his virtuous ministers: Guoshu 虢叔, Hong Yao 閎夭, San Yisheng 散宜生, Tai Dian 泰顛 and Nangong Kuo 南宮括, ministers who, he further notes, also stayed on after King Wen's death to assist King Wu in his conquest of the Shang. Indeed, the Duke of Zhou even goes so far as to claim that it was these ministers "who enlightened King Wen" (*wei shi zhao* Wen *wang* 惟時昭文王), and also they who "received the Yin's mandate" (*wei shi shou you* Yin *ming zai* 惟時受有殷命哉)!

公曰:"君奭! 在昔, 上帝割申勸寧王之德, 其集大命于厥躬. 惟文王尙克修和我有夏, 亦惟有若虢叔, 有若閎夭, 有若散宜生, 有若泰顛, 有若南宮括." 又曰, "無能往來茲迪彝教, 文王蔑德降于國人. 亦惟純佑秉德, 迪知天威, 乃惟時昭文王; 迪見冒聞于上帝, 惟時受有殷命哉. 武王惟茲四人, 尙迪有祿. 後暨武王, 誕將天威, 咸劉厥敵. 惟茲四人昭武王, 惟冒, 丕單稱德."

The Duke said, "Lord Shi, in antiquity the Lord on High observed King Wen's virtue [in] the fields of Zhou.[48] Its settling the great mandate on his person was because King Wen was richly capable of cultivating and harmonizing us, the Xia, but also was because there were [men] such as Guoshu, such as Hong Yao, such as San Yisheng, such as Tai Dian, and such as Nangong Kuo." He also said, "If there were not these [men] able to go and come to conduct the fine teaching, King Wen would have had no virtue to send down upon the men of the state. These [men] also purely had and held fast to virtue. By acting to make known Heaven's awesomeness, it was these [men] who made King Wen enlightened; by acting to make [him] visible and striving to make [him] audible to the Lord on High, it was also these [men] who received the mandate of the

Yin. King Wu continued to employ these four men. Later, together with King Wu, they extended and directed Heaven's awesomeness to cut off their enemies. It was these four men who made King Wu enlightened; it was [they] who strived illustriously to uphold virtue."[49]

After concluding this argument from history, the Duke of Zhou again calls on the Grand Protector to take a long view (*yong nian* 永念). The Duke insists that they are now at a great divide and that he is as if swimming a great river, but that together with the Grand Protector he will make it across (*yu wang ji ru* Shi *qi ji* 予往暨汝奭其濟). Then, again seeming to admit his illegitimacy to govern (*xiaozi tong wei zai wei* 小子同未在位),[50] the Duke asks the Grand Protector not to demand that he retire.

誕無我責收.

Oh, do not demand that I retire.[51]

Reminding Grand Protector Shi that the past kings had commanded him, the Grand Protector, to be an exemplar to the people (*min ji* 民極) and a helpmate to the king (*ou wang* 偶王), the Duke of Zhou concludes, even more emphatically and almost obsequiously, urging Grand Protector Shi to continue their ministerialist alliance. He even seems to promise, if the Grand Protector does cooperate, that they will yield to the successor "at an opportune time" (*rang houren yu pi shi* 讓後人于丕時).

公曰: "君! 告汝朕允. 保奭! 其汝克敬以予監于殷喪大否, 肆念我天威. 予不允惟若茲誥, 予惟曰, '襄我二人.' 汝有合哉, 言曰: '在時二人.' 天休滋至, 惟時二人弗戡. 其汝克敬德, 明我俊民, 在讓後人于丕時."

The Duke said, "Lord, [I] announce to you, my elder brother,[52] Protector Shi: may you be capable of respectfully inspecting with me the great flaws of Yin's loss, and thus of considering our heavenly awe. It was very[53] sincerely that I pronounced like this: it was that I said, 'Raise up us two men!' You agreed, saying, 'It is with [these =] us two men!' That Heaven's beneficence has amply arrived is because [these =] we two men did not suppress it. May you be capable of respecting virtue, and making enlightened our prominent people in yielding to the successor at an opportune time."

However, in conclusion, the Duke of Zhou argues that no matter how well enterprises begin, their end is always in doubt. With this in mind, the Duke of Zhou calls on the Grand Protector to "go and respectfully herewith govern" (*wang jing yong zhi* 往敬用治).

The "Shao Gao": Grand Protector Shi Makes His Case

I suspect that Grand Protector Shi's answer to this request is contained in the "Shao gao."[54] That the "Jun Shi" and "Shao gao" are related by more than just the references to Grand Protector Shi in their titles was pointed out already in the Song dynasty by Lin Zhiqi 林之奇 (1112–76). In his comment on the phrase *"Jun yi yue shi wo"* 君已曰時我 ("You lord have already said, '[You] approve of me.'") in the "Jun Shi," Lin argues for the intertextuality of the two chapters.

> 「君已曰時我」指〈召誥〉所陳之言.〈召誥〉言「敬德」則「祈天永命」,「不敬」德則「早墜厥命」,命之修短不在天而在人;故周公告召公,多援〈召誥〉之言而為之言而為之反覆辯明曉人者,當如是也.

"You lord have already said, '[You] approve of me'" refers to the address delivered in the "Shao gao." The "Shao gao" says that by "respecting virtue" then one "beseeches Heaven's eternal mandate," and by "not respecting virtue" then one "prematurely loses its mandate," and that the long and short of fate do not reside with Heaven but reside with man. Therefore, in his announcement to the Duke of Shao, the Duke of Zhou frequently quotes the words of the "Shao gao" and, as in this case, turns them over to explicate them.[55]

I think it is more likely that the "Shao gao" is quoting the "Jun Shi," but, in any event, Lin is certainly correct in seeing the two texts as very closely related.

The "Shao gao" begins with an annalistic narrative of Grand Protector Shi's supervision of the construction of the Zhou eastern capital at Luo 洛. The completion of the foundation of that city was followed by a series of sacrifices conducted by the Duke of Zhou. Then, after mention of an address by the Duke of Zhou to the men of Shang engaged in the construction work, doubtless the address in the "Duo shi" 多士 chapter of the *Book of Documents*, Grand Protector Shi is then said to have led the states' rulers in presenting a *bi* 幣 insignia to the Duke. The remainder of the chapter consists of an address made by the Grand Protector to the Duke of Zhou on this occasion.[56] The dates contained in this narrative provide a firm date for the "Announcement": the day *jiazi* of the third month of a year that other sources (especially the "Luo gao") show to be the seventh—and final—year of the Duke of Zhou's regency (28 March 1036 B.C.).

The Grand Protector begins in a formal manner:

拜手稽首旅王若公

Folding my hands and touching my head to the ground, I make presentation to the royally approved duke.

The phrase *lü wang ruo gong* 旅王若公 has bedeviled all readers of the "Shao gao." Most commentators since the Song dynasty have followed the commentary of Cai Chen 蔡沉 (1167–1230), taking *ruo* 若 as a particle meaning "and"; thus, "(I) extol the king and the duke."[57] However, I know of no clear example elsewhere in the language of this period where *ruo* serves as a conjunction linking two nouns. More consistent with the basic meaning of *ruo* is the Pseudo-Kong commentary, which takes it as a full verb, "to approve of; to accord with";[58] thus, "[I] set forth how the king should accord with the duke." This gloss assumes that King Cheng was present on this occasion and was the intended recipient of the address, an assumption which the prefatory narrative clearly contradicts. But the gloss does suggest another possibility: that the king's "approval of" or "accord with" the Duke of Zhou has already taken place; that is, that the Duke of Zhou's position as regent had earlier been approved by the king. Since the purpose of the Grand Protector's address is to argue for the sole legitimacy of the kingship, this opening reference to the Duke of Zhou as being "royally approved" underscores this hierarchy; although the Duke of Zhou may be the regent, Grand Protector Shi seems to be intimating, he serves at the pleasure of the king.

The Grand Protector wastes no time in making his purpose explicit. In contradistinction to the Duke of Zhou's point in the "Jun Shi" that it was "we Zhou"—and particularly the ministers Guoshu, Hong Yao, Sanyi Sheng, Tai Dian, and Nangong Kuo—who had received Heaven's mandate, the Grand Protector states that it was the king alone, the "eldest son" (*yuanzi* 元子), who received the mandate.

皇天上帝改厥元子, 茲大國殷之命. 惟王受命.
August Heaven, the Lord on High, has changed his eldest son and this great state Yin's mandate. It is the king who has received the mandate.

After noting that the former Shang subjects have now accepted their defeat, the Grand Protector then follows the formula of citing historical precedents used by the Duke of Zhou in the "Jun Shi." He reassures the Duke of Zhou that the king will not be unmindful of this lesson. But, the king will also be able to draw lessons from a higher source. Not only will he "fathom the virtue of our ancient men" (*qi wo gu ren zhi de* 稽我古人之德), as the Duke of Zhou would wish, but, more important, he will be able to "fathom the plottings from Heaven" (*neng qi mou zi tian* 能稽謀自天, presumably because of his unique virtue as "Son of Heaven" [*tianzi* 天子]).

> 相古先民有夏, 天迪從子保; 面稽天若, 今時既墜天命. 今相有殷, 天迪格保; 面稽天若, 今時既墜厥命. 今沖子嗣, 則無遺壽耇; 曰, 其稽我古人之德, 矧曰其有能稽謀自天.
>
> Examining the ancient prior people, the Xia, Heaven led [them] to follow and protected [them], and they faced and fathomed Heaven's approval; [yet], now they have already lost their mandate. Now examining the Yin, Heaven led [them] to approach and protected [them], and they faced and fathomed Heaven's approval; [yet], now they have already lost their mandate. Now if the young son succeeds, there will be no neglect of the elders.[59] If it be said, "May he fathom the virtue of our ancient men," how much more so should it be said, "May he be able to fathom plottings from Heaven!"

As if to ensure that the force of the final rhetorical question not be lost, the Grand Protector then follows with the ejaculation:

> 嗚呼! 有王雖小, 元子哉!
>
> *Wuhu!* Although the king is young, he is the eldest son!

Pressing the argument to its conclusion, the Grand Protector finally requests that the king be allowed "to come to succeed the Lord on High,[60] and himself serve in the center of the land" (*wang lai shao shangdi, zi fu yu tu zhong* 王來紹上帝自服于土中).

The Grand Protector then quotes the Duke of Zhou as apparently having promised (the consistent use of the word *qi* 其 renders the passage ambiguous) to yield to King Cheng once the "great city" at Luo had been built.

> 且曰: 其作大邑, 其自時配皇天. 毖祀于上下, 其自時中乂.
>
> You, Dan, had said, "[We] will build a great city, and from it comport with august Heaven. Carefully sacrificing to (the spirits) above and below, [he] will administer from this center."

To this, the Grand Protector responds that the king is now of age, "having a completed mandate" (*you cheng ming* 有成命), and should "respectfully take (his) place" (*jing zuo suo* 敬作所).

After another briefer review of history in which the Grand Protector grants the Duke of Zhou's premise that men have a hand in their own fate, he returns again to the unique nature of the king in repeating his request that the king be allowed to reign.

嗚呼! 若生子, 罔不在厥初生; 自貽哲命. 今天其命哲, 命吉
凶, 命歷年. 知今我初服宅新邑, 肆惟王其疾敬德.

Wuhu! It is like giving birth to a son: there is nothing that is not in
his initial birth; he himself is bequeathed his wisdom and his mandate. Now Heaven will command wisdom, command fortune, and
command a set number of years. Knowing that now we have for
the first time undertaken to inhabit this new city, may it be that the
king quickly respects his virtue.

Seemingly in response to the Duke of Zhou's repeated exhortations that he
"take a long view," the Grand Protector defines the function of the king's
virtue as "beseeching Heaven's eternal mandate" (*qi tian yong ming* 祈天永
命). Whereas the Duke of Zhou hopes the Zhou will compare with the Xia
and Shang in terms of longevity, the Grand Protector "wishes" (*yu* 欲) that
the king will, "with the small people" (*yi xiaomin* 以小民), "receive Heaven's
eternal mandate" (*shou tian yong ming* 受天永命). Indeed, he repeats this
construction in his conclusion, in which he declines the Duke of Zhou's
blandishments to continue in power, averring that he wishes only to serve the
king.

予小臣, 敢以王讎民、百君子、越友民, 保受王威命明德.
王末有成命, 王亦顯. 我非敢勤, 惟恭奉幣, 用供王, 能祈天
永命.

I, the small minister, together with the king's adversarial people,
the hundred lords, and the friendly people, dare to protect and receive
the king's awesome command and bright virtue. The king finally
has a completed mandate. The king is indeed brilliant. I do not
dare to be diligent, but only reverently offer this *bi* insignia with
which the king may be able to beseech Heaven's eternal mandate.

I think there can be no question as to the difference in tone between
these two addresses and these two ministers. Whereas the Duke of Zhou sees
the Zhou conquest and rule as a result of a collective mandate, Grand Protector
Shi sees it as uniquely bestowed upon the king, who is, after all, the "Son of
Heaven"; and whereas the Duke of Zhou suggests that Heaven's mandate is
earned, the Grand Protector seems to suggest that it is freely given. Whereas
the Duke of Zhou sees the successes of the Xia and Shang, and even of such
ancestors of the Zhou as King Wen himself, as owing to wise ministers, Grand
Protector Shi makes no mention of ministers at all, even declining to accept
credit for his own "diligence"; and whereas the Duke of Zhou refers constantly

to the "virtue" of all of these ministers, Grand Protector Shi reserves this attribute for just the king alone.

While the egalitarianism of the Duke of Zhou's politics will doubtless be as sympathetic to modern Western men and women as it was to later Confucians, it appears to have been less persuasive at the Zhou court. The most compelling evidence of the Duke's failure is that he did indeed step down as regent shortly after Grand Protector Shi announced his "wish" that King Cheng be allowed to rule. Even this act of yielding, for which tradition has accorded him so much merit, apparently did not return the Duke of Chou to favor at court. Instead, he seems to have left the capital in disgrace, dying shortly thereafter all but disregarded by his own countrymen.

THE QUESTION OF THE DUKE OF ZHOU'S RETIREMENT

I realize that the interpretation given above of the "Jun Shi" and "Shao gao" chapters of the *Book of Documents*, and of the relationship between the Duke of Zhou and Grand Protector Shi, is quite novel. I think, however, it can be corroborated by a consideration of one final facet of the Duke of Zhou's career: his retirement.

Among the voluminous hagiography devoted to the Duke of Zhou, there is a subcurrent of tradition that he found himself in disfavor at the court of King Cheng—so much so, indeed, that several texts state that he went into some form of exile. The earliest indication of this is in the "Jin teng" 金藤 or "Bronze Coffer" chapter of the *Book of Documents*, but it is also found in such texts as the *Mozi* 墨子, *Shiji*, and *Lunheng* 論衡. In the following section, I will review these sources, beginning with the "Jin teng." I hope that showing what happened to the Duke of Zhou after he turned over the government to King Cheng might shed light on why he was so little mentioned in Western Zhou sources.

The "Jin Teng": The Duke of Zhou Encounters Political Censure

The "Jin teng" can be divided into two parts on the basis of both content and language. An introductory section recounts how, when King Wu was ill after his conquest of Shang, the Duke of Zhou divined on his behalf, offering his own life for that of the king, and then placed the record of this divination in a bronze coffer. Then, after a puzzling passage which refers to the Duke of Zhou going to reside in the east, a second section describes fantastic meteorological events ostensibly influenced by relations between the Duke and King

Cheng. The first section, written in a language clearly more archaic than that of the second section, might be important evidence for the use of divination during the Western Zhou,[61] but it merely serves as a pretext for the concluding section, and thus need not be recounted here. On the other hand, the second section, which Creel has referred to appropriately as perhaps "the first Chinese short story,"[62] was obviously concocted by the hagiographers of the Duke of Zhou tradition. Since their work must have consisted in large part of reworking earlier stories about the Duke, I believe it may be possible to read through this reworking to find some hints, ambiguous to be sure, regarding the Duke's actual life.

The short story begins by noting that King Wu did, in fact, die, and that after his death, Guanshu, the next eldest of the royal brothers, and his several younger brothers circulated rumors in the state saying that the Duke of Zhou was not acting in the best interest of the "young son," King Wu's eldest son, King Cheng. The Duke of Zhou thereupon announced to Grand Protector Shi and to the Grand Duke Wang 太公望, the two highest ranking figures other than himself residing at the Zhou capital, that "if I were not to govern, I would have no means by which to report to our prior kings" (*wo zhi fu bi, wo wu yi gao wo xian wang* 我之弗辟, 我無以告我先王). There then follows the very vexing sentence:

周公居東二年, 則罪人斯得.
The Duke of Zhou dwelled in the east for two years, and then these guilty men were caught.

Two interpretations of this line have been proposed. The Pseudo-Kong commentary relates it, apparently consistently with the preceding context, to the Duke of Zhou's suppression of the Wu Geng rebellion (which was joined, and probably led, by the royal sibling Guanshu). According to this interpretation, the "guilty men" (*zui ren* 罪人) refers to the rebels, whose leaders traditional accounts say were either killed or exiled. However, more than a century earlier than the time of the Pseudo-Kong commentary, Zheng Xuan 鄭玄 (A.D. 127–200) had given a very different interpretation: that the Duke of Zhou went into exile and the guilty men who were caught were those of his subordinates and associates at the capital who were apprehended by King Cheng.[63]

Inconsistent though this interpretation would seem to be with the obvious intent of the "Jin teng" to glorify the Duke of Zhou, it does seem to be supported by the rest of the story. The next line says that the Duke then presented the king, King Cheng, with a poem, "Chixiao" 鴟鴞 or "The Owl."

This poem is currently found in the *Book of Poetry* (Mao 155).[64] Because it was supposedly written by the Duke of Zhou, the mainline exegetical tradition of the *Book of Poetry* has sought to see in the poem a manifestation of the Duke's virtue. However, it is hard to see any such virtue in this poem. Instead, it seems clearly to be the plaint of one who feels that his efforts have not been recognized. The poem reads in full:

Chixiao 鴟鴞 *(Mao 155)*

鴟鴞鴟鴞	Oh owl, oh owl,
既取我子	Having taken my sons
無毀我室	Do not destroy my house.
恩斯勤斯	Kindly and diligent,
鬻子之閔斯	Was my concern for rearing sons.
迨天之未陰雨	When heaven had not yet clouded and rained,
徹彼桑土	I scraped those mulberry roots
綢繆牖戶	And twined them for the window and door.
今汝下民	Now of you lower people,
或敢侮予	Some dare to despise me.
予手拮据	My hands are chafed
予所捋荼	By the bitterherb that I have plucked
予所蓄租	By the couchgrass that I have gathered.
予口卒瘏	My mouth is scarred with sores,
曰予未有家室	From saying, "I do not yet have a house and home."
予羽譙譙	My wings are tattered,
予尾翛翛	My tail clipped,
予室翹翹	My house in the air;
風雨所漂搖	The sweeping and tossing of the wind and rain:
予維音曉曉	My sound is "Yeow! Yeow!"

Regardless of whether this poem were originally associated with the Duke of Zhou in any way, which I think it almost certainly was not, it must certainly be the case that the author of the "Jin teng" thought that it represented the duke's comment on his own situation. Particularly revealing in this regard is the concluding couplet of the second stanza: "Now of you lower people, some dare to despise me." It seems clear that the duke was mistrusted and disliked by more than just his rebellious brothers, even after their rebellion had been suppressed.

The "Jin teng" concludes with the account of a great thunderstorm which had battered the autumn grain before it could be harvested. Terrified and seeking to understand the cause of the storm, King Cheng opened the bronze coffer containing the divination records. He discovered therein the text of the Duke of Zhou's offer to substitute himself for the ill King Wu. The king is then described as clutching the text and, in tears, proclaiming:

其勿穆卜. 昔公勤勞我家, 惟予沖人弗及知. 今天動威以彰
周公之德, 惟朕小子其 (新:) 親逆. 我國家禮, 亦宜之.

> We need not respectfully divine. Formerly, the duke labored dili-
> gently on behalf of the royal house. It was that I, a young man, did
> not know it, but now Heaven has moved awesomely in order to
> make manifest the Duke of Zhou's virtue. I, the little son, will
> personally meet his return. Our state and family's rituals will also
> be made fitting for him.

With that, a counterwind blew, raising up all of the flattened grain stalks and giving rise to a great harvest.

While there are again two different interpretations of the statement "I, the little son, will personally meet his return. Our state and family's rituals will also be made fitting for him," the context leaves no doubt that King Cheng was initially among those who "despised" the Duke of Zhou. One interpretation has it that King Cheng went outside of the city to meet the Duke on his return from exile.[65] The other has it that the Duke had already died and been buried according to his rank as just one among the many dukes; when the king realized the efforts the Duke had made on behalf of the royal house, he reinterred him with the rites of a king.[66] In either event, even this most hagiographical story concerning the Duke of Zhou strongly sug-gests that he was out of favor, and perhaps even in exile at some point in time.

Surprising though it may seem, given the Duke of Zhou's exalted place in Chinese tradition, there is a rather consistent tradition that he did go into exile. For instance, the interpretation that King Cheng reinterred the Duke with the rites of a king can be traced back at least to Wang Chong 王充 (A.D. 27–c. 97) in the first century A.D. In his discussion of this reburial, Wang notes that "old text" (*guwen* 古文) scholars of his time held that after the Duke of Zhou assumed the regency and his brothers Guanshu and Caishu 蔡叔 circulated rumors about him, King Cheng became suspicious of him and the duke fled to the state of Chu 楚. In fact, it was not only "old text" scholars who believed this. Sima Qian stated it explicitly in two places in his *Shiji*, once even in the genealogy of the Duke of Zhou's own state of Lu. In both of these accounts, which contain variations on the story contained in the "Jin teng," it seems that the Duke of Zhou's exile came after he had returned power to King Cheng. The "Lu Zhougong shijia" 魯周公世家 account reads as follows:

> 及七年後還政成王, 北面就臣位, 匔匔如畏然. 初, 成王少時病, 周公乃自揃其蚤沈之河, 以祝於神曰: 王少未有識, 奸神命者乃旦也. 亦藏策於府. 成王病有瘳. 及成王用事, 人或譖周公, 周公奔楚. 成王發府, 見周公禱書, 乃泣, 反周公.

> After seven years [the Duke of Zhou] returned governance to King Cheng, facing north and assuming the position of a minister, respectfully as if awestruck. At first when King Cheng was young he had been sick; the Duke of Zhou then pared his fingernails and submerged them in the River, in order to pray to the spirits, saying: "The king is young and not yet knowledgable. The one who has offended the spirits' mandate is none other than Dan." [He] again stored the slips in the repository. King Cheng's sickness was cured. Coming to the time when King Cheng acted on his own, someone libeled the Duke of Zhou and the Duke of Zhou fled to Chu. King Cheng opened the repository, saw the text of the Duke of Zhou's prayer, and then, crying, caused the Duke of Zhou to return.[67]

These references to an exile in the southern state of Chu seem not to be consistent with the ambiguous reference in the "Jin teng" to the Duke "residing in the east" (*ju dong* 居東) for two years, but I think it may well be possible to reconcile them.

Perhaps the earliest textual references to the Duke of Zhou, aside of course from those in the Western Zhou sources, are found in the *Mozi*. The first, in the "Fei ru" 非儒 chapter, is extremely oblique, comparing the Duke to several contemporary rebels and saying simply:

> 周公非其人也邪? 何爲舍其家室而託寓也?
> Was Duke Dan of Zhou not that [sort of] man? Why did he depart his home and take up a new abode?[68]

A similar passage in the "Geng zhu" 耕柱 chapter adds the information that the Duke "located in the east in the Shang state of Gai."[69]

古者周公旦非關叔, 辭三公, 東處於商蓋. 人皆謂之狂. 後
世稱其德, 揚其名至今不息.

In ancient times, Duke Dan of Zhou negated Guanshu and taking
leave of the Three Dukes, located in the east in the Shang state of
Gai. Men all called him crazy. [Yet], later generations' praising his
virtue and raising up his name have not ceased to the present.

The state of Gai 蓋 mentioned in this passage is almost certainly the same
state that the "Qin *gui*" inscription says the Zhou attacked in the course of
suppressing the Wu Geng rebellion. However, as alluded to in the discussion
of that inscription above (p. 106), Chen Mengjia 陳夢家 (1911–66) has
presented considerable textual evidence to show that there was confusion
about the name of this state, with other texts, such as the *Zuo zhuan* 左傳
and *Mencius* 孟子, referring to it as Yan 奄.[70] The vacillation between these
two names doubtless arises from their phonetic similarity in archaic Chinese
(*gai*/*kadh v. *yan*/*?jiamx).[71]

The graph for the name of the state of Gai seems also to have led to
some confusion. For example, Guo Moruo 郭沫若 (1892–1978) has identified the graph on the "Qin *gui*," 𦣻, as Chu 楚.[72] I am reasonably certain that
this identification is mistaken.[73] However, the archaic graphs (𦣻 vs. 𦣻) are
quite similar, and it is not difficult to imagine how one might be written for
the other. This is important because it suggests the possibility that the Chu in
the *Shiji*'s accounts of the Duke of Zhou's exile is a garble for an original Gai,
consistent with the passage from the "Geng zhu" chapter of the *Mozi*.

When we remember that Gai was located very near to Qufu in present-
day Shandong, that is, within the state of Lu which was the fief of the Duke
of Zhou's eldest son Qin, it becomes easier to imagine why the Duke would
have gone into "exile" there. It seems to me to make no sense to think that the
Duke of Zhou, meeting with disfavor at court, would have gone off to the far
southern state of Chu; it is quite understandable, however, that he would
have retired to the fief of his eldest son.

Further evidence that this is so comes from several parallels between
this Gai and another state called Feng 豐. First, just as Gai (or Yan) was
attacked during the suppression of the Wu Geng rebellion, so too was Feng.
In the inscription on the "Ran *fangding*," mentioned above, the Duke of
Zhou is said to have attacked the Eastern Yi, the Elder of Feng (Fengbo 豐),
and Pugu. Second, both Gai and Feng seem to have been located very near
present-day Qufu in Shandong.[74] Third, just as there are indications that the
Duke of Zhou went to live at Gai, so too are there records that he went to live

at Feng. Indeed, several sources say that the Duke of Zhou died in Feng. For instance, the *Shiji* genealogy of the state of Lu provides the following account of the Duke's death:

周公在豐. 病將沒曰: 必葬我成周以明吾不敢離成王. 周公既卒, 成王亦讓, 葬周公於畢, 從文王, 以明予小子不敢臣周公也.

The Duke of Zhou *was at Feng*. Sick and about to die, he said, "You must bury me at Chengzhou [i.e., the city Luo], in order to show that I do not dare to separate myself from King Cheng." When the Duke of Zhou had died, King Cheng also yielded, burying the Duke of Zhou at Bi, alongside King Wen, in order to show that "I, the little son, do not dare to treat the Duke of Zhou as a minister."[75]

It is generally assumed that the Feng at which the Duke of Zhou died was the Feng near present day Xi'an that served as the Zhou capital. However, this would seem to render his concern that he "not dare to separate [him]-self from King Cheng" unintelligible. Moreover, the *Bamboo Annals*, for the tenth year of King Cheng, says that the Duke "*went out* to dwell in Feng" (*chu ju yu* Feng 出居於豐).[76] If the Duke "went out" to this Feng, it must have been some place other than the Zhou capital Feng. Since it would seem that the Duke did go east to somewhere near present-day Qufu when he retired, and since there appears to have been a Feng located in that same area, it is possible that it was to this eastern Feng that the Duke of Zhou "went out," and at which he died.

Further support for this speculation may be gained from a consideration of the date of the Duke of Zhou's death. The only specific date given for his death is in the "Current" *Bamboo Annals*, which places it in the twenty-first year of King Cheng. However, as Lei Xueqi 雷學淇 and others have noted, the same text states that in the sixth month of the thirteenth year of King Cheng, "Lu conducted a great *di* 禘-ancestral sacrifice in the temple of the Duke of Zhou."[77] This certainly suggests that the duke was already dead at this time. Lei suggests that this sacrifice must have been conducted at the end of the twenty-seven month mourning period for the duke, and therefore that his death must have come in the eleventh year of King Cheng. Whatever the merits of this mourning-period thesis, there is independent corroboration that the duke did in fact die in this eleventh year. The "Preface to the *Documents*" for the now lost "Jun Chen" 君陳 chapter states:

周公既沒,命君陳分正東郊成周.
The Duke of Zhou having died, Lord Chen was commanded to divide and govern the eastern suburb and/of Chengzhou."[78]

This is apparently the command recorded in the *Bamboo Annals* under the eleventh year of King Cheng:

王命周平公治東都.
The King commanded Duke Ping of Zhou to rule the eastern capital" [Duke Ping of Zhou 平公 being another name for Lord Chen, the second eldest son of the Duke of Zhou].[79]

Thus, if the Duke of Zhou went to Feng in the tenth year of King Cheng, as both the *Bamboo Annals* and *Shangshu dazhuan* 尚書大傳 agree that he did, and if he died in the eleventh year, as the correlation between the "Preface to the *Documents*" and the *Bamboo Annals* would suggest, then, in the chronicle style of Chinese history-writing, the duration of his exile would have been two years, consistent with the passage in the "Jinteng" stating that he "dwelled in the east for two years."

CONCLUSION

This glimpse of the historical Duke of Zhou and of his failure in life, if the sort of political setback he suffered constitutes failure in any meaningful sense, does not, I believe, diminish the value of his legacy—the notion that virtue is a trait not restricted just to royalty—which has long been on view. True, the Duke of Zhou's own elaboration of this notion probably owed more to political expediency and self-interest than to any philosophical idealism. True, too, the legacy was magnified by Confucians and other philosophers of the Warring States period who were interested in promoting their own positions as ministers vis-à-vis the then declining royalty. Nevertheless, it cannot be denied that the Duke of Zhou was the first person in Chinese history to elaborate this ideal, and for this reason was an appropriate choice to be the patron saint of those later ministers. To the extent that the ideal is universalizable, the Duke of Zhou should remain an inspiration to all who wish to become virtuous.

NOTES

This is a revised and expanded version of my "Zhougong ju dong xinshuo: Jianlun Shao gao Jun Shi zhuzuo beijing he yizhi" 周公居東新說: 簡論召誥君奭著作背景和意旨, in *Xi-Zhou shi lunwenji* 西周史論文集, ed. Shaanxi Lishi bowuguan (Xi'an: Shaanxi Renmin jiaoyu chubanshe, 1993), 872-887. This version was edited for *Early China* by David N. Keightley.

1. *Analects* 7/5. All translations in this paper are my own.
2. For a detailed substantiation of the chronology of the Western Zhou dynasty given here, see Edward L. Shaughnessy, *Sources of Western Zhou History: Inscribed Bronze Vessels* (Berkeley: University of California Press, 1991), 217–87.
3. In addition to the Duke of Zhou's frequent mention together with kings Wen and Wu in writings of various schools, his elevation can also be seen in the prominent role given him in such comprehensive works of political philosophy of the time as the *Yi Zhou shu* 逸周書; for a study of the *Yi Zhou shu* showing that its core chapters—those in which the Duke of Zhou figures most prominently—must have been composed toward the end of the fourth century B.C., see Huang Peirong 黃沛榮, "Zhou shu yanjiu" 周書研究 (Ph.D. diss., National Taiwan University, 1976).
4. For a concise survey of this notion in the various schools of the period, see A. C. Graham, *Disputers of the Tao: Philosophical Argument in Ancient China* (La Salle, IL: Open Court Press, 1989), 292–99.
5. This point is made, for instance, in Gu Jiegang 顧頡剛, "Zhougong zhi zheng cheng wang—Zhougong dong zheng shishi kaozheng zhi er" 周公執政稱王—周公東征史事考證之二, *Wenshi* 文史 23 (1984): 1–30, especially 9–12. It is also acknowledged by Michael Loewe, who, on the basis of a survey of Han dynasty sources, concluded, "My impression remains that you have to wait for Wang Mang and Later Han before much attention is paid to Zhou Gong's qualities"; personal communication, 15 October 1991.
6. For the story of how the aging Han Wudi (r. 140–87 B.C.) presented to Huo Guang a picture of the Duke of Zhou supporting the young King Cheng (r. 1042/35–1006), implying that Huo was to serve as regent for the young Zhaodi (r. 86–74 B.C.), see *Hanshu* 漢書 (Beijing: Zhonghua shuju, 1962), 68.2932. For a similar illustration from the Eastern Han, see Martin J. Powers, *Political Expression in Early China* (New Haven: Yale University Press, 1991), 43 fig. 21, and for discussion, pp. 156–63.

7. For the text of this proclamation, generally referred to as the "Mang gao" 莽誥, see *Hanshu*, 84.3428–3434.

8. The first explicit indication of this belief that the Duke of Zhou had ruled as "king" seems to be in Zheng Xuan's 鄭玄 (127–200) commentary on the "Da gao" chapter of the *Shangshu*, where, at the first usage of the word *wang* 王, "king," Zheng notes, "the 'king' is the Duke of Zhou; when the Duke of Zhou resided in command of the great affairs, he appropriated the title 'king'"; quoted at *Shangshu zhengyi* 尚書正義 (Sibu beiyao ed.), 13.9b.

9. See David McMullen, *State and Scholars in T'ang China* (Cambridge: Cambridge University Press, 1988), 33. McMullen remarks that "in this way, the dynasty used the cult to maintain a difference in status between the imperial house, symbolized by the duke of Chou, and the officials and scholars, whose symbol and ideal was Confucius."

10. Zhang Xuecheng 章學誠 (1738–1801) was one of the first philosophers of history to elevate the Duke of Zhou over even Confucius; see David S. Nivison, *The Life and Thought of Chang Hsüeh-ch'eng (1738–1801)* (Stanford: Stanford University Press, 1966), 146–49. At about the same time, many "Han Studies" commentators on the *Shangshu*, citing Zheng Xuan's "Da gao" gloss, argued that the Duke of Zhou was called king, and therefore was the author of most of the royal proclamations of the *Shangshu*; see, for instance, Jiang Sheng 江聲, *Shangshu jizhu yinshu* 尚書集注音疏 (1793 Jinshiju kan ed.), 6.17a; Wang Mingsheng 王鳴盛, *Shangshu houan* 尚書後案 (Sibu congkan ed.), 14.1a–b; Sun Xingyan 孫星衍, *Shangshu jinguwen zhushu* 尚書今古文注疏 (Sibu congkan ed.), 14.1a. Even the *jinwen* 今文 (New Text) scholar Pi Xirui 皮錫瑞 shared this view; see his *Jinwen Shangshu kaozheng* 今文尚書考證 (1897 Shifutang ed.), 12.1a–b.

11. King Wen, nominal founder of the dynasty, is said to have had ten direct-line sons: Kao 考, who predeceased his father; Fa 發, who was to become King Wu; Guanshu Xian 管叔鮮, Zhougong Dan; Caishu Du 蔡叔度; Caoshu Zhenduo 曹叔振鐸; Chengshu Wu 成叔武; Huoshu Chu 霍叔處; Kangshu Feng 康叔封; and Danji Zai 聃季載; see *Shiji* 史記 (Beijing: Zhonghua shuju, 1959), 35.1570. There were also secondary sons (i.e., sons by secondary consorts), among whom, as we will see, Shaogong 召公 or Grand Protector (*taibao* 大保) Shi 奭 was the most important.

12. It is worth noting that of the two earliest texts that purport to describe the events of the conquest, the "Ke Yin" 克殷 and "Shi fu" 世俘 chapters

of the *Yi Zhou shu*, the "Ke Yin" ascribes a prominent role to the Duke of Zhou while the "Shi fu" does not mention him at all. As I argued in chapter 2 above, the "Shi fu" is almost certainly a Western Zhou text if not a contemporary account of the conquest. On the other hand, the "Ke Yin" betrays numerous anachronistic linguistic usages (most notable of which is the mention of a *qing lü* 輕呂, almost certainly the transcription of a Central Asian word for the type of curved sword known to the Greeks as *akinakes*, a type of weapon which could not have been introduced to China much earlier than about 300 B.C.). For philosophical reasons, however, Sima Qian 司馬遷 (145–c. 86 B.C.) adopted the "Ke Yin" account of the conquest in his *Shiji* (4.124–26), and it is through the *Shiji* that most historians have come to view the Duke of Zhou's role in the conquest.

13. Among numerous textual sources indicating that Guanshu and Caishu were suspicious of their brother's motives, see *Shiji*, 4.132.

14. Wang Guowei, "Yin Zhou zhidu lun" 殷周制度論, in *Guantang jilin* 觀堂集林, 4 vols. (1923; rpt. Beijing: Zhonghua shuju, 1984), vol. 2, 456 (10.3b). Wang does not explain, however, why the Zhou succession before the conquest of Shang seems to have been based on father-son inheritance (if not primogeniture), passing from Gugong Danfu 古公亶父 through Wang Ji 王季, to King Wen, and then to King Wu. Nor does he explain why it should have been the Duke of Zhou rather than his elder brother Guanshu Xian who succeeded King Wu.

15. For one of Gu's earliest explicit expressions of this view, see Gu Jiegang, "Shangshu Da gao jin yi" 尚書大誥今譯, *Lishi yanjiu* 歷史研究 1962.4, 26–51, especially 50–51.

16. See above, n. 5.

17. Of course, Gu basically presented evidence he regarded as supportive of his position that the Duke of Zhou served as king. There is, however, other evidence that Gu did not cite—evidence that is earlier and clearer than that which he did cite—which states unequivocally that the Duke of Zhou did not serve as king. For instance, in *Mencius* 5A/6, in a famous discussion of the prerequisites of kingship, Mencius states:

繼世以有天下, 天之所廢, 必若桀紂者也. 故益, 伊尹, 周公不有天下.

When the world (*tianxia*) is ruled on the basis of [succeeding generations =] heredity, those that Heaven deposes must be like Jie and Zhou. Therefore, Yi, Yi Yin, and the Duke of Zhou did not come to rule the world.

18. For this inscription, see Shirakawa Shizuka 白川靜, *Kinbun tsūshaku* 金文通釋, 56 fascicles, *Hakutsuru bijutsukan shi* 白鶴美術館誌 4.14 (1963):141–60 (Western Zhou bronze inscriptions studied by Shirakawa will hereafter be cited in the form: Sh 4.14:141). The translation given here represents my own understanding of this difficult inscription, which Gu simply transcribes without explanation. However, since he refers to it as the "Mei *Situ* Yi *gui*," his interpretation of the critical issue of who cast the vessel—Kanghou 康侯 or Mei *Situ* Yi 渣嗣土送—must be roughly the same as mine.

19. I am aware that many scholars would take exception to *my* use of the word "enfeoffment" here. While I certainly agree that the word should be used cautiously, it seems to me that it is not inappropriate for the sorts of land-grants made to royal relatives during the early Western Zhou.

20. The *Shu xu* 書序 (Preface to the *Documents*) explicitly states in several places that King Cheng participated in the suppression of the Wu Geng rebellion; see James Legge, *The Chinese Classics*, vol. 3, *The Shoo King or the Book of Historical Documents* (1865; rpt. Hong Kong: Hong Kong University Press, 1960), 9, 10, 11, 12. Among other texts that at least imply his participation (by way of placing him in Yan 奄 at the time that that state was being defeated) are the *Shiji* (4.133) and the *Zhushu jinian* 竹書紀年 (Bamboo annals; see Legge, *The Shoo King*, Prolegomena 145).

21. A similar argument is given in Matsumoto Masaaki 松水雅明, "Shūkō sokui kō—shoki Shōsho seiritsu ni tsuite no kenkyū" 周公即位考—初期尙書成立についての研究, *Shigaku zasshi* 史學雜誌 77.6 (1968): 1–37.

22. As noted above (n. 21), several texts explicitly place King Cheng in Yan, which, as I will show below (p. 106), was located at at this time at present-day Qufu 曲阜, Shandong.

23. This graph, 敊, transcribed by Shirakawa (following Ruan Yuan 阮元, *Jiguzhai zhongding yiqi kuanzhi* 集古齋鐘鼎彝器款識 [1804 Baoshi Houzhi Buzuzhai ed.], 5.28) as *chen* 敊, obviously refers to some type of sacrifice, but which type is not clear to me.

24. See Gao Ming 高明, "Guwenzi de xingpang ji qi xingti yanbian" 古文字的形旁及其形體演變, *Guwenzi yanjiu* 古文字研究 4 (1980): 71–72.

25. *Han Feizi* (Sibu beiyao ed.), 7.10b.

26. For more discussion of this identification between Gai and Yan, see below, p. 123.

27. *Shuo wen jie zi Duan zhu* 說文解字段注 (Sibu beiyao ed.), 6B.34a; the *Shuo wen* writes the graph as 郇.

28. See above, n. 20.

29. For this translation, and those that follow, see Shaughnessy, *Sources of Western Zhou History*, 185–86.

30. Herrlee G. Creel, *The Origins of Statecraft in China*, vol. 1: *The Western Chou Empire* (Chicago: University of Chicago Press, 1970), 74.

31. The Duke of Zhou is also mentioned posthumously on several vessels: the "Rong 榮 *gui*" (Sh 11.59:591), "Ling 令 *yi*" (Sh 6.25:276), "Shenzi Ta 沈子它 *gui*" (Sh 15.78:7), and the above-mentioned "Shi Qiang *pan*."

32. The Dong Yi and Pugu are recorded in traditional texts as targets of the suppression campaign; for a detailed survey of these texts, see Gu Jiegang, "San jian ji dongfang zhuguo de fan Zhou junshi xingdong he Zhougong de duice" 三監及東方諸國的反周軍事行動和周公的對策, *Wenshi* 文史 26 (1986), 1–11. Although Feng is not as prominent in the traditional record as are the Dong Yi and Pugu, I will adduce evidence below (p. 123) showing that it was located near them.

33. I here follow Chen Mengjia's 陳夢家 explication of the graph 戉 as *jue* 掘, by way of *ku* 厒; see "Xi-Zhou tongqi duandai" 西周銅器斷代, I, *Kaogu xuebao* 考古學報 1955.9: 160. It is worth noting that in this inscription, as in the "Qin *gui*" inscription, both the king—who is the subject for this "later digging out and conquest of Shang"—and the Duke of Zhou—who makes an award at the "Cheng Garrison" 成𠂤—are mentioned in the same inscription. If the "king" here refers to King Cheng, as Chen Mengjia and Shirakawa both argue it does, and as the description of a "later" (*hou* 後) conquest of Shang would seem to require (as would, perhaps, also the setting of the award ceremony at the Cheng Garrison—presumably the site at Luoyang 洛陽 later known as Cheng Zhou 成周), then this would once again demonstrate that King Cheng was very much involved in the suppression of the Wu Geng rebellion, and was recognized as "king" during it.

34. I believe that we can now lay to rest the sorts of suspicions Noel Barnard raised a generation ago about these inscriptions involving the Duke of Zhou. For Barnard's comments, see his "Chou China: A Review of the Third Volume of Cheng Te-k'un's *Archaeology in China*," *Monumenta Serica* 24 (1965): 337–54. For a detailed critique of Barnard's methodology, see Shaughnessy, *Sources of Western Zhou History*, 43–62.

35. For a representative discussion of the dating of the various chapters of the *Book of Documents*, see Creel, *The Origins of Statecraft in China*, 447–63. Creel accepts twelve chapters as being of Western Zhou date, nine of them as being from the time of the Duke of Zhou: the five "Announce-

ments" ("Da gao" 大誥, "Kang gao" 康誥, "Jiu gao" 酒誥, "Shao gao" 召誥, and "Luo gao" 洛誥), the "Zi cai" 梓材, "Duo shi" 多士, "Jun Shi" 君奭, and "Duo fang" 多方. David Keightley has criticized this dating of these chapters, suggesting that they may have been composed toward the end of the Western Zhou and thus reflect retrospective and idealizing tendencies; review, *Journal of Asian Studies* 30.3 (1971): 656. Another attempt to date the five Announcements, as well as the "Duo shi," to the opening years of the Western Zhou, that of W. A. C. H. Dobson (*Early Archaic Chinese* [Toronto: University of Toronto Press, 1962], 123–30), is similarly open to question; while Dobson argues that these chapters of the *Book of Documents* are linguistically "of a piece" with a sample of fourteen bronze inscriptions that he studies, in fact, at least one of these inscriptions, that of the "Maogong 毛公 *ding*" (Sh 30.181:637), dates to late in the dynasty, while others (e.g., the "Ling 令 *gui*" [Sh 6.24:255] and "Ban 班 *gui*" [Sh 15.79:34] certainly date to the reigns of kings Zhao (r. 977/75–957 B.C.) and Mu (r. 956–918 B.C.). Thus, even if Dobson's linguistic analysis is correct, the most one could conclude from his sample is that these chapters date from the Western Zhou.

It is not my purpose here to try to resolve this important question. Of the two chapters of the *Book of Documents* that I will examine in detail below, the "Jun Shi" and "Shao gao," I think there can be no doubt that they long predate the hagiographical traditions that, by about the time of Confucius, developed around the Duke of Zhou; they thus almost certainly reflect historiographical concerns of the Western Zhou period.

36. See, for example, the inscriptions on the "Taibao 大保 *gui*" (Sh 2.3:58), "Chuo 征 *you*" (Sh 4.16:173), and "Lü 旅 *ding*" (Sh 2.5:72). For English translations of all three of these inscriptions, as well as a study of their historical context and implications, see below, chapter 5.

37. For the "*Zuoce* Da *fangding*," see Sh 8.42:440; see below, p. 146–7. Other King Kang period inscriptions that similarly portray the Grand Protector include those on the "Jin 董 *ding*" (Sh 51.1:449), "Shu 叔 *tuoqi*" (Sh 2.6:77), and the recently discovered "Ke 克 *he*" (for which, see Yin Weizhang 殷瑋璋, "Xin chutude Taibao tongqi ji qi xiangguan wenti" 新出土的太保銅器及其相關問題, *Kaogu* 考古 1990.1: 66–77; Yin Weizhang and Cao Shuqin 曹淑琴, "Zhou chu Taibao qi zonghe yanjiu" 周初太保器綜合研究, *Kaogu xuebao* 考古學報 1991.1: 1–21.

38. The Duke of Zhou is mentioned in only two poems: "Po fu" 破斧 (Mao 157) of the Bin *Feng* 豳風 section, and "Bi gong" 閟宮 (Mao 300) of the Lu *Song* 魯頌 section. This latter poem, probably composed in the seventh

century B.C., recounts the history of the state of Lu, of which the Duke of Zhou was the titular founder. Nevertheless, mention of the Duke of Zhou in it is extraordinarily restrained; he is cited only as one of the ancestors of the current duke of Lu.

39. Some recognition of his role is found in Creel, *The Origins of Statecraft in China*, 69–78. See, too, below, chapter 5.

40. For translations of the "Jun Shi" into English, see Legge, *The Shoo King*, 474–86; and Bernhard Karlgren, *The Book of Documents* (Stockholm: Museum of Far Eastern Antiquities, 1950), 59–62; for Karlgren's annotations, see his *Glosses on the Book of Documents* (1948–49; rpt. Stockholm: Museum of Far Eastern Antiquities, 1970), nos. 1859–1903.

41. It should be noted, however, that the present arrangement of the *Book of Documents* seems to be faulty at this point. In the present arrangement, the next *jinwen* 今文 or "new text" chapter following the "Jun Shi" is the "Duo fang" 多方. As has often been noted, this placement is almost certainly incorrect. The "Duo fang," putatively an address by the Duke of Zhou to the leaders of the many (eastern) states, begins with a sort of "great event" notation dating it to the year that the king returned from Yan (*wei wuyue dinghai wang lai zi* Yan *zhi yu* Zongzhou 惟五月丁亥王來自奄至于宗周, "It was the fifth month, *dinghai* [day 24], the king returned from Yan, arriving at Zongzhou"). The *Bamboo Annals* places the king's return from Yan to Zhou in the fifth year of the regency, a date which the text of the "Duo fang" itself seems to corroborate, quoting the Duke of Zhou as saying to the leaders of the eastern states, "Now you have scurried and run about ministering to our overseers for five years" (*jin er ben zou chen wo jian wu si* 今爾奔走臣我監五祀). If the "Duo fang" is out of place in this way, it is possible that the "Jun Shi" is similarly out of place.

42. Cai Chen 蔡沉, *Shu jizhuan* 書集傳 (Siku quanshu ed.), 5.24b.

43. Legge, *The Shoo King*, 11.

44. *Shiji*, 34.1549.

45. For interpretations of this phrase, see Karlgren, *Glosses*, no. 1860. Karlgren notes (albeit in disagreement) that the Pseudo-Kong commentary takes *shi* 時 as *shi* 是, interpreting it as a request (apparently reading the *yi* 已, "already," as an ejaculation) by the Duke of Zhou that Grand Protector Shi "approve" of him so that he might remain in power. This reading is followed also in *Shangshu zhengyi* 尚書正義 ([Sibu beiyao ed.], 16.11a) and in Wang Xianqian's 王先謙 *Shangshu Kong zhuan canzheng* 尚書孔傳參正 ([1904 Xushoutang ed.], 25.2b) among other commentaries.

46. It is also possible that *bu* 不, "not," here should be read *pi* 丕, "very," as is common in Western Zhou texts, but there is no independent verification for such an emendation.

47. I emend *ning* 寧 to *wen* 文, as is common in the *Book of Documents*. It would seem that the Grand Protector's point in this quotation is to stress the primacy of kingly succession.

48. With Karlgren and others, on the basis of a quotation in the "Ziyi" 緇衣 chapter of the *Liji* 禮記 ([Sibu beiyao ed.], 17.18a), I read *ge shen quan ning wang* 割申勸寧王 as *zhou tian guan wen wang* 周田觀文王. For a discussion, see Karlgren, *Glosses*, no. 1879.

49. I here follow Ma Rong's 馬融 (79–166) reading of *mao* 冒 as *mian* 勉, "to strive," for which, see Karlgren, *Glosses*, no. 1624 (though note that Karlgren rejects this reading). For *pi dan* 丕單, I assume *pixian* 丕顯, "illustrious."

50. The *xiaozi* 小子 of this phrase is traditionally interpreted as referring to King Cheng, but as Karlgren (*Glosses*, no. 1885), following Sun Yirang 孫詒讓 (*Shangshu pianzhi* 尚書駢枝 [Beiping: Harvard-Yenching Institute, 1929], 42a–b), notes, the same term is used in the preceding sentence as a reference to the Duke of Zhou himself and it would be extremely unusual for it to have a different referent here.

51. Karlgren (*Glosses*, no. 1886), following Jiang Sheng 江聲, *Shangshu jizhu yin shu* 尚書集注音疏 ([1793 Jinshiji ed.], 8.25a–b), explains the context of this elliptical line as follows: "Chou Kung pleads with Shao Kung that he himself is no usurpator, but an ordinary minister, just as before the regency: Shao Kung should not urge him to retire, but on the contrary encourage him to achieve his work."

52. In the "Three Styles Stone Classics" (*Santi shijing* 三體石經) version of this line, *yun* 允 is written *xiong* 兄, "elder brother," which is obviously correct; see Karlgren, *Glosses*, no. 1893.

53. I here read *bu* 不, "not," as *pi* 丕, "very," as is common in Western Zhou texts.

54. For previous translations into English of the "Shao gao," see Legge, *The Shoo King*, 420–33; Karlgren, *The Book of Documents*, 48–51; and, for Karlgren's annotations, *Glosses*, nos. 1715–45.

55. Lin Zhiqi, *Shangshu quanjie* 尚書全解 (Tongzhitang jingjie ed.), 33.7a.

56. Karlgren (*Glosses*, no. 1718), following Yu Xingwu 于省吾 (*Shangshu xinzheng* 尚書新證 [1934; rpt. Taipei: Songgao shushe, 1985], 158–63 [3.1b–4a]), departs from all traditional interpreters in taking the address as being that of the Duke of Zhou. Both Karlgren and Yu argue that since the Duke was the recipient of the *bi* insignia, it would be he who would

be expected to "fold his hands and touch his head to the ground" (*bai shou qi shou* 拜手稽首), the phrase that introduces the chapter's address. While it is true that Western Zhou bronze inscriptions routinely describe gift recipients as doing this, the "Luo gao," the sister chapter to this "Shao gao," shows this phrase, repeatedly used by both the king and the Duke of Zhou, to be a conventional opening to any address respectfully delivered. Although Karlgren's glosses to this chapter remain as valuable as those for other chapters, I believe that this initial mistake causes him to misinterpret the entire thrust of the chapter.

57. Cai Chen, *Shu jizhuan*, 5.2b.

58. Not only is "to approve" the normal sense of *ruo* in Shang oracle-bone inscriptions, but it is also its sense later in the "Shao gao" in the expression "*mian qi tian ruo*" 面稽天若, "to face and fathom Heaven's approval."

59. The translations of both Legge and Karlgren treat the *wu* 無 of this line as the imperative *wu* 勿, and neglect entirely the conditional *ze* 則, suggesting that the "young son" has already succeeded and that he is being admonished not to neglect the elders. Not only is this grammatically unfounded, but more important it misses the intent of Grand Protector Shi: this is his admonition to the Duke of Zhou that if the king is given power, he will not be an autocrat but will accept advice from his ministers.

60. The expression *shao Shang di* 紹上帝, "to succeed the Lord on High," obviously refers to royal succession, but it is curious that the king should be said "to succeed" the Lord on High, especially if the "Lord on High" is to be construed as the high god known from Shang religion. I wonder if it might not refer to "the fathers on high," as suggested in Robert Eno, "Was There a High God *Ti* in Shang Religion?" *Early China* 15 (1990): especially 20–26.

61. See, for example, the contrasting interpretations of this divination rite offered by Qiu Xigui in "An Examination of Whether the Charges in Shang Oracle-Bone Inscriptions are Questions," *Early China* 14 (1989): 113–14, and by David S. Nivison in his response, pp. 154–55.

62. Creel, *The Origins of Statecraft in China*, 458.

63. Cited at *Maoshi zhengyi* 毛詩正義 (Sibu beiyao ed.), 8/2.1a.

64. For other English translations of this poem, see James Legge, *The Chinese Classics*, vol. 4, *The She King or The Book of Poetry* (1871; rpt. Hong Kong: Hong Kong University Press, 1960), 233–35; Arthur Waley, *The Book of Songs* (1937; rev. ed. New York: Grove Press, 1987), 235; Bernhard Karlgren, *The Book of Odes* (1950; rpt. Stockholm: Museum of Far Eastern Antiquities, 1974), 99–100.

65. See, for instance, Cai Chen, *Shu jizhuan*, 4.34b.

66. See, for instance, *Lunheng* (Sibu beiyao ed.), 18.17b.

67. *Shiji*, 33.1519–20. The second account, in the "Meng Tian liezhuan" 蒙
恬列傳 (88.2569), differs only slightly. It reads:

> 及王能治國, 有賊臣言: 周公旦欲爲亂久矣, 王若不倫, 必
> 有大事. 王乃大怒, 周公旦走而奔於楚. 成王觀於記府, 得
> 周公旦沈書, 乃流涕曰: 孰謂周公旦欲爲亂乎! 殺言之者
> 而反周公旦.

> Coming to the time when the king was able to rule the state, there
> was a thieving minister who said, "Duke Dan of Zhou has long
> wished to create havoc. If the king is not careful, there will cer-
> tainly be great trouble." The king was then greatly angered, and
> Duke Dan of Zhou fled and went into exile in Chu. King Cheng
> made inspection in the Note Repository, gained the text of Duke
> Dan of Zhou's submersion [of his fingernail parings], and then
> with tears flowing said, "Who said that Duke Dan of Zhou wished
> to create havoc?" He killed the one who had said it and caused
> Duke Dan of Zhou to return.

68. *Mozi* (Sibu beiyao ed.), 9.16a–b.

69. *Mozi*, 11.11b–12a.

70. Chen Mengjia, "Xi-Zhou tongqi duandai" 西周銅器斷代, II, *Kaogu
xuebao* 考古學報, 1955.10: 75. The original references are *Zuo zhuan*,
Ding 定 4; *Mencius*, 3B/9.

71. For these reconstructions, see Axel Schuessler, *A Dictionary of Early Zhou
Chinese* (Honolulu: University of Hawaii Press, 1987), 185, 712. This
phonetic similarity was pointed out to me by William G. Boltz, who
explains that the vacillation is probably akin to that between the sur-
names Tian 田 and Chen 陳 in the state of Qi 齊.

72. Guo Moruo, *Liang-Zhou jinwenci daxi kaoshi* 兩周金文辭大系考釋
(Tokyo: Bunkyudo shoten, 1935), 11b.

73. The graph for Chu 楚 appears quite frequently in Western Zhou bronze
inscriptions, in all cases clearly written with the central element *xu* 疋
rather than the *qu* 去 of the "Qin *gui*"; see *Jinwen bian* 金文編, ed. Rong
Geng 容庚, with Zhang Zhenlin 張振林 and Ma Guoquan 馬國權
(4th rev. ed.; Beijing: Zhonghua shuju, 1984), 408–9 no. 0967. The reasoning behind Guo's identification of the "Qin *gui*" graph 𣥂 with *chu*
楚 is really quite transparent: by showing that the Zhou had attacked the
state of Chu during the reign of King Cheng, Guo was hoping thereby to

substantiate his position in the well-known debate over the periodization of the "Ling *yi*" and "Ling *gui*" vessels (on which, see Shaughnessy, *Sources of Western Zhou History*, 193–216). His position in that debate is now generally regarded to be mistaken, and the association he drew between it and the "Qin *gui*" inscription is surely irrelevant.

74. Although there is no direct evidence regarding the location of this Feng, most commentators on the "Ran *fangding*" inscription assume that it was located near Pugu, which at this time was certainly near Qufu. For a discussion of these locations, see Gu Jiegang, "Zhougong dongzheng he dongfang gezude qianxi" 周公東征和東方各族的遷徙, *Wenshi* 27 (1986): 8–9.

75. *Shiji*, 33.1522.

76. See Legge, *The Shoo King*, prolegomena 146. This record is corroborated by the *Shangshu dazhuan* 尚書大傳, which states, apparently after describing the duke's return of governance to King Cheng, "three years later the Duke of Zhou retired to Feng" (*sannian zhi hou Zhougong lao yu Feng* 三年之後周公老於豐); *Shangshu dazhuan* (Congshu jicheng ed.), 4.2b.

77. Lei Xueqi, *Zhushu jinian yizheng* 竹書紀年義證 (1810; rpt. Taipei: Yiwen yinshuguan, 1976), 282–83.

78. Legge, *The Shoo King*, 12.

79. Ibid., prolegomena 146.

5

The Role of Grand Protector Shi in the Consolidation of the Zhou Conquest

Although most of the inscribed Western Zhou bronze vessels discovered in recent years have come out of the earth of Shaanxi province, the homeland and capital area of the Zhou people, this has not been the only area in which bronzes have come to light.[1] One of the most important of these discoveries, or, perhaps, better in this case, rediscoveries, was made in Washington, D.C. The "Taibao 大保 *gui*" (Sh 2.3:58), originally discovered in Liangshan 梁山, Shandong, during the first part of the Daoguang emperor's reign (r. 1821–50) in the Qing dynasty, had long since disappeared.[2] Then, in 1969, Mrs. Agnes E. Meyer donated to the Freer Gallery of the Smithsonian Institution what she described as a "Chou dynasty *kuei*" that had long been stored at her summer house in Mount Kisco, New York.[3] When the Freer curators received the vessel, they were astonished to find themselves the possessors of what many regarded at that time as the earliest vessel of the Western Zhou dynasty.[4]

Even though the discovery in 1976 of the "Li 利 *gui*" (Sh 50.*Ho*14:321), a vessel which refers to King Wu's *jiazi* day conquest of Shang and commemorates an event that took place just eight days later, has now certainly preempted this distinction,[5] the "Taibao *gui*" remains an extremely important source for the history of the early Western Zhou. Indeed, it could be argued from both historical and historiographical perspectives that the "Taibao *gui*" is still the more important of these two vessels. Whereas the maker of the "Li *gui*" is apparently unmentioned elsewhere in the historical record,[6] the "Taibao *gui*" was cast for one of the founding fathers of the dynasty, Grand Protector (*taibao* 大保) Shi 奭, the Duke of Shao 召, a figure already well known from the traditional literature of the period.[7] Moreover, the Grand Protector also plays

137

prominent roles in the inscriptions of at least five other important bronze vessels cast during the reigns of King Cheng (r. 1042/1035–1006) and King Kang (r. 1005/1003–978),[8] the second and third reigns of the dynasty. In this way, it is a source that illustrates well one of the most important methodologies of bronze studies: the association of two or more bronzes by virtue of a shared personal name.[9] For both of these reasons, it seems useful to reexmaine the recently rediscovered "Taibao *gui*," its inscription and historical background, together with other vessels either cast by or mentioning its maker, the Grand Protector.

In many ways, the "Taibao *gui*" resembles the "Li *gui*." Like the "Li *gui*," the vessel is decorated with a very pronounced and forceful animal-mask design. Its two large handles are crowned with horned animal heads and have large rectangular pendants descending from the lower curve. Although the "Taibao *gui*" does not rest on a rectangular base as the "Li *gui*" does, the foot of the vessel is still relatively high, making the vessel appear elevated. The inscription, too, greatly resembles the inscription of the "Li *gui*." It is comprised of thirty-four graphs in four columns. The graphs appear elongated and are of varying sizes. Finally, like the "Li *gui*," the "Taibao *gui*" inscription also relates a Zhou attack on Shang. In this case, however, the attack is not that led by King Wu against Di Xin (r. 1086–1045), the attack that resulted in the original conquest, but rather a second attack occurring some years later, after the death of King Wu, and directed against a rebellion led, at least nominally, by Di Xin's son Lufu 祿父, better known by his post-humous reign title Wu Geng. Although the inscription has been previously translated, it certainly warrants detailed reconsideration.[10]

TAIBAO GUI

王伐彔子耴叡厥反王

The king attacked Luzi Sheng[11] and suppressed[12] his rebellion. The king

降征令于大保克

sent down [a/the] campaign command to the Grand Protector. The Grand Protector was capable

苟亡遣王伐大保易休

of being respectful and not having any mistake.[13] The king immortalized[14] the Grand Protector, granting a benefice

宋土用彝對令

[of] Song-land;[15] [he] uses this vessel to respond to the command.

According to the relatively abundant historical sources pertaining to the establishment of the Western Zhou dynasty, after having defeated the Shang at the battle of Muye 牧野, King Wu quickly moved to organize his family into a royal administration. His next eldest brother, Guanshu Xian 管叔鮮, was deputed to the former Shang capital where he was to oversee the vanquished Shang people and their nominal ruler, Lufu or Wu Geng. Guanshu was joined in this important task of maintaining order in the conquered territories by two younger brothers, Caishu Du 蔡叔度 and Huoshu Chu 霍叔處, the fifth and eighth of the ten direct-line sons of King Wen.[16] King Wu's second eldest brother, Zhougong Dan 周公旦, the famous Duke of Zhou, was appointed to remain in the Zhou capital and serve as "Grand Captain" (*taishi* 大師), tantamount to a royal chancellor. In this, he was to share authority with his elder half-brother, Duke Shi of Shao, who was named "Grand Protector."[17]

Although this administration was already in place when King Wu died just two years after the conquest, his eldest son and heir-apparent, to be known as King Cheng, had not yet reached maturity.[18] Given the still precarious circumstances of the young dynasty, the Duke of Zhou, apparently acting on his own initiative, assumed full royal authority.[19] Many of the sources for this period are colored by the legend that was to develop around the Duke of Zhou and portray all of his actions in the most favorable of lights.[20]

Still, there is little doubt that the Duke's elder brother Guanshu Xian regarded this move as a usurpation and, in concert not only with his brothers stationed in the east but also with Wu Geng and former allies of the Shang, revolted against the Western court. The court responded quickly and decisively to this. Under the combined leadership of the Duke of Zhou, Grand Protector Shi and, at least nominally, King Cheng, the revolt was thoroughly suppressed within three years. In addition to executing Guanshu Xian and Wu Geng, and exiling the other rebel siblings, the court took further steps to lessen the chances of another such revolt. One of these was to carry the campaign beyond just the territory of the Shang to attack and subjugate the independent states situated further east in present-day Shandong. These states were then colonized by other royal relatives, who were rewarded for their allegiance and military exploits with grants of land. One of the first such grants seems to be that commemorated by the "Taibao *gui*," which also confirms the Grand Protector's role in suppressing this rebellion.

While Grand Protector Shi was only a half-brother of King Wu and the Duke of Zhou, the merit he achieved in the campaigns of conquest and suppression, coupled with an incredible longevity,[21] made him one of the most important of the dynasty's founding fathers. Indeed, were the history of this period to be written solely on the basis of bronze inscriptional evidence, the Grand Protector would probably be considered as more important than even the Duke of Zhou.[22] Some outline of his career, both at the height of his military activity and later in his old age, is preserved in a number of other early Western Zhou inscribed bronze vessels that can be associated with the "Taibao *gui*" by virtue of their mention of the Grand Protector. Two of these are closely contemporary with the "Taibao *gui*," dating probably to the third or fourth years of King Cheng's reign, and provide further information regarding the Grand Protector's role in the suppression of the Wu Geng rebellion, while three others, all of which display characteristics dating them to the reign of King Kang, portray him in his later years as something of an *eminence grise*, the power behind the king.[23] In addition to supplying information regarding the career of this important figure, this set of vessels also serves an important methodological role by illustrating the evolution of bronze styles over the first two generations of the dynasty.

In many ways the most interesting member of this group is a pair of vessels generally known as the "Bao 保 *you*" (Sh 4.16:173) and "Bao *zun*," though they should instead probably be called the "Chuo 𧾷 *you*" and "Chuo *zun*."[24] Discovered in 1948 in Luoyang, the *you* is now in the Shanghai Museum and the *zun* is in the Henan Provincial Museum in Zhengzhou. The inscription, which is nearly identical on both the vessels and covers of both vessels, presents a number of linguistic features that require more than the usual explication.

Chuo you

乙卯王令保及
Yimao (day 52), the king commanded the Protector[25] to apprehend[26]
殷東或五侯征
the Yin eastern states' five lords.[27] Chuo[28]
兄六品蔑曆于
was given six types[29] and had martial accomplishments praised[30] by[31]
保易賓用作文
the Protector and was awarded an audience; [he] herewith makes [for his] cultured
父癸宗寶障彝遘
Father Gui's temple [this] treasured, sacrificial vessel; meeting

亏 四方迨王大祀袚
with the four regions convoking at the king's great sacrificial offering
亏 周才二月既望
in Zhou; in the second month, after the full moon.[32]

Were it not for the reference to the (Grand) Protector, the mention of
the king's sacrificial offering "in Zhou," and the dating notation "after the
full moon," it would be easy to confuse this inscription with precedents cast
during the final years of the Shang dynasty. Chen Mengjia has pointed out
eight features in it that are usually associated with Shang rather than Zhou
inscriptions.[33] These divide evenly between orthographic and syntactic points.
Chen notes four graphs whose shapes are similar to Shang examples and/or
different from Zhou examples: *guo* 或 in line 2, (*xiong* 兄:) *kuang* 貺 in line
4, *han* 曆 (/*li* 曆) in line 4, and *wang* 望 in line 7. He further notes four
syntactic similarities between this and Shang inscriptions:

1. The addition of the word *zong* 宗, "temple," to the ancestor
   appellation;
2. The use of *gou* 遘 "to meet," to introduce the "great event" year
   notation;
3. The use of *he* 迨 in the sense of "convocation;"
4. The splitting of the date notation, with the *ganzhi* day placed at
   the head of the inscription and the (year and) month placed at
   its end.

To these, it could be added that the dedication of the vessel to "Father Gui" is
indicative of a Shang (or at least eastern) caster not only by virtue of the use
of a *tiangan* name,[34] but also due to the use of the word *fu* 父 for "father"
instead of *kao* 考, "deceased-father," which is standard in Zhou inscriptions.

While the reference to the king's sacrifice in Zhou is conclusive evidence
that the vessel was cast during the Zhou period,[35] all of these Shang features
of the inscription suggest that the maker of the vessel must have been of
eastern origin. This point, overlooked in most studies of this inscription, is
confirmed by the proper interpretation of the benefice record, "Chuo *kuang
liu pin, mie han yu* Bao, *xi bin*" 征兄六品蔑曆亏保易賓. The grammar of
this sentence is rather complex but the postverbal *yu* 亏 certainly indicates a
passive sentence.[36] Since the words *mie han* 蔑曆, "to praise martial accomplishments," before this *yu* are generally taken to be a verb-object compound,
there is no subject in this clause. Therefore, the complete sentence must include
the previous clause as well and have a compound structure, with *chuo* 征

being the subject of two different verb-object compounds, *kuang liu pin* 兄 六品 (to give six types) and *mie han*. Thus understood, *chuo*, must be the recipient of these awards and can only be a proper noun. In support of this, there are a number of other inscribed bronze vessels attesting to the existence of a Shang clan named Chuo in the vicinity of Luoyang.[37] Thus, the correct interpretation of this inscription on the "Chuo *you*" demonstrates that not all of the former Shang people joined in Wu Geng's revolt; some, at least, served under Grand Protector Shi in his suppression of it and were appropriately awarded by him for their aid.

The third of the vessels deriving from the eastern campaign to suppress the Shang rebellion was also cast by a subordinate of the Grand Protector in order to commemorate an award made by him. The "Lü 旅 *ding*" (Sh 2.5:72) is an extremely representative example of a King Cheng-period *ding*. Maintaining the *taotie* 饕餮 design of Shang vessels, the "Lü *ding*" also has long, tubular legs and a tripartite lobing of the belly, both traits particularly associated with this period.[38] The inscription, though somewhat effaced, displays the same type of calligraphy, with elongated, narrow graphs, as found in the "Li *gui*" and "Taibao *gui*."[39]

Lü ding

佳公大保來
It was the year that the duke Grand Protector came from[40]
伐反夷年才
attacking the rebelling Yi; in
十又一月庚申公
the eleventh month, *gengshen* (day 57)[41], the duke
才盩官公易
was at the Zhou garrison;[42] the duke awarded
旅貝十朋旅用
Lü cowries, ten strands; Lü herewith
旅父障彝
makes [for his] father [this] sacrificial vessel.

After the momentous events of this rebellion and its suppression, King Cheng apparently grew into his office and succeeded in consolidating Zhou rule throughout both the Zhou western territories and the eastern lands formerly ruled by Shang. But, with the exception of documents pertaining to the establishment of the eastern capital at Luoyang, which have recently been supplemented by the important inscription on the "He 阿 *zun*" (Sh

48. *Ho*1:171),[43] and occasional notices of royal appointments to lords of newly established states,[44] the historical record is largely blank for the remainder of King Cheng's reign. In traditional historiography, this period and extending into the first part of King Kang's reign was characterized succinctly, and apparently accurately, by Sima Qian 司馬遷 (c. 145–86 B.C.): "The world was at peace and for more than forty years punishments were not used."[45] Indeed, the fuller record contained in the *Bamboo Annals* also shows that through the remainder of King Cheng's thirty-seven-year rule (including the seven years when the Duke of Zhou acted as regent), royal authority went unchallenged.

With the death of King Cheng in 1006, however, the royal court was faced with the need to institute a routine succession. The founding fathers still on the scene, paramount among whom was Grand Protector Shi, surely recalled the devestating consequences of the irregular transfer of power following King Wu's death. It is therefore not surprising to find in the *Book of Documents* a detailed account of the ceremonies legitimating King Kang's succession. And since it shows in a singularly impressive fashion the preeminence to which Grand Protector Shi had risen, the "Gu ming" 顧命 (translated by James Legge as "The Testamentary Charge") chapter deserves to be cited at length.[46]

> It was the fourth month, on the growing brightness; the king was not well. On *jiazi* (day 1), the king then washed his hands and face. The attendants dressed him in cap and clothes and leaned him on a jade armrest. They then assembled Grand Protector Shi of Shao, the Elder of Rui, the Elder of Tong, the Duke of Bi, the Lord of Wei, the Duke of Mao, the captains, tiger (ministers=) braves, the hundred governors and the controllers of affairs. The king said:
>
> > Wuhu! The illness greatly advances; it is critical. The pains come daily and [now] constantly remain. I fear that I will not be able to make an oath to discuss the succession. Here I will command you [with] detailed instructions. The former rulers King Wen and King Wu manifested their doubled brightness and established their beauty. Arraying the teachings they toiled, but toiling they did not transgress, thereby being able to pierce Yin and gather the great mandate. I, the stupid one who has come after them, have respectfully met the awe of heaven and successively maintained the great instructions of Wen and Wu, never daring blindly to change them. Now heaven sends down

[this] illness. It is perilous that I will not arise, will not recover. Would that you understand these words of mine, therewith respectfully protecting the eldest son Zhao and vasting helping him over difficulties. If pliant with the distant ones, you will be able to cause them to draw near and you will bring peace to and encourage the many states, small and great. Think how a man disorders himself in the trappings of power and you will not take Zhao to covet tribute in what is not critical.

These [officials] having received the command, then returned and brought out the stitched garments in the courtyard. On the next day *yichou* (day 2), the king died.

The Grand Protector commanded Zhong Huan and Nangong Mao to serve and assist Lu Ji, Lord of Qi, with two shields and dagger-axes and one-hundred tiger braves to meet son Zhao outside of the southern gate and in procession to enter the solemn chamber, grievingly to dwell at the ancestral altar. On *dingmao* (day 4), he commanded the recording of the transition measures. On the seventh day, *guiyou* (day 10), the elder assistant commanded the officers to prepare the materials. . . .

The king [wearing] hempen cap and embroidered robes ascended by way of the guests' stairs. The officials and lords of states [wearing] hempen caps and ant[-colored] robes entered and assumed position. The Grand Protector, Grand Scribe and Grand Master of Rites all [wore] hempen caps and red robes. The Grand Protector elevating the large ritual-tablet and the [High =] Grand Master of Rites presenting the chalice[47] ascended by way of the main stairs. The Grand Scribe holding the document ascended by way of the guests' stairs. Standing before the king he intoned the command, saying:

> The august deceased-king leaning on a jade armrest announced his final command, commanding you to succeed to the instructions, to look over and be lord of the state of Zhou, to follow and comply with the great laws, and to bring peace to the world, thereby in answer extolling the bright instructions of [kings] Wen and Wu.

The king twice bowed. Arising, he answered, saying:

> Insignificant am I, the small child, last [of our line]; would

that I be able to govern the four quarters so as respectfully to dread the awe of heaven.

Then he received the chalice. The king thrice strained [the wine], thrice sacrificed and thrice drank. The Grand Master of Rites said, "It is enjoyed." The Grand Protector received the chalice, descended and washed his hands. Taking a different chalice, he held a demi-ladle so as to pour the sacrifice and drink.[48] Giving the chalice to an altar man, he bowed. The king bowed in answer. The Grand Protector descended and with the many lords exited the temple gate and waited.

The king exited, being within the Response Gate. The Grand Protector led the many lords of the western lands to enter the left of the Response Gate. The Duke of Bi led the many lords of the eastern lands to enter the right of the Response Gate. They all [wore] brocades and knee-covers, yellow and red.[49] The guests raised and presented their tablets together with their presents saying, "[We] the [one or two =] several ministers and defenders dare to hold the offerings of our fields." All twice bowed and touched their heads to the ground. The king, being the proper successor, bowed in answer to each in turn.[50] The Grand Protector and the Elder of Rui together advanced and saluted each other. Both twice bowed and touched their heads to the ground and said:

> We dare respectfully to announce to the son of heaven: august heaven changed the great state Yin's mandate. It was Wen and Wu of Zhou who received guiding approval and were able to be solicitous of the western regions. It was the newly deceased king [i.e., King Cheng] who completed the moderation of awards and punishments and consolidated their efforts, thereby expansively bequeathing beneficence to the heirs. Now the king must respect it! Spread the august six armies and do not corrupt our high ancestor's unique mandate.

The king said to the effect:

> Lords, husbandmen, males and defenders of the many states; I, the one man, Zhao, announce in return: Formerly, the rulers Wen and Wu grandly brought peace and prosperity, did not bring hardship or misfortune and caused there to come to be an equal trust, thereby manifesting their brightness in the

world. Then, they also had bearlike officers and ministers without two hearts to protect and govern the royal house, thereby first being commanded by Shang Di. August heaven therewith instructed its way and gave them the four quarters. Then they commanded them to establish the lords as trees and curtains among us, the heirs. Now, my [one or two =] several elder uncles, would that you assist in looking back to make concordant your ministers of the former dukes who served the former kings. Although your persons be on the outside, your hearts should never not be at the royal chamber. Therewith present solicitude of their approval and do not bequeath shame on me, the stripling.

When the multitude of dukes had all heard the command, they saluted each other and hurriedly exited. The king removed his cap and restored his mourning clothes.

The ceremonial role that the "Gu ming" attributes to Grand Protector Shi, from leading the many lords into the final audience with King Cheng, to making the matching libation to the ancestors during King Kang's coronation, to announcing the command to the new king, clearly shows him to have been the most honored official at this time, already some thirty years removed from the events commemorated by the "Taibao *gui*." Moreover, not only did the Grand Protector live to ensure this smooth transition from the reign of King Cheng to that of King Kang, but, if the *Bamboo Annals* is correct, he lived almost to the end of this next reign. Although this requires a life span of nearly one hundred years for him, it is at least partially substantiated by three more inscribed bronze vessels, all of which mention him and all of which almost certainly date to the reign of King Kang. Indeed, one of the three, the "Zuoce Da 作冊大 *fangding*" (Sh 8.42:440), serves as a "standard" for this reign by virtue of its posthumous reference to King Cheng.[51]

ZUOCE DA FANGDING

公束鑄武王
The duke came[52] from casting the King Wu
成王異鼎隹四
and King Cheng *yiding*.[53] It was the fourth
月既生霸己
month, after the growing brightness, *ji-*

丑公賞乍冊
chou (day 26), the duke awarded Recorder
大白馬大揚
Da a white horse; Da extolled
皇天尹大保
august Heaven's assistant the Grand Protector's
宜用乍祖丁
grace, herewith making [for his] Grandfather Ding
寶障彝鼎
[this] treasured, sacrificial vessel. Family-sign.

The Grand Protector is extolled in this inscription as "heaven's assistant" (*tian yin* 天尹). In the other two vessels dating from this period, he does not receive quite such an honorific accolade, but his actual treatment is perhaps even more honored. In both cases, highly placed officials dispatch subordinates to serve him, and he responds by awarding them gifts.

The first of the two vessels, the "Jin 堇 *ding*" (Sh 51.1:449), a vessel that is almost an exact duplicate of the King Kang "standard" "Da Yu 盂 *ding*" (12.61:647), commemorates one such mission initiated by the Lord of Yan, a son or grandson of the Grand Protector.[54]

JIN DING

匽侯令堇餯
The Lord of Yan commanded Jin to feast
大保于宗周庚申
the Grand Protector in Zongzhou. On *gengshen* (day 57),
大保賞堇貝用乍
the Grand Protector granted Jin cowries; [he] herewith makes
大子癸寶障彝中
[for] his eldest son Gui [this] treasured, sacrificial vessel. Family-sign.

The second of the vessels, an oddly shaped vessel called the "Shu 叔 *tuoqi*" (Sh 2.6:77),[55] is important as the record of a similar mission initiated by one Wang Jiang 王姜. The identity of this Wang Jiang is central to one of the most important periodization problems in the study of early Western Zhou inscribed bronzes. While it is a question too complex to be resolved here, it seems safe to say that she was the queen of a Zhou king, probably King Kang.[56]

SHU TUOQI

隹王萒于宗周
It was when the king made ritual-entreaty at Zongzhou;
王姜史叔吏于大
Wang Jiang caused Shu to be deputed to the Grand
保賞叔鬱乩白
Protector, [who] granted Shu sweet wine, white
金㲋牛叔對大保
metal and a *zhu*[?][57] ox. Shu responds to the Grand Protector's
休用乍寶搏彝
beneficence, herewith making [this] treasured, sacrificial vessel.

It is worth reiterating here that these last three vessels are important not only historically for the evidence they provide concerning the later career of Grand Protector Shi, but also historiographically for the development in bronze styles they manifest over the course of the Grand Protector's life, which, as we have seen, spanned the first two full generations of the young dynasty. Just as the Grand Protector helped to ensure a regular political succession, so too might this stylistic development be best characterized as a movement toward regularity. It is perceptible in both the calligraphy of the inscriptions and the shape and decor of the vessels. For instance, the disproportionately elongated graphs of the first years of the dynasty show evidence already by the reign of King Kang of evolving into a more nearly square, blocklike shape. Consistent with this attention to the proportions of individual graphs, there is also a definite tendency toward proportional spacing of the inscription as a whole; in addition to well-defined vertical columns, horizontal rows also begin to emerge in the later inscriptions. With respect to vessel shape and decor, a comparison of the "Lü *ding*," one of the earlier vessels of this set, and the "Jin *ding*," perhaps its latest member, also clearly displays this tendency towards regularity. It can be seen in at least three areas: first, the pronounced *taotie* design covering the entire body of the "Lü *ding*" gives way to a single band of decor under the lip of the later vessel; second, the extremely long, slender legs of the "Lü *ding*" are replaced with shorter, sturdier legs; and third, the tripartite lobing of the "Lü *ding*" belly is also smoothed into one continuous curve. It is by allowing comparisons such as these to be made that the association of several vessels into a single set has become one of the most important methodologies in the study of Western Zhou bronzes, and the "Taibao *gui*" and its associated vessels rightfully have pride of place as perhaps the single most important set from the beginning of the dynasty.

NOTES

1. In addition to the vessels to be discussed here, important pieces found in locations other than the Zhou Shaanxi homeland include the "Yihou Ze 宜侯夨 *gui*" (Sh 10.52:529; for this notation style, see note 2), discovered in Dantu 丹徒, Jiangsu; the "Kanghou 康侯 *gui*" (Sh 4.14:141), discovered in either Jixian 汲縣 or Junxian 濬縣, Henan; the "Ling 令 *gui*" (Sh 6.24:255) and "Ling *yi*" (Sh 6.25:276), discovered near Luoyang 洛陽, and various pieces cast by the Lord of Xing discovered throughout Hebei and Liaoning provinces (for which, see below, n. 44). It bears noting that almost all of these vessels date to the first reigns of the dynasty. Discoveries of late Western Zhou bronzes, with only a few insignificant exceptions, have been restricted to the area of modern Shaanxi. This distribution might suggest a diminished capacity on the part of the later Zhou kings to project their authority.

2. The vessel and its inscription were first published in Xu Zonggan's 徐宗干 (1796–1866) *Jizhou jinshizhi* 濟州金石志 (preface dated 1843), and the inscription at least had been mentioned in most of the more important studies of Western Zhou bronzes. For sources published through 1963, see Shirakawa Shizuka 白川靜, *Kinbun tsūshaku* 金文通釋, *Hakutsuru bijitsukanshi* 白鶴美術館志, fascicle 2 (1962), no. 3, 58ff. (subsequent references to this work, which, in addition to providing Shirakawa's own views also serves as a convenient compendium of previous research, will be in the form "Sh 2.3:58" and will follow in the text the first mention of each inscription.

3. For an account of this donation and a study of the vessel and related vessels (including references to other sources not cited by Shirakawa), see Thomas Lawton, "A Group of Early Western Chou Period Bronze Vessels," *Ars Orientalis* 10 (1975): 111–21; 190–92. For the most recent study of the vessel, see Chen Shou 陳壽, "Taibao gui de fuchu he Taibao zhu qi" 大保簋的復出和大保諸器, *Kaogu yu wenwu* 考古與文物 1980.4: 23–30.

4. The "Dafeng 大豐 *gui*," now more often referred to as the "Tian Wang 天亡 *gui*" (Sh 1.1:1), was and still is acknowledged by most scholars to date to the preceding reign of King Wu (r. 1049/45–1043), but it is also considered by many to predate King Wu's conquest of Shang and thus to be "predynastic;" see, for instance, Sun Zuoyun 孫作雲, "Shuo Tian Wang gui wei Wuwang mie Shang yiqian tongqi" 說天亡簋爲武王滅商以前銅器, *Wenwu cankao ziliao* 文物參考資料 1958.1: 57–64. The Li 利 *gui* (Sh 50.*Ho*14:321), mentioned below, had at that time not yet been discovered.

5. For excellent illustrations of the "Li *gui*" and its inscription, see, *The Great Bronze Age of China*, ed. Wen Fong (New York: Metropolitan Museum of Art, 1980), 203, 215. Among recent studies not considered in Shirakawa's *comte rendu*, the most notable are Xu Zhongshu 徐中舒, "Xi-Zhou Li gui mingwen jianshi" 西周利簋銘文簡釋, *Sichuan daxue xuebao* 四川大學學報 (*Shehui kexue* 社會科學) 1980.2: 109–10, 103, and Yan Yiping 嚴一苹, "Cong Li gui ming kan fa Zhou nian" 從利簋銘看伐紂年, *Zhongguo wenzi* 中國文字, n.s. 8 (1983): 1–22. My own study of the vessel, with a complete annotated translation of its inscription, is included in my *Sources of Western Zhou History: Inscribed Bronze Vessels* (Berkeley: University of California Press, 1991), 87–105.

6. The "Li *gui*" is dedicated to a Duke of Zhan (Zhan *gong* 擅). Tang Lan 唐蘭 has suggested that this *zhan* 擅 is equivalent to *tan* 檀, on the basis of which he identifies this Duke of Tan with the figure Elder Da of Tan (Tanbo Da) mentioned in several early texts as one of King Wu's leading lieutenants; "Xi-Zhou shidai zui zao de yijian tongqi Li gui mingwen jieshi" 西周時代最早的一件銅器利簋銘文解釋 *Wenwu* 文物 1977.8: 8. (The textual locus for Elder Da is the "Ke Yin" 克殷 chapter of the *Yi Zhou shu* 逸周書 (Sibu beiyao ed. 4.3b). For an extended discussion of his historical significance, albeit in a different context, see Kaizuka Shigeki 貝塚茂樹, "Shinshutsu Dan-haku Tatsu ki kō" 新出檀伯達器考, *Tōhō gakuhō* 東方學報 (Kyoto) 8 (1937); rpt. in *Kaizuka Shigeki chosaku shū* 貝塚茂樹著作集 (Tokyo: Chu'o koronsha, 1977), vol. 3, 171–214. Tang brings the identification full-circle by proposing that Da 達, which means "penetrating," and Li 利, the name of the caster of the "Li *gui*" and a word that means "sharp," are related to one another as name (*ming* 名) and cognomen (*zi* 字), so that Li may in fact be the historical figure Elder Da of Tan.

7. Duke Shi of Shao is best known as the namesake of two chapters of the *Book of Documents*, the "Shao gao" 召誥, which records a report made by him to King Cheng (r. 1042/1035–1006), and the "Jun Shi" 君奭, which records an address to him by the Duke of Zhou, and as the titular founder of the state of Yan 燕, for which see the "Yan Shaogong shijia" 燕召公世家 chapter of the *Shiji* 史記 (Zhonghua shuju ed. 34.1549–50). As we will see below, he also figures importantly in the "Gu ming" 顧命 chapter of the *Book of Documents*, a text that records the events surrounding the death of King Cheng and the inauguration of King Kang (r. 1005/1003–978).

8. For dates of the early Western Zhou reigns mentioned in this study, see

David S. Nivison, "The Dates of Western Chou," *Harvard Journal of Asiatic Studies* 43.2 (1983): 481–580. See, too, Edward L. Shaughnessy, "The 'Current' *Bamboo Annals* and the Date of the Zhou Conquest of Shang," *Early China* 11–12 (1985–87): 33–60. A comprehensive discussion of Western Zhou chronology is given in my *Sources of Western Zhou History*, 217–87.

9. In addition to the set of vessels organized around common reference to the Grand Protector, the "Taibao *gui*" belongs to another set as well, the vessels with which it was jointly discovered. As mentioned above, the vessel was originally discovered in the early nineteenth century in Liangshan, Shandong, one of a group of seven vessels that soon came to be known as the "Seven Vessels of Liangshan." All seven of the vessels appear to have been related to Grand Protector Shi in one way or another. The discovery included, in addition to the "Taibao *gui*," two *fangding* 方鼎 also cast by him, both of which are inscribed simply, "Grand Protector cast" (*Taibao zhu* 大保鑄). Three of the other vessels appear to be dedicated to him or to his descendants, who, like him, were referred to as lords of Shao, but who were enfeoffed with the state of Yan, centered around present-day Peking. Of these, the longest inscription is on the "Bo Xian 伯害 *ding*" (Sh 8.40:425), a vessel probably datable to two generations after the Taibao *gui*.

> It was the ninth month, after the growing brightness, *xinyou* (day 58), at Yan; the lord awarded Xian cowries and metal, (and he) extolled the lord's beneficence, herewith making (for) Father Xin, Elder of Shao (this) treasured, sacrificial vessel. (May) Xian for ten-thousand years (have) sons and grandsons to treasure (it) and gloriously (use:) sacrifice to the Grand Protector.

The final member of the "Seven Vessels of Liangshan" is certainly the earliest vessel of the group and probably also the most famous. It is the "Xiaochen Yu 小臣艅 *zun*," better known in the West as the Brundage Rhino, since it is part of the Avery Brundage Collection of the Asian Art Museum of San Francisco; see Rene Yvon d'Argence, *Chinese Treasures from the Avery Brundage Collection* (San Francisco: Asian Art Musueum, 1968), 139. This is not a Western Zhou vessel at all, dating instead to the late Shang. There is at least some suggestion that the name of the Shang subject who cast this vessel is ancestral to the name of the territory granted to the Grand Protector and commemorated by him with the "Taibao *gui*;" see below, n. 15. Whatever the merits of this suggestion might be, it is entirely plausible that the Brundage Rhino was originally taken by the Grand Protector as a spoil of war, and in this manner found its way into the group of vessels buried by his descendants. For excellent studies of the "Seven Vessels of Liangshan," see Lawton, "A Group of Early Western Chou Period Bronze Vessels," and Chen Shou, "Taibao gui de fuchu."

10. For citations of Chinese commentaries and a Japanese translation, see Sh 2.3:58. For the earliest translation into a Western language, see Max Loehr, "Bronzentexte der Chou-Zeit: Chou I (1)," *Sinologische Arbeiten* 2 (1944): 59–70; for English translations, see W. A. C. H. Dobson, *Early Archaic Chinese* (Toronto: U. of Toronto Press, 1962), 190; Lawton, "A Group of Early Western Chou Period Bronze Vessels," 119–20.

11. Most commentators agree that "Luzi" refers to Lufu, who, after the Zhou conquest, was installed by the Zhou as nominal leader of the Shang people, and who is generally referred to by the posthumous reign title Wu Geng. There is less agreement regarding the following graph, generally transcribed as *sheng* 聖. Shirakawa interprets it as the name of Luzi, citing an inscription reading, "The Son of Heaven Sheng makes [for] Father Ding [this] vessel" (for the vessel, see Wu Dacheng 吳大澂, *Kezhai jigulu* 愙齋集古錄 [1896], 21.9), and contending that only a figure of Lufu's stature would dare to appropriate the title of "Son of Heaven"; Sh 2.3:60.

12. The word *zha* 叡 occurs commonly in Western Zhou bronze inscriptions as an exclamatory particle, and its usage here is interpreted in that way by many; e.g., Yang Shuda 楊樹達, *Jiweiju jinwen shuo* 積微居金文說 (Beijing: Kexue chubanshe, 1959), 87. But the syntax suggests that it should be verbal and the meaning for the word given in the *Shuo wen* 說文, "to pluck and hold down" (*cha bei ye* 叉卑也), or, with Duan Yucai 段玉裁 (1735–1815), "to pluck that below"; *Shuo wen jiezi Duan-zhu* 說文解字段注 (Sibu beiyao ed.), 3B.13a, is appropriate here.

13. For an excellent summation of the evidence available to interpret this difficult phrase, see Lawton, "A Group of Early Western Chou Bronze Vessels," 119n45.

14. The reading of this graph is promblematic, with such suggestions as *dao* 道(:*dao* 導, "to lead"; Wu Shifen 吳式芬, *Jungu lu jinwen* 攗古錄金文 [preface dated 1895], 2,3.82); *yi* 俟 (to await; Liu Xinyuan 劉心源, *Qigushi jijinwen shu* 奇觚室吉金文述 [preface dated 1902], 3.32); *pai* 派 (to entrust; Guo Moruo 郭沫若, *Liang-Zhou jinwenci daxi tulu kaoshi* 兩周金文辭大系圖錄考釋 1935 [rev. second ed. Beijing: Kexue chubanshe, 1958], 27); and "to receive" (Lawton, "A Group of Early Western Chou Period Bronze Vessels," 119n46. However, none of these

suggestions seems graphically defensible. Shirakawa, following Takada Tadachika (Tadasuke) 高田忠周 (*Kochuhen* 古籀肩 [Tokyo: Kochuhen kankokai, 1925], 64.28b), points out that the graph has parallels with examples of *yong* 永 (eternal), which, however, is normally a modifier; Sh 2.3:63–64. Since the context of this sentence is relatively clear, requiring that this word be a verb of praise, Shirakawa's suggestion of a further parallel with the Warring States usage "eternally blessed" (*ze yong hu fu* 則 永祜福) seems appropriate, perhaps giving the verbal sense "to immortalize."

15. Not only the location but even the correct transcription of this place-name is open to question. It is generally rendered as *yu* 余 and interpreted as the original form of *xu* 徐, the name of a state anciently located in southern Shandong province. In this regard, there is an interesting suggestion by Chen Shou that the name of this state is derived from the domain of Xiaochen Yu 小臣艅, the caster of the Xiaochen Yu *zun* or Brundage Rhino (for which, see above, n. 9), which was discovered at Liangshan, Shandong together with the "Taibao *gui*"; Chen Shou, "Taibao gui de fuchu," 25. However, as Guo Moruo observes, the lower component of the graph here is "wood," and is clearly distinct from the archaic form of *yu*; *Liang-Zhou jinwenci daxi tulu kaoshi*, 27b; see, too, Loehr, "Bronzentexte," 33–34. Based on this observation, Shirakawa suggests the reading *song* 宋, which was the name of the state later associated with the Shang people; Sh 2.3:65.

16. The ten sons of King Wen, as given in the "Guan Cai shijia" 管蔡世家 chapter of the *Shiji* (35.1570) are Kao 考, who died before the conquest; Fa 發, who became King Wu; Xian; Dan 旦, the Duke of Zhou; Du 度; Zhenduo 振鐸, Lord of Cao 曹; Wu 武, Lord of Cheng 成; Chu 處; Feng 豐, Lord of Kang 康; and Danji Zai 聃季載. Although the *Shiji* and sources following it do not include Huoshu Chu among the brothers deputed to oversee the Shang domain, his commission to do so is clearly recorded in the "Zuo Luo" 作雒 chapter of the *Yi Zhou shu*, 5.7a.

17. The heritage of Grand Protector Shi has received remarkably little attention from historians, whether ancient or modern. Sima Qian 司馬遷 (c. 140–86 B.C.) remarked simply that "Duke Shi of Shao was of the same surname as Zhou"; *Shiji* 史記 34.1549. Ban Gu 班固 (A.D. 32–92) noted equally simply that "the Duke of Shao was the son of King Wen"; *Baihu tong shuzheng* 白虎通疏證 (Zhongguo zixue mingzhu jicheng ed), 383 (7.14a). Huangfu Mi 皇甫謐 (215–82) clarified this somewhat, stating that "the Duke of Shao was a secondary son (*shuzi* 庶子) of King Wen";

see *Diwang shiji jicun* 帝王世紀輯存, ed. Xu Zongyuan 徐宗元 (Beijing: Zhonghua shuju, 1964), 86. That Shi was an elder (half)-brother of the Duke of Zhou is clearly stated in the *Lunheng* 論衡 of Wang Chong 王充 (c. 27–97); 1.12a. This last statement comes in a discussion of particularly long-lived historical figures; for some indication of Grand Protector Shi's dates of birth and death, see below, p. 155, n. 21. For an excellent discussion of his career, see too Pang Huaijing 龐懷靖, "Ba Taibao yuge—jianlun Shaogong Shi de youguan wenti" 跋大保玉戈——兼論召公奭的有關問題, *Kaogu yu wenwu* 考古與文物 1986.1: 70–73.

18. The earliest standard sources state that "King Cheng was in swaddling clothes" (*zai baoqiang zhi zhong* 在襁褓之中) at the time of King Wu's death (*Huainanzi* 淮南子 [Sibu beiyao ed.], 21.6b; *Shiji*, 33.1518), however this would seem to be merely a euphemism to emphasize his youth. There are two conflicting traditions regarding his exact age at succession. In Jia Yi's 賈宜 (201–169 B.C.) *Xin shu* 新書, King Cheng's age at accession is given as six *sui* 歲; *Xin shu* (Sibu congkan ed.), 9.12a. This is possibly corroborated by Zheng Xuan 鄭玄 (A.D.127–200), who stated in one place that King Cheng was born in the year after King Wen (r. 1099–1050) died; *Maoshi zhengyi* 毛詩正義 8,1.2b. On the other hand, Zheng Xuan elsewhere gives his age at succession, after having fulfilled three years of mourning, as thirteen; *Shangshu zhu* 尚書注 (Zheng-shi yishu ed.), 7.5a. This figure is also given in Xu Shen's 許慎 (d. A.D. 146) *Wujing yiyi* 五經異義 (Han-Wei yishu chao ed.), 2.3b–4a, which quotes an "Ancient *Book of Documents*" (*Gu Shangshu* 古尚書). This debate is of some significance, bearing as it does on the recognized age of maturity in ancient China, the earlier of the two traditions suggesting a "capping" age for King Cheng of fifteen *sui*, and the latter twenty *sui*.

19. One of the more novel recent reinterpretations of Western Zhou history concerns whether the Duke of Zhou exercised this royal authority in the name of King Cheng, acting as his regent, or whether he actually arrogated unto himself the title of king. In a series of essays, Matsumoto Masaaki 松本雅明 has argued that references to the "king" (*wang* 王) in several early chapters of the *Book of Documents* actually refer to the Duke of Zhou and not to King Cheng, as traditionally understood; see, for instance, "Shū kō sokui kō" 周公即位考, *Shigaku zasshi* 史學雜誌 77.6 (1968): 1–37;. What is more, he has also suggested that the "king" mentioned in certain very early Western Zhou inscribed bronzes, such as the "Taibao *gui*," also refers to the Duke of Zhou. While this is not the place to discuss this question in detail, since there is evidence on the one hand

that King Cheng did personally participate in the suppression of the Wu Geng rebellion [see, for instance, the *Bamboo Annals* (*Zhushu jinian* 竹 書紀年) for the second through fifth years of his reign, a portion of this work that I regard as particularly reliable; see Chapter 3, esp. 99n48, and evidence on the other hand that the Duke of Zhou was regularly referred to as "Zhougong" 周公 in other inscribed bronze vessels cast in the course of this campaign (see Chapter 4, esp. pp. 106–7), I believe that it is safe to conclude that at least in the inscription on the "Taibao *gui*" the term "king" must refer to King Cheng.

20. For an interesting discussion of the career of the Duke of Zhou, and of the development of the hagiography surrounding it in later times, see Herrlee G. Creel, *The Origins of Statecraft in China, Volume One: The Western Chou Empire* (Chicago: U. of Chicago Press, 1970), 69–78.

21. The *Bamboo Annals* says that King Wu was fifty-four *sui* when he died, in 1043 B.C. (for a convenient text, see James Legge, *The Chinese Classics, Volume 3: The Shoo King or the Book of Historical Documents* [1883; rept. Hong Kong: Hong Kong U. Press, 1960], Prolegemona 144), suggesting that he was born about 1095. The Duke of Zhou, who, among the royal siblings, was third in line after King Wu, probably would have been born no later than 1085. Since Grand Protector Shi is described as an elder (half)-brother of the Duke of Zhou (*Lunheng*, 1.12a; see above, n. 17), he must have been born slightly earlier. Another entry in the *Bamboo Annals* records the death of the Grand Protector in the twenty-fourth year of King Kang (982 B.C.; Legge, *The Shoo King*, Prolegomena 149), which, if accurate, suggests that he must have lived to be slightly more than one hundred years old.

22. The Duke of Zhou's role in the suppression of the Wu Geng rebellion, the only activity with which he is connected in bronze inscriptions, is mentioned in only three contemporary inscriptions, the Xiaochen Dan 小臣單 *zhi* (Sh 3.9:89), the Qin 禽 *gui* (Sh 3.10:103) and the Ran 塑 *fangding* (Sh 3.10:115). For some discussion of the differing nature of the traditional historical sources and inscriptional sources regarding the Duke of Zhou, see Noel Barnard "Chou China: A Review of the Third Volume of Cheng Te-kun's *Archaeology in China*," *Monumemta Serica* 24 (1965): 337–54.

23. In addition to these several inscribed vessels, the Grand Protector is also mentioned on other types of artifacts from the early Western Zhou. Perhaps the best known of these is the Taibao *yu ge*, or, perhaps more properly, "Lihou 厲侯 *yu ge*," a jade *ge*-dagger-axe also in the collection of the

Freer Gallery. This artifact, apparently discovered in the late nineteenth century and said to have come from the tomb of Grand Protector Shi [Ke Changji 柯昌濟, *Jinwen fenyu bian* 金文分域編 (Yuyuan congke ed., 1930), 12.12a; for further discussion of the artifact's provenance together with interesting comments on its possible historical context, see Pang Huaijing, "Ba Taibao yu ge," 70–73], bears an inscription of twenty-seven graphs, reading:

> Sixth month, *bingyin* (day 3); the king at Feng commanded the Grand Protector to inspect the southern states, to follow the Han (River) and to go out to convene the south. (He) commanded the Lord of Li to assist, using one-hundred infantrymen of X.

There is also a bronze dagger-axe, or perhaps a *ji* 戟 (spear-axe), also in the Freer Collection that is inscribed on one side with the two graphs "*tai bao*"; see Rutherford J. Gettens, Roy S. Clarke Jr., and W. T. Chase, "Two Early Chinese Bronze Weapons with Meteoritic Iron Blades," *Freer Gallery of Art Occasional Papers* 4.1 (1971): 66–67, where, however, the inscription is mistakenly read as *tian wang zhi zi* 天王之子. For further discussion of this blade, including the suggestion that the words "*Taibao*" probably refer to a later successor to Grand Protector Shi, see Feng Zheng 馮蒸, "Guanyu Xi-Zhou chuqi Taibao shi de yijian qingtong bingqi" 關於西周初期太保奭的一件青銅兵器, *Wenwu* 文物 1977.6: 50–54.

24. By convention, inscribed vessels are named after the person for whom the vessel was cast. In this case, although the Protector (*Bao*) figures prominently in the inscription, it is clear that the vessel was not cast for him, but rather for a subordinate of his named Chuo 㣤. This point has been demonstrated conclusively by Shirakawa. In addition to his study and those cited by him, more recent studies of this inscription include Pingxin 平心, "Bao you ming xinshi" 保卣銘新釋, *Zhonghua wenshi luncong* 中華文史論 1979.1: 49–79; Sun Zhichu 孫稚雛, "Bao you mingwen huishi" 保卣銘文匯釋, *Guwenzi yanjiu* 古文字研究 5 (1982): 191–210; and Xia Hanyi 夏含夷, "Jianlun Bao you de zuozhe wenti" 簡論保卣的作者問題 *Shanghai bowuguan guankan* 上海博物館刊 5 (1990): 99–102.

25. There have been two suggestions regarding the identity of the figure referred to here simply as "Bao." Both Jiang Dayi 蔣大沂 and (Li) Pingxin argue that he is a figure who appears in other bronze inscriptions as "Ming Bao" 明保 and is described in one, the "Ling *yi*," as "the Duke of Zhou's son;" see Jiang Dayi, "Bao you ming kaoshi" 保卣銘考釋, *Zhonghua wenshi luncong* 5 (1964): 98; Pingxin, "Bao you ming xin shi," 49. Most

other scholars, however, identify Bao with Grand Protector Shi; see, e.g., Huang Shengzhang 黃盛章, "Bao you ming de shidai yu shishi" 保卣銘 的時代與史實, *Kaogu xuebao* 1957.3: 57–59. Although Grand Protector Shi is usually referred to in both bronze inscriptions and literary documents as "Grand Protector" (*taibao*) when he is not instead called "Lord of Shao," there are a number of cases where he is called simply "Protector" (*bao*). This, coupled with the evidence both inscriptional and literary concerning his suppression of the Wu Geng rebellion and especially of his attacks on the allied eastern states, clearly alluded to in this sentence, leaves no doubt that this "Bao" is indeed Grand Protector Shi.

26. Although Chen Mengjia 陳夢家 has interpreted this *ji* 及 as a conjunction, such that "the king commanded Bao and the five lords of the Yin eastern states," ("Xi-Zhou tongqi duandai 西周銅器斷代 I," *Kaogu xuebao* 1955.9: 157), Huang Shengzhang has demonstrated that the use of *ji* as a conjunction did not begin until much later; "Bao you ming de shidai yu shishi," 51–56. *Ji* is the pictograph of a hand grasping a man from behind, the original meaning being "to reach to," "to apprehend;" for a discussion showing the word clearly to have this meaning in Shang oracle-bone inscriptions, see Li Xiaoding 李孝定, *Jiagu wenzi jishi* 甲骨文字 集釋 (Taipei: Academia Sinica, 1965), 3.915–18.

27. Most commentators punctuate as given here. Shirakawa Shizuka, however, punctuates after "states," interpreting *wu* 五 as a placename, giving a figure named "Archer-lord Chuo of Wu" as the subject of the following sentence; Sh 4.16:181ff.; see, too, Sun Zhichu, "Bao you mingwen huishi," 194, and, for a slightly different interpretation, Pingxin, "Bao you ming xin shi," 62–63. Although this interpretation is one way to resolve the grammatical requirements of the next sentence, not only is there no grammatical need to regard "Chuo" as anything other than a single name, but there is no evidence of any kind for a state named Wu.

28. Many commentators have regarded *chuo* 征 here as an "empty word" with no meaning. However, such an interpretation leaves the sentence devoid of a subject. Therefore, Chuo can only be interpreted as a proper name, and as such is not only the subject of this sentence but also the name of the person for whom the vessel was cast. For further discussion of this interpretation, see below, p. 142 see, too, Xia Hanyi, "Jianlun Bao you de zuozhe wenti."

29. Guo Moruo interprets *xiong* 兄 as a phonetic loan for *huang* 荒, "waste, to lay waste," the object of which, "six types" (*liu pin* 六品), he takes to be Yin and the five lords; "Bao you ming shiwen" 保卣銘釋文, *Kaogu*

xuebao 1958.1: 1–2. A far more plausible interpretation is to read *xiong* as the original form of *kuang* 貺, "to give, to confer," as in the inscription on the "Zhe 折 *gong*" (Sh 50.*Ho*15:373): "... *ling zuoce* Zhe *kuang* Wangtu *yu* Juhou" 令作冊折兄望土于柜侯, "commanded Recorder Zhe to be given Wang Grounds by the Lord of Ju." As Guo himself demonstrates, the word *pin* 品 was commonly used in early Western Zhou inscriptions to enumerate such different types of awards as jade, men and lands. Although the referent is not specified here, it is clear that it enumerates the award given to Chuo. For the grammar of the phrase, see below, n. 31, and p. 141.

30. The graph *han* 曆 is usually transcribed as *li* 曆, but Guo Moruo has pointed out that, although the graph did later come to be written as *li*, on the basis of this inscription and Shang oracle-bone inscriptional precedents, the original graph must have been written with the phonetic *gan* 甘; "Bao you ming shiwen," 1. The exact meaning of the compound *mie han* 蔑曆, which is extremely common in early Western Zhou bronze inscriptions, remains unclear despite considerable etymological speculation; see Zhou Fagao 周法高, *Jinwen gulin* 金文詁林 (Hong Kong: The Chinese University of Hong Kong Press, 1975), 4.0495. The general meaning "to praise military achievements" is, however, fairly clear from the contexts in which the term usually appears.

31. In archaic Chinese, just as in standard classical Chinese, post-verbal *yu* 于 can serve to indicate a passive sentence, the agent of the action being the object of *yu*. For a brief study of this grammatical feature, see Yang Wuming 楊五銘, "Xi-Zhou jinwen beidong jushi jianlun" 西周金文被動句式簡論, *Guwenzi yanjiu* 古文字研究 7 (1982): 309–17.

32. The various dating notations found in this inscription combine both Shang and Zhou conventions. The "great event" year-notation "meeting with the four regions convoking at the king's great sacrificial offering in Zhou" plausibly refers to an entry in the *Bamboo Annals* for the fourth year of King Cheng, the year immediately following the final suppression of the rebellion of Wu Geng and the eastern states, which reads, "in the spring, first month, for the first time audience was held in the temple;" see, for instance, Legge, *The Shoo King*, Prolegomena 145. This inference seems to be confirmed by the month, lunar-phase, and day notations, "*yimao* (day 52) . . . second month, after the full moon," which roughly fits the calendar of 1039 B.C., the fourth year of King Cheng's official reign (inclusive of the Duke of Zhou's regency), *yimao* being the twenty-fourth day of that month.

33. Chen Mengjia, "Xi-Zhou tongqi duandai I," 159.

34. Already by the Northern Song dynasty, Lü Dalin 呂大臨 (1046–92) had observed in his *Kaogu tu* 考古圖 that Shang inscriptions could be differentiated from Zhou inscriptions by their use of *tiangan* in the names of ancestors; *Kaogu tu* (1752 Yizheng tang ed.), 1.4b, 4.26a. While it has subsequently become clear that this observation is not relevant for periodization, such dedications appearing in many vessels obviously cast during the Western Zhou period as, for instance, on the now well-known "Shi Qiang 史牆 *pan*" (Sh 50.*Ho*15:335) and other vessels of the Wei-family cache (for the discovery of this cache, see Shaanxi Zhouyuan kaogudui, "Shaanxi Fufeng Zhuangbo yihao Xi-Zhou qingtongqi kucang fajue jianbao"陝西扶鳳莊白一號西周青銅器窖藏發掘簡報, *Wenwu* 1978.3: 1–16; for an English translation, see *Chinese Archaeological Abstracts, 2: Prehistoric to Western Zhou*, ed. Albert E. Dien, Jeffrey K. Riegel, and Nancy T. Price, [Los Angeles: UCLA Institute of Archaeology, 1985], 512–29), still it does seem to manifest a deep-rooted ethnographic difference between these two peoples. A slight modification of this traditional interpretation would suggest that Shi Qiang and his *tiangan*-designated ancestors were originally descended from a Shang or related eastern people, which the inscription on the "Shi Qiang *pan*," in fact, confirms. By the same token, the dedication of the "Chuo *you*" to Father Gui would seem to suggest that Chuo, too, was of Shang or eastern ancestry.

35. It would, perhaps, be possible to suggest, as has been done in another context, that the Shang king Di Xin visited the Zhou capital and conducted sacrifices there; see, for example, Fan Yuzhou 范毓周, "Shilun mie Shang yiqian de Shang-Zhou guanxi" 試論滅商以前的商周關係, *Shixue yuekan* 史學月刊 1981.1, 15; but, against this interpretation, see Edward L. Shaughnessy, "Zhouyuan Oracle-Bone Inscriptions: Entering the Research Stage?" *Early China* 11–12 (1985–87): 159–62. Such a suggestion has, properly, never been made in the case of this inscription.

36. See above, n. 31.

37. For a convenient listing of these vessels, see Sh 4.16: 184–87. Particularly important in this regard is a "Chuo *ding*," the provenance of which is discussed in Rong Geng 容庚, *Shan zhai yiqi tulu* 善齋彝器圖錄 (Peking: Harvard-Yenching Institute, 1936), 14. Although Shirakawa properly notes the relationship between the family-name seen in these vessels and that in the "Chuo *you*," due to his curious interpretation of *wu* in line 2 of the "Chuo *you*" inscription as a place-name (see above, n. 27), he misses the obvious geographical relationship between them. For a more thorough

study of this question, see Xia Hanyi, "Jianlun Bao you de zuozhe wenti."

38. The vessel is very similar in appearance to the "Xianhou 獻侯 *ding*" (Sh 7.29:333), the inscription of which mentions King Cheng as reigning king, for which reason it serves as a "standard" for that reign.

39. Because of its uncomplicated grammar and vocabulary, this inscription has received relatively little attention. In addition to the discussion by Shirakawa, there is also an annotated translation by Loehr ("Bronzentexte," 51–58) and brief remarks at Guo Moruo, *Liang-Zhou jinwenci daxi tulu kaoshi*, 27a, and Chen Mengjia, "Xi-Zhou tongqi duandai I," 170.

40. For the archaic usage of "*lai* 來 Verb" meaning "to come from Verb-ing," see Loehr, Bronzentexte," 53; see, too, Chen Mengjia, *Yinxu buci zongshu* 殷虛卜辭綜述 (Beijing: Kexue chubanshe, 1956), 304.

41. As is customary in very early Western Zhou bronze inscriptions, a complete date notation of the sort found in later inscriptions is not recorded here. However, it is perhaps possible to combine the information that is provided with some inferences about the historical background of this vessel and the ritual practices of the early Zhou to arrive at a possible date for this vessel. In the discussion of the date of the "Chuo *you*" above (n. 32), it was pointed out that the *Bamboo Annals* records the final suppression of the eastern rebellion in the third year of the reign of King Cheng, and also a convocation of the feudal lords in the next year. If it is assumed that the Grand Protector "returned from attacking the rebelling Yi" in the year of this convocation, and that he would have chosen an auspicious day to make the award to Lü, then it may not be coincidental that *gengshen* was the *fei* 朏 day (the day on which the new moon is first visible, perhaps regarded as the first day of the month at the beginning of the Western Zhou) of the eleventh month of 1039 B.C., the fourth year of King Cheng's reign.

42. There is no agreement as to the location of this "Zhou garrison." Fang Junyi 方濬益, *Zhuiyi zhai yiqi kuanzhi kaoshi* 綴遺齋彝器款識考釋 (Shanghai: Shangwu yinshuguan, 1935), 4.2, suggests that it is to be identified with Zhouzhi 盩屋 county of Shaanxi province, located midway between the Zhou ancestral home at Qishan 岐山 and its capital at present-day Xi'an 西安, and a name that was already well attested for this area by the Han dynasty. On the other hand, Shirakawa Shizuka, without offering any historical-geographical evidence, argues that it must have been located in the just subjugated eastern region; Sh 2.5:75. The interpretation of "*lai fa*" 來伐 as "to come from attacking" in the great event year-notation would seem to support the Shaanxi location.

43. The "He *zun*" was originally excavated in 1963 but its 122-graph inscription, almost certainly the longest inscription of King Cheng's reign, was not discovered until a layer of covering patina was cleaned away in 1976. The inscription records an address made by the king upon the completion of the eastern capital at Luoyang, and is in many ways extremely reminiscent of the "Da gao" 大誥 and "Duo shi" 多士 chapters of the *Book of Documents*. Studies of this inscription, in addition to those abstracted by Shirakawa, include Ma Chengyuan 馬承源, "He zun mingwen he Zhouchu shishi" 何尊銘文初釋, in *Wang Guowei xueshu yanjiu lunji* 王國維學術研究論集, ed. Wu Ze 吳澤 (Shanghai: Huadong shifan daxue chubanshe, 1983), 45–61; Michael F. Carson, "Some Grammatical and Graphical Problems in the *Ho Tsun* Inscription," *Early China* 4 (1978–79): 41–44; *The Great Bronze Age of China*, 203–4; and Li Xueqin 李學勤, "He zun xinshi" 何尊新釋, *Zhongyuan wenwu* 中原文物 1981.1: 35–39, 45.

44. One of the first such enfeoffments is commemorated in the inscription of the well-known "Kanghou 康侯 *gui*." This vessel, reportedly discovered in 1931 either in Jixian or Junxian, Henan, and presently in the British Museum in London, became one of the first Western Zhou bronze vessels to attract attention in the West when it was displayed at the Burlington Exposition in London in 1936; see, for instance, Percival Yetts, "An Early Chou Bronze," *Burlington Magazine* 1937, 147–77; Herrlee Glessner Creel, *The Birth of China* (New York: Frederick Ungar, 1937), 234. The importance of the vessel has continued to be recognized, primarily because of the inscription's mention of the Lord of Kang, the ninth of King Wen's ten sons and a figure who also appears in several chapters of the *Book of Documents*. Studies of this inscription that have appeared since the publication of Shirakawa's *comte rendu* (Sh 4.14:141), include Zhang Guangyuan 張光遠, "Xi-Zhou kanghou gui kaoshi—jianlun Weidu didian ji Zhouchu liangci fa Shang de tongqi shilu" 西周康侯殷考釋——兼論衛都地點及周初兩次伐商的銅器實錄, *Gugong jikan* 故宮集刊 14.3 (1980): 69–96; and Zhou Yongzhen 周永珍, "Shi Kanghou gui" 釋康侯殷, *Guwenzi yanjiu* 9 (1984): 295–303.

A more detailed record of enfeoffment is available in the inscription on the "Mai 麥 *zun*" (Sh 11.60:628), apparently cast in the last years of King Cheng's reign. The inscription records the establishment of the state of Xing 邢, located at the site of present-day Xingtai 邢台 in southern Hebei province, and the appointment of the lord of a state in the vicinity of Luoyang to administer it. For a study of this inscription, including a complete translation, see Edward L. Shaughnessy, "Historical Geography and the Extent of the Earliest Chinese Kingdoms," *Asia Major*, third series, II.2 (1989): 19–20.

45. *Shiji*, 4.134.

46. For previous translations of the "Gu ming," see Legge, *The Chinese Classics*, vol. 3, 544–61, and Bernhard Karlgren, *The Book of Documents* (Stockholm: Museum of Far Eastern Antiquities, 1950), 70–74. While both of these heavily annotated translations (for Karlgren's annotations, see his *Glosses on the Book of Documents* [Stockholm: Museum of Far Eastern Antiquities, 1970]) are representative of the best scholarship of their days, it has seemed desirable here to offer a fresh translation. However, since the purpose of this citation is primarily to illustrate the role Grand Protector Shi played in the first smooth transition of Zhou rule, except for explanations of textual emendations, I forego the detailed philological apparatus that might be expected of a finished translation.

47. I here delete *mao* 瑁 as a probable commentator's gloss on *tong* 同, which, as Yu Fan 虞翻 (170–239) suggested, must originally have been written similarly to *mao*. The meaning "chalice" for *tong* follows the gloss of Zheng Xuan 鄭玄 (127–200). Karlgren's argument that this graph derives from a misreading of a putative original form of *jia* 斝 is also plausible, but the reading of *zan* 瓚, "ladle," for *mao* seems less well supported. For a thorough discussion of this problem, including the readings of previous commentators, see Karlgren, *Glosses*, 166–67, no. 1998.

48. I here emend the text to read *yi cuo ji ji* 以酢祭嚌, adding the *ji ji* 祭嚌 from the following text. I suspect that that text, which repeats almost identically this text, is the result of an inadvertant copyist's error. I suspect, too, that the word *zhai* 宅 after *ji ji* was originally a commentator's note explaining *ji* 嚌 and has been inadvertently assimilated into the text.

49. For *bu sheng* 布乘 here I read *fu fu* 黼芾, as suggested by Karlgren, *Glosses*, 170–71, no. 2009.

50. For *de* 德 here I read *te yi* 特損, as originally suggested by Yu Yue 俞越 (1821–1906) and followed by Karlgren; *Glosses*, 171–72, no. 2011.

51. The "Zuoce Da 作冊大 *fangding*" was part of the major cache discovered in 1929 just outside of Luoyang that also included the famous and controversial "Ling *yi*," "Ling *zun*," and "Ling *gui*." It is now also part of the Freer Gallery collection. For the most recent discussion of this important discovery, see Noel Barnard, "The Nieh Ling Yi," *The Journal of the Institute of Chinese Studies of the Chinese University of Hong Kong* 9.2 (1978): 585–627. For other translations of the inscription on the "Zuoce Da

fangding," see Loehr, "Bronzentexte," 81–91; John A. Pope, R.J. Gettens, J. Cahill and N. Barnard, *The Freer Chinese Bronzes*, volume 1 (Washington, DC: Smithsonian Institution, 1967), 194–95. A study of this discovery and its historiographical significance, entitled "The 'Ling *yi*' and the Kang Gong" appears as appendix 2 in my *Sources of Western Zhou History*, 193–216.

52. There is no question that the graph written here is *ci* 朿 "thorn," which both Guo Moruo and Chen Mengjia have shown to be a plausible phonetic loan for *shi* 奭, the name of the Grand Protector; Guo Moruo, *Liang-Zhou jinwenci daxi tulu kaoshi*, 33b; Chen Mengjia, "Xi-Zhou tongqi duandai III," *Kaogu xuebao* 1956.1: 88. Nevertheless, as Yang Shuda has argued, the syntax here would suggest instead the word *lai* 來, "to come," the shape of which is extremely similar; *Jiweiju jinwen shuo*, 164–65. Moreover, as Yang has also pointed out, if the "duke" is to be referred to by both title and name here, consistency would suggest that the reference to him in the fourth line, "the duke awarded Recorder . . . ," would also include his name. Since it does not, it seems reasonable to assume a slight miswriting of *lai* here. An identical case seems to occur at the beginning of the inscription on the Kanghou *gui*: *wang (ci:) lai fa Shang yi* 王朿 (朿: 來) 伐商邑, "the king came from attacking the Shang city."

53. It is not clear what the term *yiding* 異鼎 means. Guo Moruo, based on an alternative form contained in the *Shuo wen* 說文 (1A.5a), suggests that *yi* 異 is the original form of *si* 祀; *Liang-Zhou jinwenci daxi tulu kaoshi*, 33b). Chen Mengjia, on the other hand, suggests on the basis of the *Guangyun* 廣韻 (5.41a) definition of *yi* that it is a type of large *ding*; "Xi-Zhou tongqi duandai III," 87–88. Chen further suggests that the two Taibao *fangding* found among the "Seven Vessels of Liangshan" each represented the first of a pair of vessels, the second vessels of which would have read "King Wu vessel" and "King Cheng vessel," respectively, and that it was the casting of these vessels that is referred to here. In support of this, there is a Cheng Wang *fangding* in the Nelson Gallery of Art in Kansas City that is roughly similar in appearance to the one Taibao *fangding* that is still extant.

54. The "Jin *ding*" was discovered in 1975 in Liuli he 琉璃河, just to the southwest of Beijing and the site of the ancient capital of Yan, established by the family of Grand Protector Shi. For publications of this vessel, see *Zhongguo gu qingtongqi xuan* 中國古青銅器選 (Beijing: Wenwu chubanshe, 1975), 25; and Yan Wan 晏琬, "Beijing Liaoning chutu tongqi yu Zhouchu de Yan" 北京遼寧出土銅器與周初的燕, *Kaogu* 考古

1975.5: 274–79, 270. For another inscribed bronze vessel related to the state of Yan, see above, n. 9.

55. According to Chen Mengjia, in 1951 this vessel was in the possession of the Zhejiang Provincial Committee for the Management of Cultural Relics, stored together with a number of forgeries. Based upon his personal inspection, Chen determined that the vessel was in fact authentic; "Xi-Zhou tongqi duandai III," 65. Aside from Chen and Shirakawa's brief comments, however, the inscription has received no other attention.

56. In studies to date, Wang Jiang has been identified as the wife of King Wu (Guo Moruo, "Guanyu Meixian da ding mingci kaoshi" 關於郿縣大鼎銘辭考釋, *Wenwu* 1972.7: 2; Sunjoo Pang, "The Consorts of King Wu and King Wen in the Bronze Inscriptions of Early Chou," *Monumenta Serica* 33 [1977–78]: 124–35), King Cheng (Chen Mengjia, "Xi-Zhou tongqi duandai IV," *Kaogu xuebao* 1956.2: 78), King Kang (Tang Lan, "Xi-Zhou tongqi duandai zhong de 'Kanggong' wenti" 西周銅器斷代中的康宮問題, *Kaogu xuebao* 1962.1: 15–48), and King Zhao (r. 977/975–957; Tang Lan, "Lun Zhou Zhaowang shidai de qingtongqi mingke" 論周昭王時代的青銅器銘刻, *Guwenzi yanjiu* 2 [1981]: 115–18). I discuss this question in detail in my study "The 'Ling *yi*' and the Kang Gong"; *Sources of Western Zhou History*, 193–216.

57. Chen Mengjia offers the transcription *zhu*(?) 挋 for this graph without further comment; "Xi-Zhou tongqi duandai III," 65. Shirakawa notes that while the graph is unrecognizable, the context suggests that it should represent the color of the ox; Sh 2.6:82.

6

From Liturgy to Literature

The Ritual Contexts of the Earliest Poems in the *Book of Poetry*

One of the most important modern interpretive insights into the nature of ritual has come from anthropologists observing the "performance" of rites. But how is the interpreter of ancient civilizations to view the performative aspect of ritual? For ancient China, for instance, we have, on the one hand, numerous textual descriptions (often actually prescriptions) of ritual activity, and, on the other hand, an equally large body of souvenirs of actual rituals. Separately, these sources remain but echoes and shadows of rituals long since performed. No matter how detailed the prescriptions in texts like the *Liji* 禮記 or *Records of Rites*, they can be no more satisfying than reading the stage directions of a play. And artifacts such as bronze vessels and musical instruments, even when archeologically excavated from a ritual context, can give only limited evidence of the actors who once handled them. Yet, by bringing together these different sorts of evidence and combining them with the best known but nonetheless probably still most important evidence—poems in the *Shijing* 詩經 or *Book of Poetry*, it may be possible to reanimate something of the performative nature of ritual in ancient China.[1]

In this chapter I propose to examine poems of and about ritual in the earliest section of the *Book of Poetry*, the Zhou Song 周頌 or Zhou Liturgies section (Mao 266–296). I will attempt to show that the earliest of these poems, probably composed during the first century of the Western Zhou dynasty (1045–771 B.C.), were actually liturgical prayers chanted (and also danced and acted) by the celebrants of ritual, and had no function or meaning apart from that ritual context (which may account for their virtual neglect today among students of Chinese poetry and even readers of the *Book of Poetry* itself). I will also examine several poems from the same Zhou Liturgies section that linguistic and historical evidence shows to date somewhat later (probably the middle period of the Western Zhou, roughly the second half of the tenth century B.C.). These poems describe the beginnings of a different type of ritual, one performed by a specially designated celebrant before and on behalf of an audience of guests. I will conclude by suggesting that this development in ritual performance away from collective concelebration and toward a separation of celebrant and audience was paralleled by a similar development in poetic expression away from joint performance and toward a demarcation between poet and audience. With this separation, Chinese poetry moved from the realm of liturgy into that of literature.

THE "MARTIAL" SONG-AND-DANCE SUITE

The earliest evidence we have regarding the creation and performance of poems now included in the *Book of Poetry* seems to come in the "Shi fu" 世俘 chapter of the *Yi Zhou shu* 逸周書 or *Remainder of the Zhou Documents*. This text, which is an annalistic account of events surrounding the Zhou defeat of Shang and especially the victory celebrations thereafter, describes among other ceremonies held in the Shang capital area an inspection of the defeated Shang army.

甲寅謁戎殷于牧野。王佩赤白旗。籥人奏武。王入。進萬。

On *jiayin* (day 51), inspection of the armed Yin at Muye. The king suspended red and white pennants. The flutists played "Martial." The king entered, and the "Ten-thousand" [dance] was advanced.[2]

The *Zuo zhuan* 左傳 or *Zuo Tradition* (of the *Spring and Autumn Annals*) provides further detail about the creation and content of the musical piece "Martial" (*wu* 武) mentioned in the "Shi fu" chapter.

武王克商，作頌曰：載戢干戈，載櫜弓矢。我求懿德，肆于時夏。允王保之。又作武，其卒曰：耆定爾功。其三曰：鋪時繹思求定。其六曰：綏萬邦，屢豐年。夫武禁暴戢兵，保大、定功、安民、和眾、豐財者也，故使子孫無忘其章。

When King Wu had conquered Shang he made a liturgy reading:

Storing the shields and dagger-axes,
Sheathing the bows and arrows,
We seek fine virtue,
And so in this (land of) Xia,
Truly it is the king who protects it.[3]

He also made "Martial," its [final=] first[4] stanza reading: "Bringing stability to your work"; its third reading: "And spread this extensively, Our marches are to seek stability"; its sixth reading: "Comforting the ten-thousand countries, And making the abundant harvests repeat." As for "Martial," it consists of quelling the rapacious, putting away the weapons, protecting the great, stabilizing the work, bringing peace to the people, bringing harmony to the masses, and making abundant the resources, therefore causing the descendants not to forget its stanzas.[5]

The quotations here of three of perhaps an original six stanzas of the song suite "Martial" (sometimes referred to as "Great Martial" [*Da Wu* 大武]) correspond to lines from three poems currently contained in the Zhou Liturgies section of the *Book of Poetry*. "Martial" (Wu 武; Mao 285), "Gift" (Lai 賚; Mao 295), and "Outstanding" (Huan 桓; Mao 294).[6] These poems read as follows:

MARTIAL (WU; MAO 285)

於皇武王	Oh! August was King Wu,
無競維烈	Incomparable was his valor.
允文文王	Truly cultured was King Wen,
克開厥後	Capable of opening (the way) for his descendants.
嗣武受之	The heir Wu received it,
勝殷遏劉	And defeated Yin, supressing and smiting (them),
耆定爾功	Bringing stability to your work.

GIFT (LAI; MAO 295)

文王既勤止	King Wen having been diligent about it,
我應受之	We have received it
敷時繹思	And spread this extensively.

我徂維求定	Our marches are to seek stability.
時周之命	This mandate of Zhou:
於繹思	Oh! The extensiveness!

OUTSTANDING (HUAN; MAO 294)

綏萬邦	Comforting the ten-thousand countries,
屢豐年	And making the abundant harvests repeat,
天命匪解	Heaven's mandate is not dissipated.
桓桓武王	Outstanding King Wu
保有厥土	Protected his soldiers
于以四方	Throughout the four quarters,
克定厥家	And was capable of stabilizing his family.
於昭于天	Oh! Shining in heaven,
皇以閒之	Augustly therewith interposing himself.[7]

Despite their brevity and relative lack of literary elaboration, these three poems do share enough structure and content to suggest that the *Zuo zhuan* is correct in treating them as a single composition. It would also perhaps not be too impressionistic to see in them a thematic progression from defeating the Shang, through marching to extend the victory, to being capable of stabilizing families throughout the four quarters. Such, at least, has been the traditional interpretation of its significance, as the following passage from the *Records of Rites* shows.

夫樂者，象成者也。摠干而山立，武王之事也。發揚蹈厲，大公之志也。武亂皆坐，周召之治也。且夫武始而北出；再成而滅商；三成而南；四成而南國是疆；五成而分，周公左、召公右；六成復綴以崇天子。

As for music, it represents what has been completed: erecting the shields and standing like a row of hills was the business of King Wu; erupting and marching was the will of the Grand Duke; "Martial" being finished and all sitting down was the governance of [the dukes of] Zhou and Shao. What is more, "Martial" begins by starting out northward; at the second [completion:] stanza, they destroy Shang; at the third stanza, they turn south; at the fourth stanza, the southern states are delimited; at the fifth stanza, they separate—the Duke of Zhou to the left, the Duke of Shao to the right; at the sixth stanza, they rejoin again in order to exalt the Son of Heaven.[8]

Not only does this passage suggest the thematic progression of the song suite, but, perhaps more important, it also shows that the singing of "Martial" was also accompanied by ritually significant dance movements. According to the commentarial tradition, at least from Zheng Xuan 正玄 (127–200) through the *Zhengyi* 正義, "Correct Meaning," project of the early Tang dynasty, the movements of the dance corresponded to the stanzas of the poetic suite, all serving to recreate symbolically the Zhou conquest of Shang: "starting out northward," the ranks of dancers would move to the north in order to symbolize the march of the conquest campaign as it turned northward after crossing the Yellow River at Mengjin 孟津; the "destroy[ing] Shang" of the second movement obviously refers to the battle at Muye 牧野, the dancers presumably pantomiming the battle; the "turn south" of the next movement, the dance movements of which would seem obvious, represented the return of the army to Zhou; "the southern states being delimited" of the fourth movement apparently refers to the appointing of members of the royal family to rule various states; the "separation" of the Duke of Zhou 周公 and the Duke of Shao 召公, traditionally assumed to refer to the division of lands through enfeoffment,[9] must have been represented by the division of the dancers into two ranks; and the dance concluded with these ranks rejoining and acknowledging the supremacy of the king, the "Son of Heaven."

Thus, from three separate references, each fairly brief and obscure, we can get at least some sense of how some poems presently included in the *Book of Poetry*—the "Martial" song-and-dance suite—were performed and how they were understood at the time—as a ritual reenactment of the establishment of the Zhou dynasty. Including musical accompaniment, singing of songs describing the deeds of the dynastic founders, and acting out those same deeds through pantomimic dancing, this must have been a fairly complete ritual performance.

THE LITURGIES OF THE SUCCESSION RITES

As a reenactment, the effect of the "Martial" performance must have been essentially symbolic. Symbolism, to be sure, is an essential aspect of ritual. However, as has come to be well recognized since the pioneering work of J.L. Austin,[10] performative rituals also serve the effective function of enactment. The *Book of Poetry* is not lacking in evidence of this type of performance as well. Perhaps the most intriguing examples of such poetry as performative utterances are the three Zhou Liturgies poems "Pity Me, the Little Son" (Min Yu Xiaozi 閔予小子; Mao 286), "Visiting the Beginning" (Fang Luo 訪落; Mao 287), and "Respect It" (Jing Zhi 敬之; Mao 288). The *Mao Zhuan* 毛傳 or Mao Commentary indicates that these poems were sung in the temple during the installation of a new king,[11] an interpretation that is also readily apparent from the content of the poems. More recently, by comparing these poems to passages in the "Gu ming" 顧命 or "Retrospective Command" chapter of the *Shangshu* 尙書 or *Book of Documents,* a wonderfully detailed narrative of the installation of King Kang of Zhou (r. 1005/03–978 B.C.[12]), Fu Sinian 傅斯年 (1896–1950) has demonstrated a possible specific ritual context for the enactment of these poems.[13] Demonstration of this point will require extensive quotation from both the "Gu ming" chapter and the three poems from the Zhou Liturgies. (Following the lead of Fu Sinian, I present the texts of the "Gu ming" and the three poems in facing columns, the "Gu ming" to the left and the poems to the right.)[14]

The Grand Protector commanded Zhong Huan and Nangong Mao to serve and assist Lu Ji, Lord of Qi, with two shields and dagger-axes and one-hundred tiger braves to meet son Zhao [i.e., King Kang] outside of the southern gate, and in procession to enter the solemn chamber, grievingly to dwell at the ancestral altar. On *dingmao* (day 4), he commanded the recording of the transition measures. On the seventh day, *guiyou* (day 10), the elder assistant commanded the officers to prepare the materials. . . .

The king [wearing] hempen cap and embroidered robes ascended by way of the guests' stairs. The officials and lords of states [wearing] hempen caps and ant-[colored] robes entered and assumed position. The Grand Protector, Grand Scribe and Grand Master of Rites all [wore] hempen caps and red robes. The Grand Protector elevating the large ritual-tablet and the [High=] Grand Master of Rites presenting the chalice ascended by way of the main stairs. The Grand Scribe holding the document ascended by way of the guests' stairs. Standing before the king he intoned the command, saying:

> The august deceased-king leaning on a jade armrest announced his final command, commanding you to succeed to the instructions, to look over and be lord of the state of Zhou, to follow and comply with the great laws, and to bring peace to the world, thereby in answer extolling the bright instructions of [kings] Wen and Wu.

The king twice bowed.
Arising, he answered, saying:

> Insignificant am I, the small child, last [of our line]; would that I be able to govern the four quarters so as respectfully to dread the awe of heaven.

> Pity me, the little son. I have met
>   with a family unachieved,
> And am alone in distress.
> *Wuhu!* August father,
> [May] endless generations be
>   capable of being filial.
> Regard these august ancestors
> Ascending and descending at
>   court.
> It is I the little son
> Who morning and night respects
>   them.
> *Wuhu!* August kings,
> Continue the line and do not
> forget.
>
>   "Pity Me, the Little Son"
>   (Min Yu Xiaozi; Mao 286)

Then he received the chalice. The king thrice strained [the wine], thrice

sacrificed and thrice drank. The
Grand Master of Rites said: "It is
enjoyed." The Grand Protector received the chalice, descended and
washed his hands. Taking a different
chalice, he held a demi-ladle so as to
pour the sacrifice and drink. Giving
the chalice to an altar man, he bowed.
The king bowed in answer. The
Grand Protector descended and with
the many lords exited the temple gate
and waited.

The king exited, being within
the Response Gate. The Grand Protector led the many lords of the
western lands to enter the left of the
Response Gate. The Duke of Bi led
the many lords of the eastern lands
to enter the right of the Response
Gate. They all [wore] brocades and
knee-covers, yellow and red. The
guests raised and presented their tablets together with their presents saying: "[We] the [one or two=] several
ministers and defenders dare to hold
the offerings of our fields." All twice
bowed and touched their heads to the
ground. The king, being the proper
successor, bowed in answer to each
in turn. The Grand Protector and the
Elder of Rui together advanced and
saluted each other. Both twice bowed
and touched their heads to the ground
and said:

> We dare respectfully to an-
> nounce to the Son of Heaven:
> August heaven changed the
> great state Yin's mandate. It was

[kings] Wen and Wu of Zhou who received guiding approval and were able to be solicitous of the western regions. It was the newly deceased king [i.e., King Cheng] who completed the moderation of awards and punishments and consolidated their efforts, thereby expansively bequeathing beneficence to the heirs. Now the king must respect it! Spread the august six armies and do not corrupt our high ancestor's unique mandate.

Respect it! Respect it!
Heaven is lustrous,
And the mandate is not easy!
Do not say, "Those high, high up
     above
Cause their men to ascend and
     descend."
Daily scrutinize it here.

The king said to the effect:

Lords, husbandmen, males and defenders of the many states; I, the one man, Zhao, announce in return: Formerly, the rulers Wen and Wu grandly brought peace and prosperity; did not bring hardship or misfortune; and caused there to come to be an equal trust, thereby manifesting their brightness in the world. Then, they also had bearlike officers and ministers without two hearts to protect and govern the royal house, thereby first being commanded by the Lord on High. August heaven therewith instructed its way and gave them the four quarters. Then they com-

It is that I the little son
Am not perceptive [enough] to
     respect it.
As the days go and the nights lead
     on,
My study will take light from the
     radiant brightness.
Great is this burden on my
     shoulder;
Show us the motion of lustrous
     virtue.
                    "Respect It"
          (Jing Zhi; Mao 288)

Examining our loss,

manded them to establish the lords as trees and curtains among us, the heirs. Now, my [one or two=] several elder uncles, would that you assist in looking back to make concordant your ministers of the former dukes who served the former kings. Although your persons be on the outside, your hearts should never not be at the royal chamber. Therewith present solicitude of their approval and do not bequeath shame on me, the stripling.

When the multitude of dukes had all heard the command, they saluted each other and hurriedly exited. The king removed his cap and restored his mourning clothes.

I follow this shining father. *Wuhu!* Longing [am I]! I have not yet greyed. If you lead me to attend to it, My continuance will be hesitant. It is that I, the little son Have not yet borne many of the family's difficulties. I summon to the court those above and below To ascend and descend to their family. Beneficent indeed is the august father, Hereby protecting and enlightening his person.

"Visiting the Beginning" (Fang Luo; Mao 287)

The ritual significance of the "Gu ming" narrative does not require further elaboration from me. I am aware that the comparison between the direct address quoted within that narrative and the three "installation" poems is less direct than Fu Sinian may have suggested; but I believe the comparison is enlightening nonetheless. Placing these poems within their ritual context makes them more meaningful than they could ever be just within a literary context.

LITURGIES OF ANCESTRAL SACRIFICE

I believe that when this same type of interpretation is addressed to poems in the Zhou Liturgies section that concern sacrifices to the ancestors—the majority of poems in the section—it will not only help to illustrate the original function of these poems, but it will also shed important light on the development of these rituals during the Western Zhou dynasty and how that development may have affected in turn the development of poetic expression in China. In order to demonstrate this point, it will be necessary to examine rather more closely than I have done above a fairly large block of poems. I will begin by translating the first ten poems of the Zhou Liturgies section (numbers 266–75 in the Mao sequence),[15] taking care to note those places where my readings differ appreciably from those of past commentators and translators. These poems, which are grouped into a single unit in most texts of the *Shijing*, all derive from rites performed for the ancestors. Indeed, as I will try to demonstrate after presenting the translations, in most cases it is clear that these were prayers intoned as the rites were being performed.

THE CLEAR TEMPLE (QING MIAO 清廟; MAO 266)

於穆清廟	Oh, in the stately clear temple,
肅雝顯相	Solemn and harmonizing are the lustrous images.[16]
濟濟多士	Well arrayed are the many officers,
秉文之德	Holding to [King] Wen's virtue;[17]
對越在天	In response to those surpassing in heaven,
駿奔走在廟	Quickly [they] hurry about in the temple.
不顯不承	Illustrious and inestimable;
無射於人斯	Tireless with respect to men.

IT IS HEAVEN'S MANDATE
(WEI TIAN ZHI MING 維天之命; MAO 267)

維天之命	It is heaven's mandate;
於穆不已	Oh, stately, is it unending!
於乎不顯	*Wuhu*, illustrious!
文王之德之純	The purity of King Wen's virtue
假以溢我	Approaches to shower down upon us.[18]
我其收之	May we receive it;[19]
駿惠我文王	Quickly help us, King Wen's great grandsons, to make it
曾孫篤之	steadfast.[20]

THEY ARE CLEAR (WEI QING 維清; MAO 268)

維清緝熙	They are clear and continuously shining:
文王之典	King Wen's statutes.
肇禋	The beginning sacrifices
迄用有成	Are still used with success:
維周之禎	It is Zhou's fortune.

Valorous and Cultured (Lie Wen 烈文; Mao 269)

烈文辟公	Valorous and cultured are the ruling lords,[21]
錫茲祉福	Bestowing these blessings;
惠我無疆	Help us limitlessly
子孫保之	[To have] sons and grandsons to protect them.
無封靡于爾邦	There are no boundary-markers that are not in your country;
維王其崇之	May it be the king who honors them.
念茲戎功	Regard these martial works;
繼序其皇之	May the continuing of the line render him august.
無競維人	Incomparable as a man;
四方其訓之	May the four quarters regard him as a teacher.
不顯維德	Illustrious is the virtue;
百辟其刑之	May the hundred rulers regard him as a model.
於乎前王不忘	*Wuhu!* The former kings have not forgotten.

Heaven Created (Tian Zuo 天作; Mao 270)

天作高山	Heaven created the high mountain;
大王荒之	The Great King leveled it.[22]
彼作矣	That was creation indeed.
文王康之	King Wen made it vibrant:
彼岨矣岐	That precipice, indeed, of Qi.
有夷之行	There is a level road
子孫保之	For the sons and grandsons to protect.

Bright Heaven has a Successful Mandate
(Hao Tian you Cheng Ming 昊天有成命; Mao 271)

昊天有成命	Bright heaven has a successful mandate;
二后受之	The two lords received it.[23]
成王不敢康	King Cheng did not dare to be (healthy:) complacent,

夙夜基命宥密	But morning and night grounded the mandate ever more firmly.
於緝熙	Oh, continuously shining,
單厥心	Single was his heart.[24]
肆其靖之	And so may he make it (i.e., the mandate) tranquil.

WE LEAD (*WO JIANG* 我將; MAO 272)

我將我享	We lead our offerings:
維羊維牛	They are sheep; they are cows;
維天其右之	May it be that heaven [has=] accepts them.[25]
儀式刑文王之典	The rites properly take as model King Wen's statutes,
日靖四方	Daily making tranquil the four quarters.
伊嘏文王	And so blessed[26] King Wen
既右饗之	Has [had=] accepted and enjoyed them.
我其夙夜	May we morning and night
畏天之威	Revere Heaven's awe
于時保之	And protect it here.

NOW PASSING THROUGH (*SHI MAI* 時邁; MAO 273)

時邁其邦	Now passing through his country,
昊天其子之	May bright heaven treat him as a son,[27]
實右序有周	And make fruitful the line of Zhou.
薄言震之	Extensively shaking them,[28]
莫不震疊	None are not shaken and afraid;
懷柔百神	Cherishing and making pliant the hundred spirits,
及河喬嶽	As far as the River and the high peak;
允王維后	Truly it is the king who is lord.
明昭有周	Brightly shining is Zhou;
式序在位	The proper line is in place.
載戢干戈	Storing the shields and dagger-axes,
載櫜弓矢	Sheathing the bows and arrows,
我求懿德	We seek fine virtue.

| 肆于時夏 | And so in this [land of] Xia, |
| 允王保之 | Truly it is the king who protects it. |

MAY THE CULTURED (*SI WEN* 思文; *MAO 275*)

思文后稷	Would that the cultured Lord of Millet[29]
克配彼天	Be capable of joining that heaven,
立我烝民	And establishing our offering people.
莫匪爾極	Nothing is not within your reach.
貽我來牟	Bequeath to us wheat and barley;
帝命率育	The Lord commands [us] everywhere to cultivate.
無此疆爾界	Nothing here limits your borders,
陳常于時夏	Spreading constancy throughout [the land of] Xia.

These poems display several consistent linguistic and poetic features, evident on both formal and syntactic levels. On the formal level, they have neither consistent line lengths nor any consistent rhyme pattern, if they even display rhyme at all. In this, they are consistent with the poems in the "Martial" song-and-dance suite examined at the beginning of this essay, poems that, as noted there, are generally regarded as the earliest creations in the *Book of Poetry*. Inscriptions on bronze vessels suggest that rhyme was a feature that began to appear only midway through the Western Zhou dynasty,[30] so that the absence of rhyme in these poems may serve to confirm their traditional attribution to the beginning of the Western Zhou. It should also be noted that these poems provide very little description of the rites taking place. Rather, as I will try to show below, they consist for the most part of prayers addressed directly to the ancestors.

On the syntactic level, these poems also display at least two important features that show them to have been performative in nature. First, and also an important dating criterion, several of these poems (Mao 269, 271, 272, 273) use the modal auxilliary *qi* 其, familiar from the dedications of Western Zhou bronze inscriptions where it is used with the prayerful meaning "may, would that" (e.g., *zi sun qi yong bao yong* 子孫其永寶用, "may sons and grandsons eternally treasure and use [this vessel]").

維王其崇之   *May* it be the king who honors them.
            "Valorous and Cultured" (Lie Wen; Mao 269)

肆其靖之　　And so *may* he make it tranquil.
　　　　　　　　　"Bright Heaven has a Successful Mandate"
　　　　　　　　　(Han Tian you Cheng Ming; Mao 271)

我其夙夜　　*May* we morning and night
畏天之威　　Revere heaven's awe.
　　　　　　　　　"We Lead" (Wo Jiang; Mao 272)

昊天其子之　*May* bright heaven treat him as a son.
　　　　　　"Now Passing Through" (Shi Mai; Mao 273)

By contrast, poems in the Zhou Liturgies section that display consistent meter and rhyme (e.g., Mao 274, 284, 290, 291, 292) use *qi* as the third-person possessive pronoun, a usage that appears in bronze inscriptions no earlier than the middle of the Western Zhou period.[31] The modal usage of *qi* in the poems translated above would seem to indicate beyond doubt that these poems were prayers addressed to the ancestors.

In addition to introducing wishes with the modal auxilliary *qi*,[32] several of these poems also employ full verbs such as *hui* 惠, "to help," *xi* 錫, "to bestow," *yi* 貽, "to bequeath," and *qiu* 求, "to seek," to request blessings from the ancestors.

駿惠我文王　Quickly help us, King Wen's great grandsons,
　　　　　　　　to make
曾孫篤之　　　them steadfast.
　　　"It is Heaven's Mandate" (Wei Tian zhi Ming; Mao 267)

錫茲祉福　　Bestowing these blessings.
　　　　　　　"Valorous and Cultured" (Lie Wen; Mao 269)

我求懿德　　We seek fine virtue.
　　　　　　　"Now Passing Through" (Shi Mai; Mao 273)

貽我來牟　　Bequeath to us wheat and barley.
　　　　　　　"May the Cultured" (Si Wen; Mao 275)

These verbs again seem to suggest that these prayers were addressed by the celebrants of the rites directly to the ancestors to whom the rites were dedicated.

Direct address is also apparent in the use of pronouns in these poems. As in three of the examples quoted in the preceding paragraph, several of the poems (Mao 267, 269, 272, 273 and 275) use the first-person plural pronoun *wo* 我, "we, us."[33] Perhaps even more indicative of direct address is the use in two of the poems of the second-person personal pronoun *er* 爾, "you," to refer to the ancestors.

無封靡于爾邦   There are no boundary markers that are not
                       in *your* country.
                 "Valorous and Cultured" (Lie Wen; Mao 269)

莫匪爾極   Nothing is not within *your* reach.
                 "May the Cultured" (Si Wen; Mao 275)

The use of the first-person plural pronoun *wo* seems to me also to be significant in showing something of the nature of these rituals. There is no evidence in any of these poems that the rites were performed by a designated priest or representative acting on behalf of those present in the temple. Rather, the use of *wo* both as the grammatical subject of the prayers ("*We* seek fine virtue") and as the recipients of blessings ("Bequeath to *us* wheat and barley") suggests that the rites were performed, one might say concelebrated, by the collective body. I hope that the significance of this feature will become clearer as we next go on to discuss the exceptional poem within this unit, "Capturing and Competitive" (Zhi Jing 執競; Mao 274), and three other poems that I believe are analogous with it.

Unlike the other poems in the first ten-poem unit of the Zhou Liturgies, "Capturing and Competitive" consists entirely of four-character lines (14/14), and also displays a consistent rhyme scheme (nine of the first ten lines end with a *yang* 陽 class rhyme, while three of the final four lines end with an *yuan* 元 class rhyme). What is more, there is no evidence of the sort of prayers addressed directly to the ancestors seen in the other poems of the unit. Instead, this poem seems to focus on describing the rites taking place.

CAPTURING AND COMPETITIVE (ZHI JING 執競; MAO 274)

執競武王	Capturing and competitive was King Wu.[34]
無競維烈	Incomparable was [his] valor!
不顯成康	Illustrious were [kings] Cheng and Kang;[35]
上帝是皇	The Lord on High exalts them.
自彼成康	Since those [kings] Cheng and Kang
奄有四方	Covered all the four quarters,
斤斤其明	Piercing, piercing was their brightness.

鐘鼓喤喤	The bells and drums *huang-huang*,[36]
磬筦將將	The chimes and flutes *jiang-jiang*,
降福穰穰	Bring down blessings, strong-strong,
降福簡簡	Bring down blessings, long-long.
威儀反反	The awe and dignity, stern-stern;
威儀既飽	Being drunk, being sated,
福祿來反	The blessings and wealth come in return.

The most prominent descriptive feature of the poem is its use of reduplicatives as onomatopoeia to describe the sounds of the musical instruments.

鐘鼓喤喤	The bells and drums *huang-huang*,
磬筦將將	The chimes and flutes *jiang-jiang*,

This use of reduplicatives, extended throughout the poem even in cases not clearly onomatopoeic in nature (斤斤其明, "Piercing, piercing was their brightness"; 降福穰穰, "Bring down blessings, strong-strong"; 降福簡簡, "Bring down blessings, long-long"; 威儀反反, "The awe and dignity, stern-stern"), would develop into one of the characteristic features of prosody in the *Book of Poetry*.[37] However, it is important to note that it is virtually absent in the other nine poems of the ten-poem unit we have been discussing,[38] as it is also in Western Zhou bronze inscriptions before about the time of King Mu (r. 956–918 B.C.).

Bronze inscriptions suggest that these reduplicatives did, in fact, develop from onomatopoeia of the type used in this poem to imitate the sounds of musical instruments. The inscription on the famous "Hu *zhong*" (also known as the "Zongzhou *zhong*" 宗周鐘; Sh 18.98:260), commissioned by King Li (r. 857/53–842/28), provides an excellent example of this onomatopoeia.

Hu *Zhong*

朕猷有成亡競。我唯司配皇天王對作宗周寶鐘。倉 ₌戠
₌雝雖 ₌用邵洛丕顯祖考先 ₌王 ₌其嚴在上象 ₌數 ₌降
余多福 ₌余孫

My governance has succeeded without competition. We have succeeded in joining the august heavenly kings, and in response make for the Ancestral Zhou temple this treasured bell: *cangcang-zongzong, yingying-yongyong*. I herewith summon the illustrious ancestors and deceased father and the former kings to come. The former kings will be sternly on high. *Bobo-pengpeng!* Send down on me many blessings; bless me, the obedient grandson.

In this regard, it is important to note that it was not until about the time of King Mu that bells were introduced into the Zhou area from regions to the south and east.[39] Thus, in addition to its use of onomatopoeia, the explicit reference to bells in "Capturing and Competitive" (i.e., "The *bells* and drums *huang-huang*") also serves as an excellent dating criterion for the poem, showing that it could have been composed no earlier than about the middle of the Western Zhou dynasty.

At least three other features of the poem "Capturing and Competitive" support this dating. First, the fifth line of the poem, 自彼成康, "Since those [kings] Cheng and Kang," almost certainly refers—posthumously—to kings Cheng (r. 1042/35–1006 B.C.) and Kang, suggesting that the poem could date no earlier than the reign of King Zhao (r. 977/75–957 B.C.), the son of King Kang. Second, the first line of the poem, 執競武王, "Capturing and competitive was King Wu," is extremely reminiscent of the epithets used to describe Zhou kings in the inscription on the "*Shi* Qiang 史墙 *pan*" (Sh 50.*Ho*15:335). The section of that inscription dedicated to King Wu begins "Capturing and controlling (*suo yu* 鬣圉) was King Wu." Since the "*Shi* Qiang *pan*" dates to the reign of King Gong (r. 917/15–900 B.C.), the similar use of this epithet style in the poem "Capturing and Competitive" may signal a similar date for the creation of the poem. Third, the poem does not employ the modal *qi* noted above to be a feature of many of the other poems in the ten-poem unit under discussion, but instead employs the pronominal *qi*: 斤斤其明, "Piercing, piercing was their brightness." As I mentioned above (p. 179), this usage first appears in bronze inscriptions, and even then only exceptionally, only in the middle of the Western Zhou dynasty.

All of this serves, I believe, to show that the poem "Capturing and Competitive" is not of a piece—poetically or linguistically—with the other nine poems of the first ten-poem unit of the Zhou Liturgies. I would like to suggest that neither does it stem from the same ritual context, in which a group of people concelebrates the rites. Instead, I believe that it derives from a context in which there was a clear separation between a ritual officiant and observers. To demonstrate this ritual difference, it will be helpful to examine three other Zhou Liturgies poems concerning ancestral rites: "There are Blind-Drummers" (You Gu 有瞽; Mao 280), "Harmonious" (Yong 雝; Mao 282), and "Now Appearing" (Zai Xian 載見; Mao 283), all three of which share the same poetic and linguistic features as "Capturing and Competitive." I will begin by translating "There are Blind-Drummers" and "Now Appearing." After discussing salient features of their prosody and ritual performance, I will then return to the poem "Harmonious."

There are Blind-Drummers (*You Gu* 有瞽; Mao 280)

有瞽有瞽	There are blind-drummers, there are blind-drummers
在周之庭	In the court of Zhou.
設業設虡	Erecting stands, erecting racks
崇牙樹羽	With high flanges and mounted wings.
應田縣鼓	The echo-drums, kettle-drums, suspended drums,
鞉磬柷圉	Little-drums, chimes, rattles, and clappers
既備乃奏	Being ready then are played.
簫管備舉	The pan-pipes and flutes are all raised:
喤喤厥聲	*Huang-huang*, their sound.
肅雝和鳴	Solemn and harmonizing the concordant sound.[40]
先祖是聽	The prior ancestors hear this.
我客戾止	Our guests arrive and stop,
永觀厥成	Long viewing their performance.

Now Appearing (*Zai Xian* 載見; Mao 283)

載見辟王	Now appearing is the ruling king,
曰求厥章	Daily seeking his pattern:
龍旂陽陽	The dragon banner is *yang-yang*,
和鈴央央	The jingle-bells and tinkle-bells *yang-yang*,
鞗革有鶬	The reins are metal-studded,
休有烈光	The beneficence resplendent;
載見昭考	Leading to see the Shining Deceased-father,[41]
以孝以享	To be filial, to make offering,
以介眉壽	To strengthen long life,
永言保之	Eternally to protect it.
思皇多祜	Hoping for august and many blessings;
烈文辟公	The valorous and cultured ruling lords
綏以多福	Comfort with many blessings
俾緝熙于純嘏	And make continuous brightness in pure blessings.

The first thing to notice about these two poems is that, like the poem "Capturing and Competitive," they display consistent meter (all thirteen lines of "There are Blind-Drummers" have four characters, as do thirteen of the fourteen lines of "Now Appearing"[42]) and rhyme (the rhyme schemes of both poems alternate between *dong* 東 or *yang* 陽 class rhymes and *yu* 魚 or *zhi* 之 class rhymes[43]). Also like "Capturing and Competitive," both poems employ onomatopoeia. I think these formal features demonstrate beyond much doubt that the poems derive from a somewhat later poetic context than do the poems of the first ten-poem unit of the Zhou Liturgies.

Going on to examine the content of these two poems, perhaps the most striking contrast with those earlier poems is the complete absence of direct address to the ancestors who are the recipients of the rites. Instead of being part of the liturgy of the rites, these poems describe the actions of the rites. What is more, instead of first and second-person pronouns, we find the ritual participants, their activity, and the ancestors all modified by the third-person pronoun *jue* 厥, "his, their."

> 喤喤厥聲 　*Huang-huang, their* sound.
> 　　　　　　"There are Blind-Drummers" (You Gu; Mao 280)

> 先祖是聽　　The prior ancestors hear this.
> 我客戾止　　Our guests arrive and stop,
> 永觀厥成　　Long viewing *their* performance.
> 　　　　　　"There are Blind-Drummers" (You Gu; Mao 280)

> 載見辟王　　Now appearing is the ruling king,
> 日求厥章　　Daily seeking *his* pattern.
> 　　　　　　"Now Appearing" (Zai Xian; Mao 283)

It is clear to see that such description entails a separation between the poem and its context.

This separation between poem and context seems to parallel a separation within the very performance of the rites themselves. In an extremely important observation, Jessica Rawson has suggested that changes in ritual bronze vessels that appeared over the course of the middle of the Western Zhou dynasty imply a a radical reform in the way that rituals were performed. Rawson's remarks are deserving of quotation *in extenso*.

> A society that in 950 B.C. required sets of wine vessels as well as food vessels and in 880 B.C. had abandoned most of them, replacing them by extended sets of food vessels, must have effected major changes in ceremonies and even in beliefs. There was also, visible still today, a major change in the presentation of the bronzes. Early Western Zhou vessels were comparatively small and intricate. To

appreciate them fully they must have been viewed from close quarters, at least on occasions. It seems reasonable to suggest that the ritual may have been a relatively private matter, celebrated by a small number of people who were close to the bronzes. Later Western Zhou vessels achieved their impact from a distance, by sheer numbers and mass. Their surfaces were no longer decorated with minute detail. Indeed the prevalent motifs of ribbing or wave bands offered no advantage to close inspection. Their relatively coarse designs could just as well be seen from further off. In addition, bells introduced a new element—the expenditure of bronze to make music. Both the spectacle of rows of large bronzes and the impact of bell music seem to imply that at this date a larger number of people than previously witnessed the ritual, standing perhaps at a respectful distance.[44]

I believe that this ritual reform in which there developed a separation between ritual officiant or officiants and observers is also implied in the poems "There are Blind-Drummers" and "Now Appearing." In "There are Blind-Drummers," after describing the sights and sounds of the musical instruments, the poem concludes by referring to "our guests" (*wo ke* 我客) who "observe" (*guan* 觀) the musical and ritual performance.

> 我客戾止 Our *guests* arrive and stop,
> 永觀厥成 Long *viewing* their performance.
> "There are Blind-Drummers" (You Gu; Mao 280)

In the case of "Now Appearing," the officiant is specified as the king himself, while the word "appearing" (*xian* 見) seems to require some oberver or observers apart from him.

> 載見辟王 Now *appearing* is the ruling *king*.
> "Now Appearing" (Zai Xian; Mao 283)

This status of the king as the perhaps solitary performer of ritual is especially evident in the last of the Zhou Liturgies poems that I propose to consider: "Harmonious" (Yong; Mao 282). As I mentioned above, this poem is formally of a piece with "There are Blind-Drummers" and "Now Appearing." All sixteen of its lines are of four characters; it has a rhyme scheme that alternates between *dong* 東 or *yang* 陽 class rhymes and *yu* 魚 or *zhi* 之 class rhymes; it employs onomatopoeia; it describes the performance of the rites, and within that description refers to the ancestors with the third-person pronoun *jue*. It differs somewhat from the other two poems in that, like many of the poems in the first ten-poem unit of the Zhou Liturgies, it contains, sand-wiched between descriptions of the ritual activities, some direct address. However, unlike those earlier poems, this direct address is that of the king alone, explicitly marked by the use of the first-person singular pronoun *yu* 予.

HARMONIOUS (YONG 雝; MAO 282)

有來雝雝	There are those who come *yong-yong*;
至止肅肅	Arriving and stopping *su-su*.[45]
相維辟公	The images are the ruling lords.
天子穆穆	The Son of Heaven is stately, stately.[46]
於薦廣牡	"Oh, presenting the fatted bull,
相予肆祀	Assist me in presenting the sacrifice.[47]
假哉皇考	Approach, oh, august deceased-fathers;
綏予孝子	Comfort me, the filial son."
宣哲維人	Far-reaching and wise as men,
文武維后	Cultured and martial as lords:
燕及皇天	The feast reaches to august heaven,
克昌厥後	And is able to give rise to their descendants.
綏我眉壽	"Comfort us with long life
介以繁祉	In order to strengthen the maniform blessings."[48]
既右烈考	Having made offering to the valorous deceased-fathers,
亦右文母	(He) also makes offering to the cultured mothers.[49]

If Rawson is correct, and I am confident that she is, that the manifest changes in ritual paraphernalia that appeared over the course of the middle Western Zhou entailed "major changes in ceremonies and even in beliefs," then we should not be surprised to find those major changes reflected as well in the poetry of the times. While the present study is but a first step in trying to trace the changes in the earliest poetry, I think it is already clear that these changes were of two sorts: formal and conceptual. I have already treated the formal developments at some length. In short, we find a development from loose meter and little or no rhyme in the earliest poems (probably composed within the first century of the Western Zhou) to a consistent meter and rhyme scheme in poems that linguistic and historical features suggest must have been created no earlier than the second half of the tenth century B.C. (i.e., about the time of King Mu).

The conceptual changes are perhaps more important. I have suggested that the earliest poems were liturgical prayers, chanted by the concelebrants of the rites. It is hard to imagine that these poems could have had any role or meaning outside of the context of the rites. The later poems, on the other hand, are not parts of the rites but rather descriptions of the rites, and thus reflect already a separation between the rites and the poem—and the poet responsible for it. Indeed, I believe this separation reflects the rise of professionalization, a tendency evident also in other aspects of mid-Western Zhou society.[50] Just as the rites came to be performed by a ritual specialist before an observing audience, so too must these later poems have been performed (and doubtless have been created, also) by a solitary poet before a listening audience. The more distant these poems grew from that original communal ritual context, the more they would reflect the inner views of the poets themselves. Such surely must be a key ingredient in the rise of literature.

NOTES

1. A first draft of this chapter was delivered to the conference "Court Ritual in China" (7 April 1993, Cambridge, England); I would like to express my gratitude to all of the participants in that conference for a stimulating discussion. I have revised the paper—quite extensively—while in residence at the Center for Chinese Studies, Taipei, Taiwan. I would like to express my gratitude to the Center for its hospitality and support.

2. *Yi Zhou shu* (Sibu beiyao ed.), 4.10b; for a translation, though somewhat different from that given here, see above, chapter 2, p. 34.

3. These five lines are from the *Book of Poetry* poem "Now Passing Through" (Shi Mai 時邁; Mao 273; here and hereafter, poems in the *Book of Poetry* will be referred to first by an English title, then, within parentheses, by the Chinese title and the number of the poem in the standard sequence [indicated as "Mao"]); for a translation of the complete poem, see below, p. 177.

4. In his commentary on the poem "Martial" (Wu 武; Mao 285) in the *Book of Poetry*, Zhu Xi 朱熹 (1130–1200) states that the "*Chunqiu zhuan*" 春秋傳 (i.e., *Zuo zhuan*) gives the poem as the "first stanza" (*shou zhang* 首章) of the complete "Martial" suite (see Zhu Xi, *Shijing jizhu* 詩經集註 [Guoxue congshu ed.], 183), leading Ma Ruichen 馬瑞辰 (1782– 1853) to surmise that a text of the *Zuo zhuan* available in the Song dynasty must have read *shou zhang*, "first stanza," instead of the *zu zhang* 卒章, "final stanza," of the present text; see Ma Ruichen, *Maoshi zhuan jian tongshi* 毛詩傳箋通釋 (Sibu beiyao ed.), 29.16b.

5. *Zuo zhuan* Xuan 宣 12; for a text and translation, see James Legge, *The*

Chinese Classics, vol. 5, *The Ch'un Ts'ew with the Tso Chuen* (1872; rpt. Hong Kong: Hong Kong University Press, 1960), 315/320. However, all translations in this chapter are my own.

6. There is a consensus that two other poems now found at the end of the Zhou Liturgies section were also originally part of this suite: "Toast" (Zhuo 酌; Mao 293) and "Revolving" (Pan 般; Mao 296; the translation of these titles, which do not occur in the poems themselves, is extremely problematic). There have been numerous suggestions concerning the identification of the possible sixth stanza; for probably the most comprehensive discussion of this question, see Sun Zuoyun 孫作雲, "Zhouchu Da Wu yue zhang kaoshi" 周初大武樂章考釋, in *Shijing yu Zhoudai shehui yanjiu* 詩經與周代社會研究 (Beijing: Zhonghua shuju, 1966), 239–72.

7. Despite the traditions noted above that the "Martial" song suite was first performed in the presence of King Wu shortly after his victory over Shang, these final lines of "Outstanding" (Huan; Mao 294) seem to refer to King Wu as already deceased. For this reason, I translate descriptions of his actions here in the past tense.

8. *Liji Zheng zhu* 禮記鄭注 (Sibu beiyao ed.), 11.21a–b.

9. I have argued in chapter 4, a study of the "Shao gao" 召誥 and "Jun Shi" 君奭 chapters of the *Shangshu* 尚書 or *Book of Documents*, that the dukes of Zhou and Shao, principal lieutenants of King Wu (r. 1049/45–1043 B.C.), took two very different views of government after the king's death, the Duke of Zhou representing a ministerialist viewpoint and the Duke of Shao a royalist position. I maintained that the Duke of Shao's support for the legitimate authority of the king, the "Son of Heaven," carried the day, which may be consistent with the *Records of Rites'* characterization of the sixth and final movement of the "Martial" dance, the ranks of dancers "rejoining and acknowledging the supremacy of the king, the 'Son of Heaven.'"

10. See, e.g., J. Austin, *How to Do Things with Words* (London: Oxford University Press, 1962).

11. *Mao Shi Zheng jian* 毛詩鄭箋, (Sibu beiyao ed.), 19.11b–12b. Zheng Xuan specifies here that these were sung in the installation of King Cheng (r. 1042/35–1006 B.C.). However, it seems more likely that they were integral to installations of all kings in the Western Zhou.

12. Throughout this chapter, dates of reign for the various Western Zhou kings are as given in Edward L. Shaughnessy, *Sources of Western Zhou History: Inscribed Bronze Vessels* (Berkeley: University of California Press, 1991), xix, 217–87.

13. Fu Sinian, *Fu Sinian quanji* 傅斯年全集, 5 vols. (Taipei: Lianjing shuban shiye gongsi, 1980), vol. 1, 218–20.

14. For a convenient text of the "Gu ming," see James Legge, *The Chinese Classics*, vol. 3, *The Shoo King or the Book of Historical Documents* (1865; rpt. Hong Kong: Hong Kong University Press, 1960), 544–61. The partial translation given here is taken from the more extensive (though still not complete) translation given above in Chapter Five. Because of the extensiveness of the quotation, the ready availability of all of the texts, and the essentially derivative nature of the quotation, I here present just the English texts and also refrain from any textual notations.

15. I will first translate nine of these ten poems, reserving the translation of one exceptional poem ("Capturing and Competitive" [Zhi Jing 執競; Mao 274]) until the discussion of that poem in particular.

16. *Xiang* 相 is usually understood as "assistants," referring to those who assist with the sacrifice. I suspect that it refers instead to "images" of the ancestors in the temple (the word is certainly cognate with *xiang* 想, "to imagine," and doubtless also with *xiang* 象, "image, figure"). In support of this interpretation, I would point to the identification of the *xiang* with the "ruling lords" (*bi gong* 辟公) in the poem "Harmonious" (Yong 雝; Mao 282): 相維辟公, "The *xiang* are the ruling lords." Although here too traditional commentaries interpret the "ruling lords" to refer to the leaders of the various states who have come to court to assist in the sacrifices, comparison with the use of the same term in the poems "Valorous and Cultured" (Lie Wen 烈文; Mao 269): 烈文辟公，錫茲祉福, "Valorous and cultured are the ruling lords, Who bestow these blessings," and "Now Appearing" (Zai Xian 載見; Mao 283): 烈文辟公，綏以多福, "Valorous and cultured ruling lords, Who comfort [us] with many blessings," clearly shows that the "ruling lords" are ancestors capable of bestowing blessings.

17. *Wen zhi de* 文之德 is glossed by the Mao commentary as "cultured virtue," but Zheng Xuan fills it out to be *wen wang zhi de* 文王之德, similar to the occurrence in the poem "Valorous and Cultured" (Lie Wen; Mao 267).

18. Although the translation given here reflects the traditional parsing of these two lines, breaking them between *chun* 純, "pure," and *jia* 假, "approach," I suspect that *jia* should read *gu* 嘏, "blessing," and be modified by *chun*, to form the common Western Zhou idiom *chun gu*, "pure blessings." I refrain from this emendation primarily because it would expose the *yi* 以 of the second line, leaving it with neither an object nor a verbal complement.

19. The *qi* 其 opening this line is the modal "may, would that" so ubiquitous in the dedications of Western Zhou bronze inscriptions. For further discussion of its significance, see below, p. 178.

20. This line is usually broken between the words "King Wen" and "great grandsons," the first line then being read as an equational sentence: 駿惠我交王, "The one who quickly helps us is King Wen." However, in such a reading the final pronominal *zhi* 之 refers back to King Wen, such that the great grandsons "make steadfast" (*du* 篤) "him," i.e., King Wen, which would seem to be quite unnecessary. Instead, I believe that "King Wen's great grandsons" stands in apposition modifying "us" (*wo* 我), so that the *zhi* refers back to the "purity" of King Wen's virtue mentioned in line 4, just as does the *zhi* of line 6.

21. As noted above (n. 16), "ruling lords" (*bi gong* 辟公) here is usually interpreted to refer to the many lords (*zhuhou* 諸侯) of the various Zhou states, equivalent to the "hundred rulers" (*bai bi* 百辟) in the twelfth line of this poem. That this interpretation is mistaken here can be seen from two points. First, both *lie* 烈, "valorous," and *wen* 文, "cultured," are epithets almost always reserved for deceased ancestors, who were also routinely referred to with the honorific *gong* 公, "lord." Second, the "ruling lords" here are the agents who "bestow" (*xi* 錫) these "blessings" (*zhi fu* 祉福), which is certainly something of which only the ancestors were capable.

22. The "high mountain" (*gao shan* 高山) of line 1 is generally understood to refer to Qishan 岐山, which is specifically mentioned in line 5 below and which was the ancestral homeland of the Zhou people in central Shaanxi province. The "Great King" (*tai wang* 大王) of line 2 refers to Gugong Danfu 古公亶父, the leader of the Zhou people who led their migration to Qishan. The "leveling" (*huang* 荒) of the mountain, the cutting down of the trees on it, is understood by the commentaries—and was doubtless intended within the poem—as a salutary act, a necessary first step to bringing it under cultivation.

23. The "two lords" (*er hou* 二后) refers to kings Wen and Wu.

24. "Single was his heart" (*dan jue xin* 單厥心) refers to King Cheng's resolve, as we might say, his "single-mindedness." For a contrast, compare the description in the "Gu ming" chapter of the *Book of Documents* (quoted above, p. 173) of the ministers of kings of kings Wen and Wu as being "without two hearts" (*bu er xin* 不二心).

25. The graph used to write the word *you* here is 右, "right," which has given rise to much discussion about the sides of the temple to which the gods

and the offerings were placed. However, *you* belongs to an extended word family based on the word *you* 有, "to have," which also includes many words (such as *you* 侑, "to offer," and *you* 祐, "blessings") related to the exchange of offerings and blessings between humans and spirits. I suspect that both in this line and in line 7 *you* reflects this sense of offering, and praying that heaven will accept it.

26. *Gu* 嘏, which is usually a noun meaning "blessing," is frequently read here as *jia* 假, "to approach." While the two meanings are clearly related (King Wen's approach brings blessings), the grammar here seems to require an adjective, which I have tried to approximate with "blessed."

27. I suspect that the opening of this poem is garbled, since there is no antecedent for either the *qi* 其, which I translate as "his," of the first line (which, I might also add, is the only prepositional *qi* in what I regard as the earliest poems of the Zhou Liturgies, for which see below), or for the *zhi* 之, which I translate as "him," of the second line. Although it is grammatically possible that the *zhi* of the second line could refer back to the "country" (*bang* 邦) of the first line, it would seem strange to personify the country in this way (i.e., treating it as a son). Since the poem is otherwise a paean to the reigning king ("Truly it is the king who is lord"; "Truly it is the king who protects it"), it seems to me that both *qi* and *zhi* here must refer to the king.

28. The antecedent of this *zhi* 之, which I here translate as "them," is also unclear, though I suspect that the traditional commentaries are correct in understanding it to refer to the lords of the various countries, grammatically referring back to the *bang* 邦, "country," of line 1. Also unclear here is the agent of this "shaking" (*zhen* 震). It is of course possible that the agent is the "heaven" of line 2, in which case this line and those following would read as a prayer (i.e., "Extensively shake them," etc.). However, consistent with my suspicion above (n. 27) that an initial reference to the reigning king has somehow fallen out of the poem, I understand this and the following lines also to refer to the king, and to be the results of his actions.

29. The initial *si* 思 is generally glossed as an initial particle without meaning. However, I believe that this is an excellent example of its use in Zhou texts of several genres introducing prayers, with the sense "we hope that, would that, may." For a study of its use in divinatory contexts, see Xia Hanyi 夏含夷, "Shilun Zhouyuan buci si zi—jianlun Zhoudai zhenbu zhi xingzhi" 試論周原卜辭𢀖字——兼論周代貞之性質, *Guwenzi yanjiu* 古文字研究 17 (1989): 304–8.

30. For studies of rhyme in Western Zhou bronze inscriptions, see Guo Moruo 郭沫若, *Jinwen yu shi zhi yu* 金文餘釋之餘 (Tokyo: 1932), 127a–149b; Chen Shihui 陳世輝, "Jinwen yundu xuji yi" 金文韻讀續輯一, *Guwenzi yanjiu* 古文字研究 5 (1981): 169–90; and Chen Banghuai 陳邦懷, "Xi-Zhou jinwen yundu jiyi" 西周金文韻讀輯遺, *Guwenzi yanjiu* 9 (1984): 445–62. Shirakawa Shizuka 白川靜, "Seishu shiryaku" 西周史略 (*Kinbun tsūshaku* 金文通釋, 47: 1100–9) proposes that the earliest Western Zhou inscriptions that display rhyme, dating to about the time of King Mu (r. 956–918 B.C.; e.g., the "Shenzi Ta 沈子它 *gui*" [Sh 15.78:7] and "Ban 班 *gui*" [Sh 15.79:34] used an interlocking rhyme with *zhi* 之 and *yu* 魚 class rhymes interspersed with *dong* 東 class rhymes, and that this is similar to the rhyme scheme seen in some Zhou Liturgies poems such as "Harmonious" (Yong 雝; Mao 282). I will suggest below that other linguistic features also show that the poem "Harmonious" could have been created no earlier than about the time of King Mu.

31. The earliest usage of *qi* 其 as the third-person possessive pronoun seems to come in the inscription of the "Yu *ding* 寓鼎" (Sh 17.89:177): 對揚其父休, "In response extolling *his* father's beneficence, herewith making this treasured *ding*-caldron." The "Yu *ding*" inscription, the vessel of which is no longer extant, seems to date to the time of King Mu (r. 956–918 B.C.). The only other third-person possessive pronominal uses of *qi* that I know of in Western Zhou bronze inscriptions come on the "Hu *zhong* 鐘" (Sh 18.98:260) and on the "Xi Jia *pan* 兮甲盤" (Sh 33.191:785), vessels dating to the reigns of King Li (r. 857/53–842/28) and King Xuan (r. 827/25–782) respectively.

32. One should note here too the analogous use of *si* 思, "hope that; would that, may," in the poem "May the Cultured" (Si Wen 思文; Mao 275); for this usage, see above, n. 29.

33. For the plural usage of *wo* 我 as seen in Shang oracle-bone inscriptions, see Chen Mengjia 陳夢家, *Yinxu buci zongshu* 殷墟卜辭綜述 (Beijing: Kexue chubanshe, 1956), 96. Wang Li 王力, *Hanyu shigao* 漢語史稿 (Beijing: Kexue chubanshe, 1959), 267, suggests that this original plural usage became less rigorously distinguished throughout the Western Zhou, so that *wo* eventually could be used for either the plural or the singular. At the risk of circularity, I would suggest that the usage of *wo* in the poems translated here seems in all cases to be plural, perhaps attesting to an early Western Zhou date for these poems.

34. "Capturing and competitive" (*zhi jing* 執競) is reminiscent of the types of epithets used in the inscription on the "*Shi* Qiang *pan*" 史墻盤 (Sh

50. *Ho*15:335) to characterize deceased Zhou kings. In that inscription, King Wu is praised as being "capturing and controlling" (*suo yu* 縶圉).

35. Although the Han commentators regarded *cheng* 成 and *kang* 康 as adjectives meaning "successful" and "vibrant," it seems clear from context that they refer to the second and third kings of the Western Zhou dynasty. The further reference in line 5, "Since those [kings] Cheng and Kang," in which "those" (*bi* 彼) serves to distance the two kings (temporally), suggests that the poem could have been created no earlier than the following reign of King Zhao (r. 977/75–957 B.C.), a dating which, as I will discuss below, seems consistent with several of the linguistic and poetic features of the poem.

36. *Huang-huang* 喤喤, like *jiang-jiang* 將將 in the following line, is onomatopoeia for the sounds of musical instruments. Although the *rang-rang* 穰穰, *jian-jian* 簡簡, and *fan-fan* 反反 of the next three lines are all linguistically similar, and the chanting of which may have been syncopated with the bell and drum beats, I suspect that the words used were intended to be syntactically significant.

37. For a discussion of the use of reduplicatives in *Book of Poetry*, including a table of statistics showing that they appear in virtually every poem in the Da Ya 大雅 and Xiao Ya 小雅 or Greater and Lesser Epics and in the Guo Feng 國風 or Airs of the States sections, see Zhou Manjiang 周滿江, *Shijing* 詩經 (1980; rpt. Taipei: Sanmin shuju, 1990), p. 29. In the Zhou Liturgies section, reduplicatives are found in the following poems: 266, 274 (6x), 276 (2x), 280, 282 (3x), 283 (2x), 284 (2x), 288, 290 (5x), 291 (2x), 292, 294. Those poems that display multiple reduplicatives are precisely those poems that also display consistent meter (274: 14/14 four-character lines; 276: 15/15; 282: 16/16; 283: 13/14; 284: 12/12; 290: 31/31; 291: 23/23) and rhyme. This would seem to suggest that the use of reduplicatives is one excellent criterion by which to distinguish the dates of poems in the Zhou Liturgies section.

38. There is one reduplicative, *ji ji* 濟濟, "well arrayed," in the poem "The Clear Temple" (Qing Miao 清廟; Mao 266), however, this is certainly not onomatopoeic.

39. For the introduction of bells into the Zhou area, and a comprehensive discussion of their use there, see Lothar von Falkenhausen, *Suspended Music* (Berkeley: University of California Press, 1994), 159–62.

40. *Su* 肅, "solemn," and *yong* 雝, "harmonious," occur reduplicated in "Harmonious" (Yong 雝; Mao 282) presumably as onomatopoeia for the sounds of flutes and drums. Although the words are not reduplicated here, and

thus I translate them as full words, I suspect that they are used as much for their onomatopoeic value as for their syntactic sense.

41. It seems to me likely that this *zhao* 昭, "shining," deceased-father may well refer to King Zhao (a possibility which I attempt to reflect obliquely by capitalizing Shining and Deceased-father). If so, the creation of this poem could then date no earlier than the time of King Mu, a dating not inconsistent with the poem's linguistic and poetic features.

42. For further discussion of this feature, see above, n. 37.

43. For further discussion of this feature, see above, n. 30.

44. Jessica Rawson, "Statesmen or Barbarians? The Western Zhou as Seen through their Bronzes," *Proceedings of the British Academy* 75 (1989): 89–91.

45. As pointed out above (n. 40), *yong* 雝 and *su* 肅 occur together, but not reduplicated, in the poem "There are Blind-Drummers" (Mao 280), and are interpreted there as full words meaning "harmonious" and "solemn." Although commentators also gloss the separate and reduplicated occurrences of these words here with the same full meanings, it is clear that they are primarily onomatopoeia for the sounds of drums and flutes respectively.

46. Although it is of course possible that this term "stately, stately" (*mu mu* 穆穆) could be used to describe any Zhou king, it is nonetheless the case that it does not appear in any Western Zhou bronze inscription before the time of King Mu (r. 956–918 B.C.). I suspect that its occurrence here may well refer to King Mu, a dating of this poem that is consistent with the other linguistic and poetic features of the poem.

47. Here I follow the traditional reading of *xiang* 相 as "to assist," although I believe it is also possible to maintain the reading offered in line 3 above (as also in the poem "The Clear Temple"; see above, n. 16) in which *xiang* refers to "images" of the ancestors in the temple. In the direct address of this line, this interpretation would suggest a reading: "Images, I present the sacrifice."

48. I suspect that *jie yi* 介以 here must originally have read *yi jie* 以介, as in the similar lines in "Submerged" (Qian 潛; Mao 281): 以介景福, "In order to strengthen the great blessings," and "Now Appearing" (Zai Xian; Mao 283): 以介眉壽, "In order to strengthen long life." It is also worthy of mention, if only in passing, that there are eighteen occurrences of *yi* 以 in the Zhou Liturgies section, almost all of them in poems that display the latest linguistic and poetic features seen in the section.

49. As in the poem "We Lead" (Wo Jiang; Mao 272) above (see above, n. 25),

the word *you* 右 here must stand for another word in the same word family; in this case, I suspect that the proper word should be *you* 侑, "to offer."

50. For a preliminary indication of this sort of development of professionalization within the bureaucracy of the Zhou court, see Shaughnessy, *Sources of Western Zhou History*, 169.

7

The Composition of "Qian" and "Kun" Hexagrams of the *Zhouyi*

Just as the *Zhouyi* 周易 or *Yijing* 易經 has been regarded by the Chinese since the time of the composition of the "Wenyan" 文言 commentary down to the contemporary philosopher Xiong Shili 熊十力 as the essence of Chinese thought and wisdom, so too has there never been an intellectual who has doubted that the essence of that essence is to be found in the first two hexagrams, "Qian" 乾 and "Kun" 坤. Regardless of the heuristic device used to interpret the text, these two hexagrams, the former pure *yang* (i.e., all six lines of the hexagram picture are unbroken) and the latter pure *yin* (i.e., all six lines are broken), are seen to be imbued with a virtue greater than just that of initial position; they are seen as a microcosm of the entire text, indeed of the entire world. Every attempt has been made in this study (i.e., "The Composition of the *Zhouyi*") to interpret the text of the *Zhouyi* contextually and without resort to the philosophical and moralistic reasoning that has produced the majority of these interpretations.[1] Yet evidence has indeed been found that the final redaction of the *Zhouyi* was not a coincidental achievement. The line Topics and their Prognostications have been shown to share an intrinsic relationship,[2] individual hexagrams display in their progressive development the unmistakable hand of an editor or editors, and in some cases pairs of hexagrams are coordinated into one complete thought. We have also seen that the final hexagram pair, "Jiji" 既濟 (63) and "Weiji" 未濟 (64), may have obtained its position as the final unit of the text by virtue of a conscious editorial decision.[3] All of this should suggest that the editor of the *Zhouyi* himself held the hexagrams he placed at the head of the text in a special regard.

Before proceeding to discuss the original meaning of and relationship between "Qian" and "Kun" hexagrams, we should begin by translating the

197

two texts. The translations given here schematically divide the texts into topics (the left column), injunctions (the middle column), and technical divination terminology (including both prognostications and verifications, combined in the right column).

"QIAN" 乾 (1)

元亨利貞
Primary receipt: beneficial to divine.

潛龍	勿用	
Submerged dragon	do not use	

見龍在天	利見大人	
See the dragon in the fields	beneficial to see the great man	

君子終日乾乾，夕惕若厲		无咎
The lordling throughout the day is vigorous, in the evening he is fearful as if there is danger[4]		no harm

或躍在淵		无咎
And now jumping in the depths		no harm

飛龍在天	利見大人	
Flying dragon in the skies	beneficial to see the great man	

亢龍		有悔
Necked dragon		there are problems

見群龍无首吉		吉
See the flock of dragons without heads		auspicious

"KUN" 坤 (2)

元亨利牝馬之貞。君子有攸往，先迷後得主。利西南得朋，東北，喪朋。安貞吉。
Primary receipt: beneficial for a mare's divination; the lordling does some travelling; first lost, then he gets his ruler; beneficial to the southwest to get a friend, to the northeast to lose a friend; divining about peace: auspicious.

履霜 Treading on frost	堅冰至 the solid ice is coming	
直方 Inspecting the borderland	（大）不習无 not timely[5]	无不利 nothing not beneficial
含章 Containing a pattern	可貞；或從王事 one may divine; and now attend to royal affairs	无成有終 without completion but with an end
括囊 Tying the sack		无咎无譽 no harm but no praise
黃裳 Yellow skirts		元吉 primary auspiciousness
龍戰于野其血玄黃 The dragon fights in the wilds, his blood is black and yellow	利永貞 beneficial to perform a permanent divination	

Isolating just the topics of the line statements, we have for "Qian":

> Submerged dragon,
> See the dragon in the fields,
> And now jumping in the depths,
> Flying dragon in the skies,
> Necked dragon,
> See the flock of dragons without heads,

and for "Kun":

> Treading on frost,
> Inspecting the borderland,
> Containing a pattern,
> Tying the sack,
> Yellow skirts,
> The dragon fights in the wilds, his blood is black and yellow.

It has been the images of these topics that have generated the greatest interest among *Yijing* exegetes, and which will also be our focus in the present discussion.

The dragon imagery of "Qian" has proven to be that aspect of the *Zhouyi* most susceptible to allegorical or metaphysical interpretation. What is perhaps the dominant interpretation is well represented by Richard Wilhelm's general comment:

> The power represented by the hexagram is to be interpreted in a dual sense—in terms of its action on the universe and of its action on the world of men. In relation to the universe, the hexagram expresses the strong, creative action of the Deity. In relation to the human world, it denotes the creative action of the holy man or sage, of the ruler or leader of men, who through his power awakens and develops their higher nature.[6]

The dragon is the symbol of the sage and the six lines are interpreted to be depictions of his actions *vis-à-vis* circumstances in which he finds himself. Thus, in times of an evil and unreceptive sovereign, the sage submerges, that is, retreats to his mountain hideaway. On the other hand, given a virtuous ruler the sage not only rejoins the world of men but finds his rightful position above all men ("flying" over them, so to speak), where his moral influence can have its greatest effect. The line texts have even served as the *locus classicus* for a theory of radical anarchy. The top line (1/7), "see the flock of dragons without heads," is interpreted by Xiong Shili to refer to the innate equal goodness of all men, above whom there should be no ruler (i.e., "head").[7]

Interesting and often philosophically profound though these interpretations may be, it is the role of the context critic merely to document what the image may have originally represented. From what we know of the Western Zhou intellectual and political milieu and what we have seen elsewhere in the *Zhouyi*, it is safe to assume that the intended referent of the dragon was *not* the moralistic or metaphysical force elaborated in the later commentaries. But it is also true that the dragon is a mythological creature that is not to be found in the world of animals. Still, the attributes of the dragon were so firmly fixed in China's ancient mythology that it had to be based on some natural phenomenon. In fact, the Chinese have long seen the form of a dragon in a constellation of stars which becomes visible in the eastern quadrant of the sky in spring and finally passes out of sight beneath the western horizon in autumn. While in the West these stars are split into three constellations, Virgo, Libra, and Scorpius, the Chinese see the composite form of a dragon, marked especially by a long, curling tail and a pair of horns. Indeed, the names given to the respective star clusters are "Horn" (*Jiao* 角) and "Tail"

Fig. 7.1. The Celestial Dragon

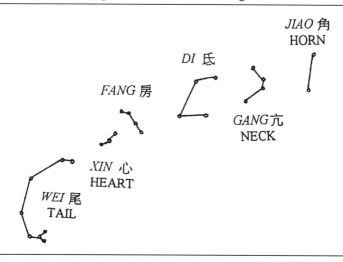

(*Wei* 尾). In between, the "neck" (*Gang* 亢) and the "heart" (*Xin* 心) of the dragon are also distinguished (see figure 7.1).

Returning now to the dragons of "Qian" hexagram, we can see that the various lines depict the seasonal positions of the celestial dragon. The bottom line (1/1), "submerged dragon," represents the dragon constellation at about the time of the winter solstice, designated in the Chinese calendar as the *zi* 子 month. At this time, the horns of the dragon have still not appeared above the eastern horizon and the entire dragon is invisible in what the Chinese considered to be the watery depths beneath the horizon (see figure 7.2).[8] Coming to the second line, the statement "see the dragon in the fields" suggests the first appearance of the dragon's horns above the horizon, a phenomenon that occurred in early March (modified for precession; see figure 7.3). From the perspective of one looking toward the horizon, it would indeed appear as if the dragon were lurking in the distant fields. Skipping over the third line (1.3), a line that does not share the literary structure or imagery of the hexagram's other lines, the fourth line (1.4), "and now jumping in the depths," continues the description of the dragon's progress across the night sky. From the first appearance of the horns in early March until late in April only the horns and neck are yet visible. But in about twenty-five days from late April until mid-May, the entire torso of the dragon (the lunar-lodges *Di* 氐, *Fang* 房, and *Xin* 心), including the Fire Star (*Huo* 火 or *Dahuo* 大火;

Fig. 7.2. Submerged Dragon

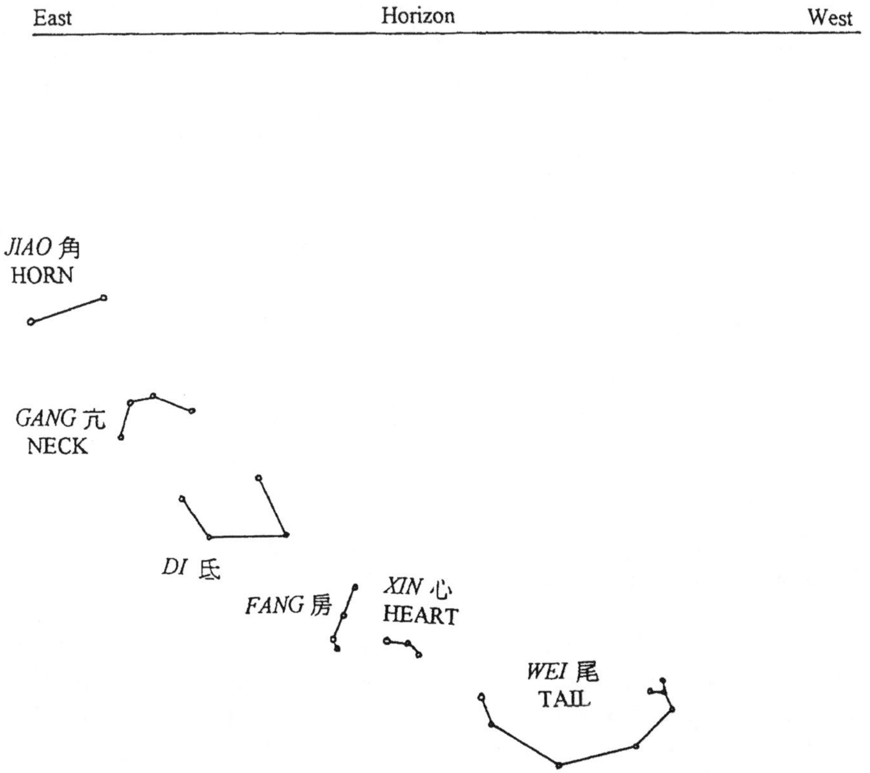

East	Horizon	West

JIAO 角
HORN

GANG 亢
NECK

DI 氐

FANG 房

XIN 心
HEART

WEI 尾
TAIL

(The position of the Dragon constellation at dusk at winter solstice, 800 B.C.)

i.e., Antares), known to have been in ancient China an important marker of the beginning of the growing season,[9] suddenly becomes visible above the horizon, leaving only the tail still submerged (see figures 7.4 and 7.5). "And now jumping in the depths," although not specifically mentioning the dragon, is certainly evocative of the dragon's sudden emergence.[10] By the fifth line (1.5), corresponding to the summer solstice in late June, the entire dragon is now arrayed across the night sky (see figure 7.6). It is thus not surprising that the line statement here reads "flying dragon in the skies." The final two lines (1.6 and 1.7), "necked dragon" and "see the flock of dragons without heads," appear to represent one and the same astronomical situation. As figure 7.7 shows, as of mid-August the star cluster *Gang* (i.e., "Neck") is located on the

Fig. 7.3. See the Dragon in the Fields

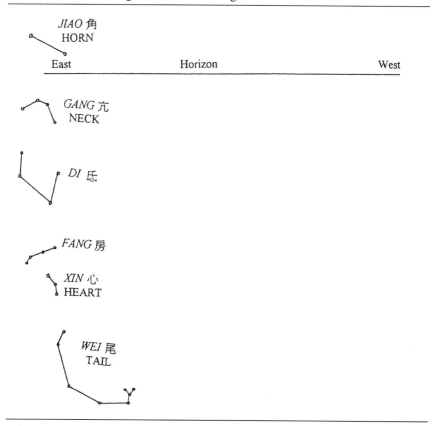

(The position of the Dragon constellation at dusk in early March, 800 B.C.)

western horizon, just about to sink once again into the depths. It cannot be coincidental that the dragon of "Qian"'s top line is referred to as the "*gang*" ("necked") dragon, using the same word as the name of the star cluster poised on the horizon. This leads quite naturally to the statement "see the flock of dragons without heads," for at this point only the body and tail of the dragon remain visible in the dusk sky, while the horns and head (i.e., Jiao) have already sunk from sight.[11]

Explicit as this astronomical imagery is, it has passed remarkably unnoticed by Chinese commentators.[12] For them, much more important has been the calendrical implications of this astronomy. The period of visibility of the Dragon constellation coincides so perfectly with the agricultural growing season

Fig. 7.4 and 7.5. And Now Jumping in the Depths

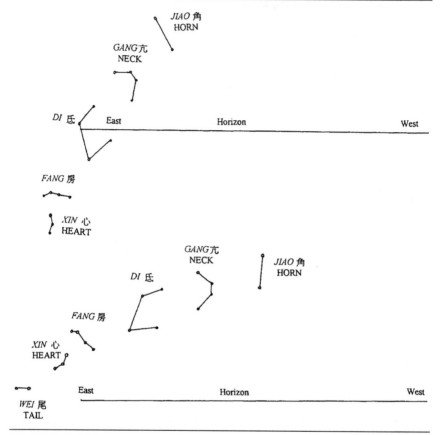

(The positions of the Dragon constellation at dusk in late April [*top*] and mid-May [*bottom*], 800 B.C.)

in China that the progress of the dragon is equated with the maturation of the crops. In this regard, the "Tuan" 彖 commentary states:

> 大哉乾元。萬物資始乃統天；雲行雨施，品物流形。大
> 明終始，六位時成。時乘六龍以御天。
>
> Great indeed in the primalness of Qian. The ten-thousand things materially begin and it is arrayed across the skies; the clouds move and the rain falls and all things take shape. The Great Brightness [i.e., the moon] ends and begins again; the six positions are seasonally formed. The seasons ride the six dragons across the skies.

Fig. 7.6. Flying Dragon in the Skies

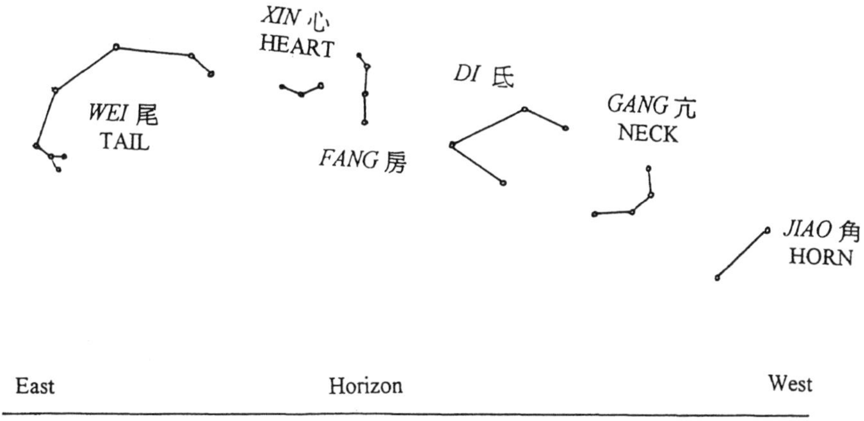

(The position of the Dragon constellation at dusk at summer solstice, 800 B.C.)

While a certain astronomical significance can be detected in this passage, there is no doubt that its author was more interested in "Qian"'s seasonal implications. To him, "Qian" was important insofar as it relates to the growing season; the birth of things in the spring, their growth through the summer, and final maturity in the fall.

This calendrical significance becomes explicit in "Kun" hexagram. The bottom line of the hexagram (2.1) reads, "treading on frost: the solid ice is coming." This is certainly an evocation of the period shortly after the autumn equinox when the first frosts of autumn bring the reminder that winter is soon to arrive.[13] Several "stars-and-seasons" almanacs confirm that "frost" is a natural phenomenon associated with the ninth month. The *Lüshi chunqiu* 呂氏春秋 states in its description of the last month of autumn, "In this month the frost begins to descend,"[14] and the *Huainanzi* 南淮子 says, "If in the third month there is a loss of government, then in the ninth month the frost will not come down."[15] That this association was also current at the time of the *Zhouyi*'s composition can be seen in the poem "Qiyue" 七月 (Mao 154) of the *Shijing*. "In the ninth month there is shrivelling [of plants] and frost."[16] But before winter does arrive, there is still much to be done in an agricultural society. The overseers of the land must go out and inspect the harvest, which gives rise to the second line (2.2), "inspecting the borderlands."[17] The third line (2.3), "containing a pattern," requires more study but seems to be an evocation that the crops are ripe and ready for harvesting (compare the fifth

Fig. 7.7. Necked Dragon, See the Flock of Dragons without Heads

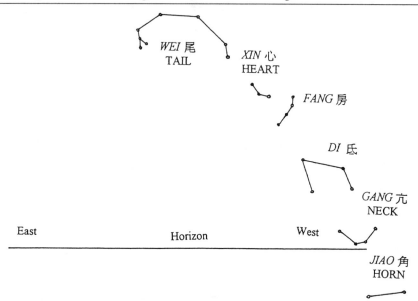

WEI 尾
TAIL

XIN 心
HEART

FANG 房

DI 氐

GANG 亢
NECK

East

Horizon

West

JIAO 角
HORN

(The position of the Dragon constellation in dusk in mid-August, 800 B.C.)

line of "Gou" 姤 [44.5]: "*Yi qi bao gua: han zhang; you yun zi tian*" 以杞包瓜；含章，有隕自天, "With willow wrap the gourd: containing a pattern; there is something fallen from heaven.") The fourth line (2.4), "tying the sack," can be compared with the following line in the *Shijing* poem "Gong Liu" 公劉 (Mao 250).[18]

乃積乃倉，乃裹餱糧，于橐于囊
He collected, he stored, he tied up provisions in bags, in sacks.

From this it would seem to indicate the storing of the harvest. The fifth line (2.5), "yellow skirts," perhaps signals the ritual celebration of the harvest's completion and the continuing preparations for winter. Here again a comparison with the poem "Qiyue" may be instructive:

八月載績，載玄載黃
我朱孔陽，爲公子裳
In the eighth month we spin, both black and yellow; Our red-dye is very bright; we make skirts for the young noblemen.[19]

But it is the top line (2.6), "the dragon battles in the wilds, his blood is black and yellow," resuming as it does the dragon imagery of "Qian," that climactically brings these two hexagrams to full circle.

The natural phenomenon to which the line refers is far from straightforward. Traditionally, two methods of interpreting this line have predominated. The first is based on *yin-yang* and "line position" (*yao wei* 爻位) theory. This broken line in the top position of the pure *yin* hexagram "Kun" represents *yin* at its extreme, which is in the tenth, or *hai* 亥, month. According to *yin-yang* theory, whenever either *yin* or *yang* reaches its extreme it invariably reverts to its opposite. Here the reversion is accomplished by way of the *yang* force's (i.e., the dragon's) battling to regain its prominence. That there is both black and yellow blood is interpreted to imply that both primal forces have suffered some injury.

The other major interpretation of this line finds its *locus* in the *Shuo wen jie zi* 說文解字 of Xu Shen 許慎. This line is quoted in Xu's definition of the word *ren* 壬:

壬位北方也，陰極陽生，故易曰：「龍戰于野。」戰者接也。家人衷壬之形，承亥壬以子生之敘也。

The position of *ren* is to the north with *yin* at its extreme and *yang* coming to life; therefore, the *Changes* says, "The dragon *zhan*'s in the wilds." *Zhan* means "to couple." It is the form of a pregnant woman and is based on the exposition of *hai* and *ren* giving birth to a child.[20]

In his gloss to this definition, Duan Yucai 段玉裁 states, "The reason for the allusion to the line statement of the top line of 'Kun' is that the top line of 'Kun' is in *hai*," and also notes that the apocryphal Han dynasty work *Qian zuo du* 乾鑿度, somewhat in anticipation of normative *yin-yang* theory (which holds that *yang* begins in the *zi* month), states: "*Yang shi yu hai, qian wei zai hai*" 陽始于亥，乾位在亥, "*Yang* begins in *hai*; the position of "Qian" is in *hai*." While the underlying meaning of this interpretation of the line statement is functionally identical with that of the *yin-yang* theorists, it views the transformation from *yin* to *yang* as being one of production rather than destruction. When *yin* has reached its peak, *yang* stirs back to life, much like an embryo growing in a mother's womb.

Both of these interpretations, however, derive from theories popular during the Han dynasty, nearly a millennium after the composition of the *Zhouyi*. While the context critic certainly cannot ignore these traditions, it is his responsibility to attempt to discover the natural phenomena underlying them. Since the dragon imagery of "Qian" hexagram has been shown above

Fig. 7.8. *Bi* (Turtle) Constellation

to be astronomical in origin, it is logical here also to turn to the skies for an understanding of the dragon imagery of this line and the background for these later interpretations. As noted by the *Shuo wen* scholiasts, the heavenly stem *ren* is paired with earthly branch *hai*, which corresponds to the tenth month, the month before that containing the winter solstice. In addition to its calendrical associations with the rebirth of *yang*, the tenth month is also the time of an astronomical phenomenon that bears on this theme of draconian paternity. The historian of Chinese astronomy Gustave Schelgel notes that the *Erya yi* 爾雅翼 remarks:

> 介潭生先龍，先龍生元黿
> The great pond gives birth to the first dragon;
> The first dragon gives birth to the primal turtle.

Schlegel adds the observation, "The tail of the dragon touches the head of the celestial turtle, a fact which, without any doubt, has given birth to this fiction that 'Water produces the dragon and the dragon the turtle.'"[21] In a similar manner, Schlegel quotes the *Shishi xingjing* 石氏星經, purported to date from the fourth century B.C.:

> 北方玄武七宿斗有龍蛇蟠結之象
> In the seven lunar lodges of the Dark Warrior of the northern quadrant, (the lunar lodge) *Dou* has the appearance of a dragon and snake coiled together.

To this, he adds, "It is easy to know the astronomical reason for this explanation, because the head of the constellation of the turtle, *Dou* or φ Saggitarius, touches the tail of the constellation of the dragon, *Wei* or the tail of Scorpius, and has probably given birth to the popular belief in the carnal union of the dragon with the turtle."[22]

    Although the Turtle or Black Warrior is identified generally with the seven lunar lodges of the northern quadrant, it would seem that this characterization

Fig. 7.9. The Dragon Fights in the Wilds, His Blood Is Black and Yellow

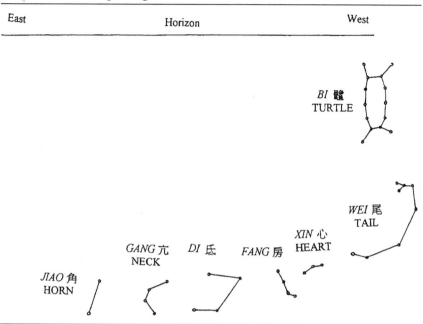

(The position of the Dragon and Turtle constellations at dusk in October, 800 B.C.)

derives from the configuration of one prominent constellation found on its northeastern border. As illustrated here, the constellation Bi ZZ (Turtle), comprised of stars in Corona Australis bears a striking resemblance to an earthly turtle (figure 7.8). Moreover, as can be seen in figure 7.9, the relationship between the Dragon and this celestial Turtle takes on a particular significance in the tenth month. This is precisely the time when the Turtle rejoins the Dragon in the watery depths beneath the western horizon. This presumably marks both the proper time and the proper place for the consummation of their amorous tryst.[23]

While the conjoining of Scorpius and Saggitarius may well be the *locus* for Xu Shen's gloss of *jie* 接, "to join," for the word *zhan* 戰, "to battle," in this line statement, mythological accounts of dragons doing battle suggest that such an interpretation of this phenomenon is unnecessary. Perhaps the most important of the battles in which dragons engaged was that between the Yellow Emperor and Chi You 蚩尤. In that battle, a dragon (specified as a "responsive dragon" [*ying long* 應龍]) was one of the two principal lieutenants of the Yellow Emperor. Chi You, described in one source as having the feet of a turtle and the head of a snake,[24] met the Yellow Emperor on the field of Zhuolu 涿鹿, said to be situated in the wilds of the north (*Jizhou zhi ye* 冀州之野). At the beginning of the battle Chi You marshalled his forces of wind and rain and caused a great fog to descend over the field, throwing the forces of the Yellow Emperor into confusion. The Yellow Emperor is said to have thereupon looked up and regarded heaven. Inspired by the astral dipper (*dou* 斗), he invented the compass-chariot. When even with this celestial guide he could gain only a stalemate, a "dark woman" (*xuan nü* 玄女) named Drought (*Ba* 魃) was sent to the aid of the Yellow Emperor. With her arrival, the rain finally ceased and Chi You was killed.

Mythological sources are not in agreement as to who finally killed Chi You; while general credit goes to the Yellow Emperor, at least one source credits the Dragon. The *Shan hai jing* 山海經 says:

大荒東北隅中有山名曰凶犁土丘。應龍處南極，殺蚩尤
與夸父，不得復上，故下數旱

In the great wastes of the northeast corner there is a mountain called the Earth Mound of Inauspicious Plowing. The Responsive Dragon was situated to the extreme south; he killed Chi You and Gua Fu but was not able to rise up again. Therefore, below there was a long drought.[25]

The consequences of this action for the dragon are clarified in Guo Pu's 郭僕 comment on this passage: "*Ying long sui zhu dixia*" 應龍遂住地下, "The Responsive Dragon thereupon lived under the ground." But the specification of the dragon as Chi You's killer is relatively unimportant, for the Yellow Emperor is himself but the incarnation of a dragon. In addition to his common association with dragons,[26] the "Astronomical Treatise" (*Tianguan shu* 天官書) of the *Shiji* 史記 informs us that the constellation Xuanyuan 軒轅 (another name of the Yellow Emperor) "has the body of a yellow dragon."[27] Nor is the Yellow Emperor the only combatant in this mythological struggle who is to be found in the skies. Several sources attest that after Chi You died he ascended into the skies and became a comet.[28]

Although it would be premature to associate this myth with any particular astronomical phenomenon, that the general tenor of its imagery is astronomical is undeniable.[29] Of particular importance to our discussion of the dragon's battle in the top line of "Kun" is the fact that during the Han dynasty the cult to Chi You was conducted during the tenth month.[30] Moreover, this corresponds well with the climatic descriptions of his battle with the Yellow Emperor. In China, autumn marks the rainy season. The beginning of winter—the tenth month—brings dryness that lasts until the next spring.

This is certainly the reason why the Yellow Emperor required the aid of the goddess Drought to vanquish Chi You, the master of the rains. Likewise, this is why the dragon is said to have had to remain under the ground after killing Chi You; astronomically, the dragon would not be able to rise again until the following spring. And finally, directly pertinent to the conclusion of the *Zhouyi* line statement "his blood is black and yellow," this same phenomenon is undoubtedly why both black blood (i.e., Chi You's; recall his association with the turtle and snake, the Dark Warrior) and yellow blood (i.e., the yellow dragon's) was shed.

I have reviewed above two tentative solutions to the mystery of the dragon's battle in the wilds. Whichever is the original source of the image, and it is possible that nuances of both apply, there is one important point that they have in common. They are both related to events of the tenth month, the beginning of winter. As noted above, Han dynasty *Yijing* scholars were unanimous in also attributing this top line of "Kun" to the tenth month. Typical of them is Xun Shuang, who in his comment on them says:

消息之位；坤在於亥，下有伏龍，爲兼于陽，故稱龍也。

It is the position of destruction and growth; "Kun" is in *hai* and below there is the hidden "Qian" which links it [i.e., this line] with *yang*, and therefore it refers to the dragon.[31]

More important perhaps is evidence contemporary with the composition of the *Zhouyi* that the tenth month, which after all marked the end of the "living season," was indeed considered as the end of the year. The oldest of China's "stars-and-seasons" almanacs is the poem "Qiyue" in the *Shijing*. With regard to the tenth month it states:

In the tenth month the cricket is under our bed; the holes being stopped up, we smoke out the rats; we block the northern windows and plaster the door; Oh, you wife and children: it is all for the [changing of the year=] passing into a new year; let us enter into this house and dwell there.[32]

With this calendrical conception in mind, it is easy to recognize the complementarity of "Qian" and "Kun." But, unlike the paradigmatic hexagram pairs "Tai" 泰 (11) and "Pi" 否 (12), and "Jiji" (63) and "Weiji" (64), the complementarity here is only incidentally one of structure or imagery. While they share one astromythological image, the deep structure is entirely calendrical. "Qian" makes use of the image of the celestial dragon to characterize the various periods in the growing season of the agricultural year, the time when the crops germinate and grow to maturity. The "Tuan" commentary, though written at a time when the original astronomical foundation of the hexagram was largely forgotten, leaves no doubt about this "living" aspect of "Qian."

> Great indeed is the primalness of "Qian!" The ten-thousand things materially begin and it is arrayed across the skies; the clouds move and the rain falls and all things take shape.

"Kun," on the other hand, marks the culmination of this agricultural and calendrical process and the passage into the "dead" season of winter. Unlike "Qian" which refers to astronomical phenomena spanning ten months, "Kun" is concentrated in just two months of the year. But these two months possess an importance deserving of such concentration for they represent the time of the harvest, certainly the most significant time in the agricultural calendar. Here again the "Tuan" commentary signals the proper interpretation.

> Extreme indeed is the primalness of "Kun"! The ten-thousand things come to life and then, following the heavens, "Kun" broadly supports [all] things. Its virtue coalesces without bounds, containing great brightness, and all living things come to fruition.

Important though the growing season is, without the harvest it remains incomplete. So too, important though "Qian" is, without "Kun" its promise remains unfulfilled. This complementarity is a certain proof that their juxtaposition in the text was the result of a conscious editorial decision. And whether in terms of the subtlety of their imagery, the sophistication of their poetry, or the complementarity of their calendrical associations, "Qian" and "Kun" fully deserve their place at the head of the *Zhouyi*.

NOTES

1. Shaughnessy, "The Composition of the *Zhouyi*," (Ph.D. diss., Stanford University, 1983).
2. For these terms and their use in explicating the text of the *Zhouyi*, see ibid., 139–58.
3. Ibid., 257–65.
4. An alternative reading, first suggested by Kong Yingda, *Zhouyi zhengyi*: 4.26, punctuates this line after *ruo* 若, with *li* 厲 understood in its normative *Zhouyi* prognosticatory sense (i.e., in the evening frightened-like:

danger). Whichever of these readings is adopted, this line is obviously not of a piece with the hexagram's other line statements, and I suspect that it is the remnant of an early commentarial stratum.

5. Deleting *da* 大, *apud* Gao Heng 高亨, *Zhouyi gu jing jin zhu* 周易古經今注 (Shanghai: Kaiming Shudian, 1947), 8. Traditionally, the line has been parsed as *zhi* 直, *fang* 方, *da* 大, *buxi* 不習, "straight, square, and great: not timely," but comparisons with the other lines of "Kun" [*lü shuang* 履 [*siang (GSR 731a)], *han zhang* 含章 [*tiang (GSR 723a)], (*kuo nang* 括囊 [*nang (GSR 730l)], and *huang chang* 黃裳 [*diang (GSR 725d)] leave little doubt that *zhi fang* 直方 [*piwang (GSR 740a) constitutes a single phrase. In further support of this reading, the lack of any gloss for *da* 大 in the "Xiang" 象 commentary suggests that *da* is indeed an intrusion into the text.

6. Richard Wilhelm, *The I Ching or Book of Changes*, translated by Cary F. Baynes, Bollingen Series 19 (New York: 1950), 3.

7. Xiong Shili 熊十力, *Qian Kun yan* 乾坤衍 (Rpt. Taipei: Xuesheng shuju, 1976), 419–22.

8. These star-charts are not intended to be precisely calibrated; for present purposes it suffices that the Dragon constellation's relative change of position be portrayed.

9. In addition to appearing in oracle-bone inscriptions (e.g., *Houbian*, "Xia" 9.1, *Heji* 12488), the Fire Star is said by later sources (see, e.g., *Zuozhuan* 9th year of Duke Xiang [James Legge, *The Chinese Classics*, vol. V: *The Chun Ts'ew with the Tso Chuen* (London and Hong Kong: 1872), 439]; *Shiji* 史記 [Zhonghua shuju ed.], 3.1257) to have been the object of observation by a Shang official, the *Huo zheng* 火正, specifically charged with determining the agricultural seasons; see further, Chen Zungui 陳尊媯, *Zhongguo tianwenxue shi* 中國天文學史 (Shanghai: Shanghai Renmin chubanshe, 1980), 196–97.

10. In addition to the logic of a conscientious editor of the *Zhouyi* wishing to include the appearance of the Fire Star in his outline of the dragon's celestial progress, there are three linguistic factors in support of interpreting this line as alluding to the dragon. First, the action here is specified as taking place in the watery "depths" (*yuan* 淵). Comparing the *Shuo wen* (11B.21b) definition of the dragon, "*qiu fen er qian yuan*" 秋分而潛淵, "at the autumn equinox he submerges into the depths," with the bottom line of "Qian" (1.1), "*qian long*" 潛龍, "submerged dragon," there is an obvious relationship between the words *qian*, "submerge," of line 1.1 and

yuan, "depths," of 1.4. Moreover, the *Shijing* poem "Han lu" 旱麓 (Mao 239) contains the couplet:

鳶飛戾天，魚躍于淵
The hawk flies through the skies,
The fish jumps in the depths,

wherein the contrast between "*fei tian*" 飛天 and "*yue yuan*" 躍淵 is precisely the same as that in lines 1.4 and 1.5 of this hexagram. Second, *yuan* is in the same rhyme category (*zhen* 眞 class) as *tian* 田 of line 1.2 and *tian* 天 of line 1.5. This suggests that these three lines not only belong to a common rhyme-scheme but also to a common conceptual scheme. Third, just as both lines of the couplet:

魚在于渚，或潛在淵
The fish is on the sand bar,
And now submerges in the depths,

in the *Shijing* poem "He ming" 鶴鳴 (Mao 184) refer to the fish, with *huo* 或 acting as a copula ("and now," "and then"), so too should the *huo* of this line be read as a copula grammatically linking this Topic with those of lines 1.1 and 1.2. For all of these reasons, despite the lack of an explicit reference to the dragon, line 1.4 should also be interpreted as a reference to the relative motion of the dragon constellation.

11. I suspect that the reason that there is a reference here to a "flock" of dragons is due to the ancient Chinese astromythological conception that celestial luminaries, because of their nightly rising in the east and setting in the west, had to be plural, as for example with the case of the ten suns and twelve moons. Later tradition holds that there were "six" dragons; whether this represents the original astonomical myth or is a later elaboration due to the six positions of "Qian" hexagram, I prefer not to speculate.

12. This is not to say that I am the first to have noticed the astronomical significance of "Qian's" dragon image. As early as 1911 the Swiss historian of Chinese astronomy Leopold de Saussure said of the dragon constellation, "In the course of the months a larger and larger part of the dragon emerged at twilight; by the end of Spring the entire dragon was found above the horizon and seemed to take flight in the sky," to which he appended the note, "this process of the dragon's Spring appearance is manifest in the first pages of the *Yijing*, a book in which the developments of the ethical order always repose on an astronomical canvas" and continued by citing Legge's translation of lines 1.1, 1.2, 1.4 and 1.5 of

"Qian" hexagram; Leopold de Saussure, *Les Origines de l'Astronomie Chinoise* (1909–22; rpt. Taipei: Ch'eng-wen, 1967), 378. Unfortunately, Saussure did not expand on this insight.

In China it was not until 1941 that Wen Yiduo 聞一多 made a similar association; Wen Yiduo, *Gu dian xin yi* 古典新義 (1941; rpt. in *Wen Yiduo quanji* 聞一多全集 [1948; rpt. Beijing: Sanlian shudian, 1982], vol. 2, 45–48). However, Wen did not perceive the relationship among the lines and the process they describe, but rather interpreted each line as an individual omen. Correlating them with the *Shuo wen* (11B.21b) definition, "at the spring equinox the dragon rises into the skies, and at the autumn equinox submerges into the depths," he was led to interpret the bottom line, "submerged dragon," as an omen of autumn, the second, "see the dragon in the fields," and fifth, "flying dragon in the skies," lines as omens of spring.

Twenty years later, the calendrical development of the lines was finally related systematically to the astronomical phenomena by Gao Wence; "Shilun *Yi* de chengshu niandai yu fayuan diyu" 試論易的成書年代與發原地域, *Guangming ribao* 光明日報 2 June 1961, 4. Unfortunately, again, Gao was unaware of the sidero-lunar nature of pre-Chunqiu astronomy and this led him to interpret "Qian" as being related to the winter months and "Kun" as related to the summer months. The first line of "Kun" (2.1), *"lü shuang: jian bing zhi"* 履霜堅冰至, "treading on frost: the solid ice is coming," suffices to demonstrate the incongruity of this argument. Despite this, Gao's essay was a significant step forward in interpreting this imagery; only a proper understanding of the history of Chinese astronomy is necessary to return the lines of "Qian" to their proper seasonal associations.

13. Akatsuka Kiyoshi 赤塚忠 ("'*Lü shuang jian bing zhi*' no kaishaku—ka, kō ji kōsei kaimei no kokoromi" 履霜堅冰至の解釋——卦爻辭成解明の試之, in *Suzuki Hakushi koki kinen tōyōgaku ronsō* 鈴木博士吉稀記念東洋學論叢, eds. Uno Seichi 宗野精一, et al. [Tokyo: Meitoku shuppanshe, 1972], 9–28) and Chow Tse-tsung ("The Child-Birth Myth and Ancient Chinese Medicine: A Study of Aspects of the *Wu* Tradition," in David Roy and T.H. Tsien, eds. *Ancient China: Studies in Early Civilization* [Hong Kong: Chinese University of Hong Kong Press, 1978], 53) have both treated the image of "treading on frost" as a symbol for spring nuptials. This totally neglects the association of "frost" with the ninth month, ubiquitous in early stars-and-seasons texts, and also disrupts the calendrical associations of "Kun" hexagram.

14. *Lüshi chunqiu* (Sibu beiyao ed.), 9.1b.

15. *Huainanzi* (Sibu beiyao ed.), 5.18a.

16. Tr. Bernhard Karlgren, *The Book of Odes* (Stockholm: Museum of Far Eastern Antiquities, 1974), 99.

17. This meaning is based on the common oracle-bone inscriptional compound 㞢方. The graph 㞢 has been subject to considerable analysis, with such transcriptions as *xing* 省, *xun* 循, and *de* 德 proposed; see Li Xiaoding 李孝定, *Jiagu wenzi jishi* 甲骨文字集釋 (Taipei: Academia Sinica, 1965), 1.563–69; see too, David S. Nivison, "Royal 'Virtue' in Shang Oracle Inscriptions," *Early China* 4 (1978–79): 52–55. While there is no doubt that all three of these words are related, both to each other and to the oracle-bone graph 㞢, there is also no doubt that a "literal" transcription of that graph would be *zhi* 直 (with ｜ → 十 and ⬭ → 目; see Paul L-M Serruys, "Towards a Grammar of the Language of the Shang Bone Inscriptions," in *Zhongyang yanjiuyuan guoji Hanxue huiyi lunwen ji* 中央研究院國際漢學會議論文集 (Taipei: Academia Sinica, 1981), 359n1. That the compound occurs here in this archaic form (i.e., *zhi fang*) rather than in the form *xing fang*, which later became common, is an interesting indication of the *Zhouyi*'s antiquity. For a discussion of this compound (albeit proposing the transcription *xing fang*), with special emphasis on its agricultural associations and meaning in this line of "Kun" hexagram, see Wen Yiduo, *Wen Yiduo quanji*, vol. 2, 41.

18. Tr. Karlgren, *The Book of Odes*, 207.

19. Tr. Karlgren, *The Book of Odes*, 98.

20. *Shuo wen jie zi Duan zhu* 說文解字段注 (Sibu beiyao ed.), 4B.16b–17a.

21. Gustave Schlegel, *Uranographie Chinoise* (Leiden: E. J. Brill, 1875), vol. 1, 64.

22. Schlegel, *Uranographie Chinoise*, vol. 1, 172.

23. I should like to clarify here that "Xuan Wu" 玄武, the Dark Warrior, is not strictly identifiable with "Bi" ZZ, the Turtle. "Xuan Wu" is generally considered to be the seven lunar-lodges of the northern quadrant (i.e., "Dou" 斗, "Niu" 牛, "Nü" 女, "Xu" 虛, "Wei" 危, "Shi" 室, and "Bi" 壁), while "Bi" ZZ, the Turtle, is but a paranatellon of "Dou." Yet, unlike the Dragon and Bird constellations, which do have a certain resemblance to the creatures for which they are named, it would be very difficult to see the shape of a turtle in the composite appearance of these seven lunar-lodges. Rather, I suspect that the entire quadrant received its name (whenever the concept of four roughly equilateral quadrants was formalized) by

virtue of this one constellation at its head, which so definitely does resemble a turtle. And it is this constellation that virtually touches the tail of the Dragon.

24. Cited in Moriyasu Tarō 一森安太郎, *Zhongguo gudai shenhua yanjiu* 中國古代神話研究, translated by Wang Xiaolian 王孝廉 (Taipei: Dipingxian chubanshe, 1979), 195.

25. *Shan hai jing* (Sibu beiyao ed.), 14.6a–b.

26. He is commonly depicted as ascending to heaven on the back of a dragon. For a complete discussion on the identification of the Yellow Emperor with the dragon, see Moriyasu, *Zhongguo gudai shenhua yanjiu*, 175–202 and 215–40.

27. *Shiji*, 27.1299.

28. See, e.g., *Lüshi chunqiu* (Sibu beiyao ed.), 6.9b, and *Shiji*, 27.1335.

29. Especially interesting here is the account of the invention of the compass, and the explicit relationship of this in the *Guanzi* 管子 ([Sibu beiyao ed.] 41.10a–b) to the succession of the seasons:

昔者，黃帝得蚩尤而明於天道 ... 蚩尤明乎天道，使爲當時。

Of old, the Yellow Emperor took Chi You and became aware of the celestial way ... Chi You made bright the celestial way and caused there to be the proper seasons.

Note too the comment by Fang Xuanling 房玄齡: "*wei zhi tian shi zhi suo chang ye*" 謂知天時之所常也, "this means that he knew the constancy of the celestial seasons." In this regard it is useful to compare the battle between the Yellow Emperor and Chi You with the other great battle of Chinese mythology, that between Yu the Great (*Da Yu* 大禹) and Gong Gong 共工. It will be recalled that in the course of losing this battle, Gong Gong butted his head against Mount Buzhou 不周, the northwestern pillar of heaven, snapping it and causing the heavens to tilt downwards in the northwest. It is commonly, if not explicitly, understood by Chinese commentators that this myth is basically astronomical in nature, being an attempt to explain the obliquity of the ecliptic. It is this obliquity of the ecliptic that causes the stars to appear at different times of the year, thus making them markpoints *par excellence* of the changing seasons. In a sense, this displacement of the ecliptic from the celestial equator could be described as the beginning of cosmic time, and is thus an especially appropriate topic for mythologization. Such myths can be found in cultures throughout the world, a number of them having been collected and discussed by Giorgio de Santillana and Hertha von Dechend. To cite just one example, they quote a popular identification of Kronos (Saturn) with Chronos (Time) by Macrobius:

> They say, that Saturn cut off the private parts of his father Caelus (Ouranos), threw them into the sea, and out of them Venus was born who, after the foam (aphros) from which she was formed, accepted the name of Aphrodite. From this they conclude that, when there was chaos, no time existed, insofar as time is a fixed measure derived from the revolution of the sky. Time begins there; and of this is believed to have been born Kronos who is Chronos, as was said before.

To this, de Santillana and Dechend add, "the fact is that the 'separation of the parents of the world,' accomplished by means of the emasculation of Ouranos, stands for the establishing of the obliquity of the ecliptic: the beginning of measurable time"; Giorgio de Santillana and Hertha von Dechend, *Hamlet's Mill* (Boston: Godine, 1977), 135.

  We should note, as do de Santillana and Dechend, that Saturn, the master of time, corresponds in China to the Yellow Emperor, who became the master of time through his battle with Chi You. This suggests that, like the battle between Yu the Great and Gong Gong, the battle between the Yellow Emperor and Chi You is but another mythological manifestation of this same astral phenomenon. In fact, Marcel Granet has pointed out several features in the myths of Chi You and Gong Gong so similar as virtually to require identification: both are gods of the eight winds, both belong to the Jiang 姜 family, both are associated with the Kong sang 空桑 tree, both were punished at Shangqiu 商丘, and most important, both were rebels said to have "*zheng wei di*" 爭爲帝, "fought to be theocrat"; see Marcel Granet, *Danses et Legendes de la Chine Ancienne* (Paris: Albin Michel, 1926), 351–60, 482ff. All of this suggests that while its astronomical associations have not been as readily recognized as those of Gong Gong's breaking the pillar of heaven, the compass-chariot fashioned by the Yellow Emperor in response to the great fog (chaos?; recall the "foam" from which Aphrodite was formed) of Chi You is also a representation of the beginning of cosmic time.

30. See *Shiji*, 1.5.
31. Quoted in Li Dingzuo 李鼎祚, *Zhouyi jijie* 周易集解 (Yijing jicheng ed.), 9.69–70, 80.
32. Tr. Karlgren, *The Book of Odes*, 98–99. It should also be noted that this

poetic almanac employs two distinct calendrical enumerations. Months designated as "*siyue*" 四月, "fourth month," through "*shiyue*" 十月, "tenth month," correspond to the Xia 夏 calendar; i.e., to the calendar that begins with the *yin* 寅 month, the seond month after the month containing the winter solstice. Other months, corresponding to the Zhou calendar; i.e., the calendar beginning with the *zi* 子 month, the month containing the winter solstice, are referred to as "*yi zhi ri*" 一之日, "the days of the first," "*er zhi ri*" 二之日, "the days of the second," and so on through "*si zhi ri*" 四之日, "the days of the fourth"; for a discussion of this poem correlating these months with natural phenomena described in other almanacs, see Hua Zhongyan 華鐘彥, "'Qi yue' *Shi* zhong de lifa wenti" 七月詩中的曆法問題, in *Shijing yanjiu lunwen ji* 詩經研究論文集 (Beijing: Renmin chubanshe, 1959), 151–62. This is interesting evidence of the simultaneous existence of dual calendars, one popular and one governmental, and also serves to underscore the rite of passage from the *hai* month, the tenth month of the Xia calendar, to the *zi* month, the first month of the Zhou calendar, which has been shown to be so important in the cycle of "Qian" and "Kun" hexagrams.

8

How the Poetess Came to Burn
the Royal Chamber

In the study of the Chinese classics, modern scholarship has made perhaps its most satisfying contribution toward the explication of the *Shijing* or *Classic of Poetry*. The poems of the *Classic of Poetry* range from temple liturgies probably sung as early as the tenth century B.C., through epics praising the founding of the House of Zhou or criticizing the depths to which it had sunk in the ninth and eighth centuries, to songs ("airs") of the various states into which Zhou divided thereafter. By no later than the time that the collection had been edited into its definitive form, sometime in the sixth century B.C., the poems were regularly cited within the context of political discourse, and were apparently understood as being inherently suited to such use. By the Western Han dynasty, when the earliest extant commentary—the Mao Commentary—was written, most readers seem to have believed that the poems derived from specific historical moments, and that they achieved their power by commenting on those moments. This historical-political interpretation dominated the next two thousand years of exegesis of the *Classic of Poetry* (though, one of course needs to add parenthetically, not without insinuations of revisionism beginning as early as the Northern Song dynasty), and continues today to influence much, if not most, Chinese readings of the text. However, it is no longer the only exegetical paradigm available. The twentieth century has brought a bold departure from the traditional exegesis, and it is almost certainly the case that the two or three best known modern interpreters of the *Classic of Poetry* are those who have departed the farthest from tradition.

This new interpretation of the *Classic of Poetry* was pioneered by the great French Sinologist Marcel Granet (1884–1940). In his *Fêtes et Chansons Anciennes de la Chine*, published in 1919, Granet proposed that the poems, or perhaps better "songs," of the *Classic of Poetry*, had originally been sung in the celebration of popular seasonal festivals.[1] Combining evidence within the poems themselves (particularly those of the "Airs of the States" portion of the collection) with evidence in later ritual texts and also with parallels from other cultures, Granet surmised that the festivals were held at the times of the spring plantings and autumn harvests. Not only were these festivals intended to seek and to celebrate the fertility of the agricultural life, but they were also designed to serve as occasions for the unmarried young men and women of the community to meet. According to Granet, these men and women, lined up in facing rows, would extemporize choruses of songs to each other, hoping to impress each other and to win each other's affections. A good example of such a ritual mating song is the poem "Zhen and Wei" ("Zhen Wei" 溱洧; Mao 95) of the notorious Airs of Zheng.

ZHEN AND WEI

溱與洧	The Zhen and Wei rivers
才渙渙兮	Are just at full flood;
士與女	The boys and girls
方秉蕑兮	Are just holding *jian*-orchids.
女曰觀乎	The girl says, "Have you looked?"
士曰既且	The boy says, "Already have."
且往觀乎	"Shall we go look!"
洧之外	Beyond the Wei
洵訏且樂	There is fun and joy.
維士與女	It is the boys and girls
伊其相謔	Who frolic with each other
贈之以勺藥	And make presents of peonies.

This poem also serves well to illustrate two particular features of these festivals for which Granet found pervasive evidence in the *Classic of Poetry*: that they were held along the banks of rivers, and that they often involved the exchange of floral love tokens.

Important as Granet's ethnographic analysis is for understanding the context in which the poems were created, his disavowal of any symbolism or subtlety within the poems was surely an over-reaction to the traditional allegorical interpretation.[2] Fortunately, this over literalism was in turn corrected (and perhaps over-corrected) by the second of the great twentieth-century *Classic of Poetry* critics—Wen Yiduo 聞一多 (1899–1946). Like Granet, Wen is also best known for interpreting many of the Airs of the States poems as popular love songs.[3] Unlike Granet, however, Wen saw symbolism throughout the poems. Whereas Granet interpreted the nature imagery that begins so many of the poems as describing the actual setting of the seasonal celebrations, Wen argued—not altogether unlike traditional commentators on the *Classic of Poetry*—that the images were intended primarily to evoke situations and sentiments within the human realm.[4] Perhaps the most famous of his interpretations of these images or evocations (*xing* 興) is that of the symbolic meaning of fish.[5]

Wen noted that most references to fish in the *Classic of Poetry* introduce poems about marital relations. The poem "The Transverse Gate" ("Heng Men" 衡門; Mao 138) is a good example.

THE TRANSVERSE GATE

衡門之下	Beneath the Transverse Gate,
可以棲遲	One can take his ease;
泌之洋洋	Where the spring gurgles,
可以樂飢	One can satisfy his hunger.
豈其食魚	In eating fish,
必河之魴	Must it be a bream of the River?
豈其取妻	In taking a wife,
必齊之姜	Must she be a Jiang of Qi?
豈其食魚	In eating fish,
必河之鯉	Must it be a carp of the River?
豈其取妻	In taking a wife,
必宋之子	Must she be a Zi of Song?

Like Granet, Wen was an enthusiast of ethnography, which enjoyed something of a craze in China during the 1930s. He compared "The Transverse Gate" to contemporary folk songs he heard while walking through southern China with his students. One such song comes from the Hakka people.

天上下雨	Heaven above pours down rain,
地下滑	and earth below is moist.
池中魚兒	In the pool's midst,
擺尾巴	the fishes sway their tails.
那天得魚	On that day that I get a fish,
來下酒	come and pour some wine;
那天得妹	On that day that I get a girl,
來當家	come and make a family.

Another was popular in Yunnan.

要吃辣子	If you want to eat a pepper,
種辣秧	plant pepper-seeds;
要吃鯉魚	If you want to eat a carp,
走長江	go to the Yangzi River.
要吃鯉魚	If you want to eat a carp,
長江走	to the Yangzi River you go;
要玩小妹	If you want to play with a young girl,
走四方	go to the four quarters.

The ubiquity of this association between the eating of fish and marital relations (in addition to these folk songs, Wen also noted the occurrence of fish as symbols of fertility in other cultures) led Wen to conclude that there must be something about fish intrinsically evocative of sexual relations (perhaps their resemblance to the male sexual organ), and that it was this evocative or symbolic significance that the poets who created the *Classic of Poetry* primarily intended when they mentioned fish.

The association between fish and marital relations would seem to be quite clear in the poem "The Transverse Gate." Even in some poems where fish are not mentioned explicitly, Wen found the same association underlying the poem's nature imagery. For instance, in the poem "Men at Waiting" ("Hou Ren" 候人; Mao 151), the title of which could equally well be translated "Waiting for a Man," the primary nature image is of a pelican; however, as Wen noted, the pelican is a fish-eating bird, and thus its mention immediately calls fish to mind.

MEN AT WAITING

彼候人兮	Oh, those men at waiting,
何戈與祋	Carrying dagger-axes and spears;
彼其之子	Those young men there:
三百赤芾	Three hundred red knee-covers.
維鵜在梁	There is a pelican on the bridge
不濡其翼	Who does not wet his wings;
彼其之子	That young man there
不稱其服	Does not match his clothes.
維鵜在梁	There is a pelican on the bridge
不濡其味	Who does not wet his beak;

彼其之子	That young man there
不遂其媾	Does not follow up his mating.

薈兮蔚兮	Oh, how dense; oh, how lush,
南山朝隮	The morning mist upon the Southern Mountain;
婉兮孌兮	Oh, how pretty; oh, how lovely
季女斯飢	This young girl who hungers.

It seems clear—and certainly was not doubted by the mainstream of traditional *Classic of Poetry* exegesis—that the image of the pelican in the second and third stanzas is intended to evoke the human situation: that the pelican does not wet his beak, which is to say that it does not eat a fish, parallels the arrogant young man who "does not follow up his mating." The difference between Wen Yiduo's approach and that of the traditional exegetes is that whereas they searched for a specific historical referent to which to tie the association, he believed that the poems addressed the general human condition, just as the Hakka and Yunnanese courtship songs obviously do.

Easy as it is for a post-Freudian reader to appreciate Marcel Granet's emphasis on communal fertility rites or Wen Yiduo's sexual interpretation of images, it is probably just as easy to understand how that interpretation would seem foreign to readers steeped in the traditional exegesis of the *Classic of Poetry*.[6] In order to come to a better understanding of the backgrounds of these two styles of exegesis, I propose to examine in some detail one of the most enigmatic poems in the entire collection of the *Classic of Poetry*: "The Bank of the Ru" ("Ru Fen" 汝墳; Mao 10). This poem is replete with the kinds of images studied by Granet and Wen (including a particularly graphic fish image), but it also contains an apparently explicit political referent (to a "royal chamber"). I believe that the differing interpretations of this one poem provide an excellent illustratation of the contrast between the traditional exegesis of the *Classic of Poetry* and that of Granet, Wen, and their more recent followers.

"The Bank of the Ru" is found in the *Nan* of Zhou 周南 section, the first section of the entire collection. This provenance informs traditional interpretations based on the Han-period "Preface to the *Poetry*," which ascribes all eleven poems in the section to a single historical context: the time of King Wen of Zhou (r. 1099/57–1050 b.c.) and the virtuous influence that he and his queen exerted not only on the Zhou people, but even on people living in areas still controlled, at least nominally, by the paradigmatically evil last king of the Shang dynasty, Di Xin (r. 1086–1045 b.c.).[7] The "Ru" 汝 of the title refers to the Ru River, a river which flows east through the central part of present-day Henan province, to the south of the Zhou eastern capital (and the Eastern Zhou capital) at present-day Luoyang. While this geographic setting has predictably stimulated no little discussion among later traditional exegetes, the particular locale would seem not to be crucial to either of the two basic interpretive approaches to the poem.[8]

The poem presents no major linguistic difficulties. It begins with two stanzas that describe a woman collecting kindling or cutting firewood along the banks of the Ru River while she awaits her lover's return from an absence (expressed in the standard *Classic of Poetry* formula "Not yet seeing my lord" [*wei jian junzi* 未見君子]). The continuation of this theme across two stanzas suggests that the absence was long. However, at the end of the second stanza, the lover returns (again expressed formulaically, "Having seen my lord" (*ji jian junzi* 既見君子). The third and final stanza departs from this formula, beginning instead with the mention of a fish. It then shifts, seemingly without association, to state that "the royal chamber is as if ablaze," and then concludes, again without any apparent association, by remarking on the proximity of the poetess's parents.

THE BANK OF THE RU

遵彼汝墳	Walking along the bank of the Ru,
伐其條枚	Cutting the slender stems;
未見君子	Not yet seeing my lord,
惄如調飢	My desire is like the morning hunger.
遵彼汝墳	Walking along the bank of the Ru,
伐其條肄	Cutting the slender sprouts;
既見君子	Having seen my lord,
不我遐棄	He didn't desert me after all.
魴魚赬尾	The bream has a reddened tail.
王室如燬	The royal chamber is as if ablaze.
雖則如燬	But even though it is as if ablaze,
父母孔邇	Father and mother are very near.

The traditional interpretation of the poem (by which I here intend the "Preface to the *Poetry*," the Mao Commentary [*zhuan* 傳], the annotations [*jian* 箋] of Zheng Xuan 鄭玄 [A.D. 127–200], and the subcommentary of Kong Yingda 孔穎達 [574–648]) begins with the premise that it, like the other poems in its *Nan* of Zhou (Mao 1–11) section, dates to the time of

King Wen of Zhou.[9] This was a time of great moral contrast. On the one hand, King Wen was the embodiment of virtue in both his public and private lives, and this inevitably transformed the mores of the Zhou people as well. Thus, the "Preface to the *Poetry*" states with respect to "The Bank of the Ru":

汝墳道化行也。文王之化，行乎汝墳之國。婦人能閔其
君子，猶勉之以正也。

The civilizing influence of the Way is in motion. With the civilizing influence of King Wen extending to the state of the banks of the Ru, the wives were capable of pitying their husbands, but at the same time of encouraging them to be upright.

However, on the other hand, the evil king Di Xin of Shang had not yet been deposed. His presence just as inevitably served to weaken the proper bonds between people—even that of husband and wife, such as the poetess and her "lord" in "The Bank of the Ru."

That the poem opens by describing the poetess as walking along the bank of the Ru River collecting kindling or cutting firewood is understood by the traditional commentaries to depict a situation in which the wife must assume the work of her absent husband.[10] The poem does not make clear why the husband is absent. The Mao Commentary implies that he is a soldier participating in the final overthrowal of the Shang capital, though this entails a certain anachronism since King Wen was certainly already then dead. Perhaps because of this, Zheng Xuan states that the husband is doing his duty in serving, reluctantly, his lord—Di Xin, despite the king's manifest evil. In any event, there is general agreement that the poem is set in the context of the death throes of the Shang dynasty.

In the absence of her husband, the wife describes herself as desirous "like the morning hunger," a description that even the prolix *Maoshi zhengyi* 毛詩正義 commentary passes over with only linguistic glosses. In the second stanza, formally parallel to the first, she is again collecting kindling. That the kindling this time is referred to as "slender sprouts" is understood to mean that another entire season has passed since the first stanza. On this walk along the bank of the Ru, however, her husband returns and she rejoices that he has "not deserted" her after all.

The final stanza then begins with the problematic fish image. The fish—a "bream," a fish normally white in color,[11] is described as having a reddened tail. The Mao Commentary states simply enough that when "a fish labors then its tail reddens," presumably evoking the belabored state of affairs under Di Xin. Zheng Xuan posits a stricter comparison, remarking that "when a lord serves in a chaotic age, his face will be drawn and pallid, like the fish's tail reddening when it labors."[12] In either event, the fish is seen to represent the difficulties brought about by Di Xin and thus to shift the poem's focus to the Shang court.

Neither the Mao Commentary nor Zheng Xuan offers a very explicit interpretation of the even more problemmatic following line: "The royal chamber is as if ablaze" (*wang shi ru hui* 王室如燬). Mao states simply that "ablaze" (*hui* 燬) means "fire" (*huo* 火), perhaps suggesting the Shang capital engulfed in flames upon the Zhou conquest.[13] Zheng Xuan, consistent with his interpretation of the poem as dating to just before the Zhou conquest, explains that it signifies the "ostentatiousness" of the Shang court. The divergence between these two historical contexts is resolved to some extent with the interpretation of the final line of the poem: "Father and mother are very near." Despite the frustration of having to serve an evil lord or even the fury and exaltation of the overthrowal of the house of Shang, the civilizing influence of King Wen (the "father" of the Zhou people) remains at hand to remind the Zhou people to maintain their own morality.

Wen Yiduo was the first to break decisively with this tradition. As might be expected from the brief remarks above on his interpretation of the fish image, Wen read "The Bank of the Ru" as a love song. Although he did not offer a sustained commentary on the poem, he did refer to several of its lines in support of his interpretations of various nature images in the *Classic of Poetry* and his understanding of it is quite clear. Moreover, this understanding has been developed by his main disciple, Sun Zuoyun 孫作雲 (d. 1978), and, more recently, by Chen Bingliang 陳炳良.[14]

In addition to the fish image and the formulaic "not yet seeing my lord" and "having seen my lord," other images in the first two stanzas also contribute to the romance of the poem. For instance, Sun and Chen both follow Marcel Granet in reading the opening couplet, "Walking along the bank of the Ru/ Cutting the slender stems," as describing the gathering of floral love tokens near the riverine site of a romantic engagement.[15] While I would not deny either the pervasiveness of this trope in the *Classic of Poetry* or its consistency with the other themes in this particular poem, I see no reason, linguistic or conceptual, to favor it over the traditional interpretation of the woman as gathering kindling or cutting firewood. Indeed, such an image has a double purpose within this poem. First, Wen Yiduo has cited evidence to show that in the *Classic of Poetry* firewood could spark flames of passion as well of heat.[16] Perhaps the best of the examples of this symbolism is the poem "The Southern Mountain" ("Nan Shan" 南山; Mao 101), a poem again explicitly concerned with marriage.

THE SOUTHERN MOUNTAIN

析薪如之何	How does one split firewood?
匪斧不克	Without an axe it can't be done.
耳妻如之何	How does one take a wife?
匪媒不得	Without a matchmaker it won't succeed.

This symbolism seems to be especially efficacious in the case of "The Bank of the Ru," evoking the central image of the final stanza: "The royal chamber is as if ablaze."

Wen's interpretation of the symbolism of "hunger" in the final line of the first stanza, "My desire is like the morning hunger," has met with greater appreciation. As already noted by him, in both "The Transverse Gate" and "Men at Waiting," both of which were translated above, hunger is clearly a euphemism for sexual desire. "The Transverse Gate," which is directed at a man seeking an appropriate wife, compares his situation to one who hungers.

泌之洋洋	Where the spring gurgles,
可以樂飢	One can satisfy his hunger.

In a similar way, the young woman snubbed by the arrogant young courtier in "Men at Waiting" is described in the end as one who "hungers."

婉兮孌兮	Oh, how pretty; oh, how lovely
季女斯飢	This young girl who hungers.

This symbolism is found not only in the *Classic of Poetry*, but also elsewhere in early Chinese poetry. Qian Zhongshu 錢鍾書 has cited the following passage from the "Tian wen" 天問 or "Heavenly Questions" of the *Chuci* 楚辭 or *Songs of the South* by way of commenting on the symbolism of "hunger" in "The Bank of the Ru."[17]

禹之力獻功	Yu labored with all his might.
降省下土日方	He came down and looked on the earth below.
焉得彼嵞山女 而通之於台桑	How did he get that maid of T'u-shan and lie with her in T'ai-sang?
閔妃匹合厥身 是繼	The lady became his mate and her body had issue.
胡維嗜不同味	Why were their appetites for the same dish,
而快鼂飽	When they sated their hunger for the morning food of love.

Indeed, it would seem that every line in the first two stanzas of "The Bank of the Ru" is designed to set the table for "the morning food of love."

While Wen Yiduo certainly regarded the fish image opening the final stanza as the main course of the poem, he had nothing to say about the rest of the stanza except to note that the "royal chamber" could be a euphemism for members of the royal house (who, "as if ablaze," were in extreme sexual excitement). Both Sun Zuoyun and Chen Bingliang have given more concrete interpretations of the "royal chamber." With only slightly different explanations, they both conclude that it is a term for an ancestral temple. Since ancestral temples would have been visited only in the course of the rites offered to the ancestors, these buildings would have been vacant much of the time, and would therefore make excellent venues for surreptitious meetings.

Vacant though the ancestral temple may have been, it would also have been situated near the family's residence. This then, according to Chen, is the reason for the final line of the poem: "Father and mother are very near." This seems to combine the admonitions that close two other famous love songs of the *Classic of Poetry*. The first, "Please, Zhongzi" ("Qiang Zhongzi" 將仲子; Mao 76), is sung by a woman to an ardent suitor who proposes to jump over the wall into her courtyard.

PLEASE, ZHONGZI

將仲子兮	Oh, please, Zhongzi,
無踰我里	Don't cross into my neighborhood,
無折我樹杞	Don't break my willows.
豈敢愛之	Could it be that I dare care about them!
畏我父母	I fear my father and mother.
仲可懷也	Zhong is one to be cherished,
父母之言	But father and mother's words
亦可畏也	Are also to be feared.

As for the second of these two poems, "In the Wilds there is a Dead Doe" ("Ye You Si Jun" 野有死麕; Mao 23), only the most politically ardent reader could fail to see that it describes a young couple in the heat of passion; in the climactic third stanza, the girl slows the boy down, so as not to "make the dog bark," and presumably alert the neighborhood.

IN THE WILDS THERE IS A DEAD DOE

野有死麕	In the wilds there is a dead doe;
白茅包之	With white madder we wrap it.

有女懷春	There is a girl who cherishes spring
吉士誘之	And a fine boy who entices her.
林有樸樕	In the woods there is a clump of saplings;
野有死鹿	In the wilds there is a dead deer;
白茅純束	With white madder we bundle it.
有女如玉	There is a girl like jade.
舒而脫脫兮	Oh, slow and easy,
無感我帨兮	Oh, don't touch my girdle;
無使尨也吠	Don't make the dog bark!

Drawing a parallel with this poem, Chen Bingliang suggests that even though the passions of the lovers of "The Bank of the Ru" are "as if ablaze," they remain alert to the proximity of their parents and the need for circumspection.

With all due respect for the importance and the subtleties of the traditional exegesis of the *Classic of Poetry* (which has been treated sensitively in two recent Western-language monographs[18]), I believe that it fails in the case of "The Bank of the Ru." It is true that read together with other poems in the collection, and especially those in its *Nan* of Zhou section the commentaries present a reasonably cogent historical and moral reading. However, it seems to me that this reading wins its cogency at the expense of the poem. When the exegetical approach causes interpreters to spend much of their time debating whether it is plausible that the wife of a high officer would cut firewood, then I would suggest that there is something wrong with the approach.[19]

The poem as read by Wen Yiduo almost comes alive. The evocative images of the poem, so consistent with but one important exception (the reference to the "royal chamber"), are part of a metalanguage of the time in which actions in the natural and human realms coincide. While these coincidences were not without their political import, they had a much wider currency than just among the scribes at court. Yet this is why Wen's interpretation is also ultimately unsatisfying: just when the poem seems to work so well as a folk love song, suddenly members of the royal family intrude. That they do so without any of the context that King Wen's influence might have supplied seems to introduce an irresolvable contradiction to the sense of the poem.[20]

It is true that some aspect of royalty now seems to be very much involved in the "The Bank of the Ru." The "royal chamber" of the third stanza is the major support for the otherwise unconvincing traditional interpretation, and the major obstacle preventing acceptance of Wen Yiduo's otherwise consistent reading. Is it possible to explain this image in a way that accounts for both of these interpretations?

I believe that the question of how the royalty got into this poem may help to resolve the final image standing in the way of Wen Yiduo's love-song interpretation. In another essay in which he discussed some of his theoretical approaches to the interpretation of the *Classic of Poetry*, Wen began with two points. First, since Confucius "edited" the *Classic of Poetry*, the text that we now have could well have been changed or "corrected." Second, a single word or character can often determine the meaning of an entire poem. In the case of "The Bank of the Ru," it is clear that the "single word or character" that could determine the meaning of this poem is the *wang* 王, "royal," of the line "The royal chamber is as if ablaze." It is less clear, but nonetheless possible, that the text of this line which we have now was changed or "corrected."

The word *wang* is now written 王; however, from midway through the Western Zhou until the Han dynasty it was written 王, with the central horizontal stroke very near to the top horizontal stroke. Throughout that same period, the word *yu*, "jade," now written 玉, was written 王, identical to the way that *wang* came to be written. What makes this coincidence particularly intriguing for the interpretation of this love song is that from at least the beginning years of the Han dynasty, *yu*, "jade," was the general euphemism for sex of all sorts and especially for the genitalia. Thus, it is well known that the *yujing* 玉莖, "jade stalk," refers to the penis; in the "Sunü jing" 素女經 or "Classic of the Pure Maiden," the vulva are either the *yumen* 玉門, "jade gate," or *yuhu* 玉戶, "jade door."[21] Although I have found no reference to a "jade chamber," the same text refers to the vagina as the *zhushi* 朱室, "red chamber." Particularly considering the developing political-moral exegesis of the *Classic of Poetry* discussed above, it is at least conceivable that when the text of the *Classic of Poetry* achieved its present form (whether at the time of Confucius or as late as the Han dynasty), an original *yu* 王 in "The Bank of the Ru" might have been—advertently or inadvertently—left unchanged such that it was read *wang* 王.[22]

It is true that the variora in the *Classic of Poetry* are typically phonetic in nature, as would be natural with the oral transmission of a poetic tradition.[23] The incidence of graphic variation within the *Classic of Poetry* tradition requires further research; however, one important case has been demonstrated, and since it is remarkably similar to that which I detect in "The Bank of the Ru" it is important to introduce it here. The poem "The Intersection of the Tenth Month" ("Shi Yue zhi Jiao" 十月之交; Mao 193), traditionally dated to the reign of King You of Zhou (r. 781–771 B.C.), contains the mention of a solar eclipse on the first day of a tenth lunar month. There are later traditions (in the *Zhushu jinian* 竹書紀年 or *Bamboo Annals*) that such an eclipse took place in the sixth year of King You's reign (i.e., 776 B.C.). There was indeed a solar eclipse on 6 September 776 B.C. However, this eclipse was not visible in the vicinity of present-day Xi'an, the site of the Western Zhou capital, and thus could not have been the eclipse mentioned in the poem. Instead, it has been shown by Pang Sunjoo 方善柱 that the eclipse mentioned in the poem must be that of 4 June 781 B.C., which was indeed visible from Xi'an.[24] This is relevant for the discussion of graphic variants in the *Classic of Poetry* because, in the Zhou calendar, 4 June would have been the first day of a *seventh* month, rather than a *tenth* month. It is well known that the numerals "seven" (*qi* 七) and "ten" (*shi* 十) were regularly confused in early Chinese texts. This is because throughout the Zhou period, *qi*, "seven," was written 十, while *shi*, "ten," was written 𠂉. However, during the Han dynasty, when the redactions of extant pre-Qin texts were produced, *shi*, "ten," came to be written with the graph, 十, originally used to write *qi*, "seven," while *qi* itself was slightly changed to 七. It would seem to be the case in "The Intersection of the Tenth Month" that the graph for an original "seventh" month was left unchanged when the definitive text of the *Classic of Poetry* was produced, causing it to be read as "tenth" month.

If, in the same way, the graph 王, read in the Han dynasty as *wang*, "royal," originally represented the word *yu*, "jade," then the problematic final stanza of "The Bank of the Ru" would read:

> The bream has a reddened tail.
> The jade chamber is as if ablaze.
> But even though it is as if ablaze,
> Father and mother are very near.

Suddenly, the imagery is so graphic as to be unmistakable. The "bream" with "a reddened tail" obviously refers to an engorged phallus, representing the just returned "lord." The "jade chamber" which is "as if ablaze" just as obviously symbolizes the poetess in the heat of sexual excitement. This serves at once to balance the male image in the first line and also to bring the poetess back into the center of the poem.

It is perhaps appropriate that the poem should end with a warning. Just as the poetess knew that her "father and mother" would frown upon such a blazing celebration, so too can we be sure that the scholars responsible for transmitting the text of the poem would find such vaginal imagery threatening. Caught between their duty to transmit the *Classic of Poetry* faithfully and their desire to imbue it with moral-political significance, they could have achieved both purposes by simply doing nothing; by not changing the graph for *yu*, "jade," and thus reading it as *wang*, "royal," they could replace the bawdy poetess with a royal chamber, even if it had to be one "ablaze."

NOTES

1. Marcel Granet, *Fêtes et Chansons Anciennes de la Chine* (Paris: E. Leroux, 1919); for an English translation, see *Festivals and Songs of Ancient China*, trans. E. D. Edwards (London: George Routledge, 1932).

2. See Granet, *Festivals and Songs*, p. 27, where Granet states that he will exclude "all interpretations which are symbolic or which imply subtlety in the poet."

3. Wen Yiduo's studies of the *Classic of Poetry*, written over a ten-year period from 1935 until his untimely death in 1946, are generally in the nature of occasional comments on single images or lines rather than sustained analyses of entire poems. Relevant observations can be found sprinkled throughout his "*Shijing* xinyi" 詩經新義 and "*Shijing* tongyi" 詩經通義, both reprinted in volume two of *Wen Yiduo quanji* 聞一多全集 (1948; rpt. Shanghai: Shanghai Guji chubanshe, 1984).

4. This nature imagery, generally termed *xing* 興 or "evocation," has been perhaps the most discussed feature in literary criticism of the *Classic of Poetry*. Although there have been scholars who have regarded the imagery as virtually devoid of meaning (for a succinct survey of their views, see Pauline Yu, *The Reading of Imagery in the Chinese Poetic Tradition* [Princeton: Princeton University Press, 1987], pp. 60–64), Pauline Yu has said of the evocation that "most traditional commentators on the *Classic of Poetry* believed that some relationship of similarity linked it with the main topic of the poem"; *ibid.*, p. 65.

5. For the most cogent presentation of this interpretation, see his study "Shuo yu" 說魚; *Wen Yiduo quanji* vol. 1, pp. 117–38.

6. For instance, Liang Shiqiu 梁實秋 pointed out: "There are people who are dissatisfied with his (i.e., Wen Yiduo) frequent use of Freudian analytical methods, and who think that he overemphasized sexual symbolism"; *Tan Wen Yiduo* 談聞一多 (Taipei: Zhonghua wenhua shiye chubanshe, 1967), p. 86; quoted at Chen Bingliang 陳炳良, "Shuo 'Ru fen': Jianlun Shijing zhong youguan lianai he hunyin de shi" 說如墳: 兼論詩經中有關戀愛和婚姻的詩, *Zhongwai wenxue* 中外文學 7.12 (1979): 150n2.

7. The traditional commentaries routinely refer to this last king of the Shang as King Zhou 紂, Zhou being his personal name. To avoid confusion with the Zhou of the Zhou people, I will refer to him in all cases by his reign title, Di Xin.

8. The interpretation of the poem given by Cui Shu 崔述 (1740–1816; *Du Feng ouzhi* 讀風偶識 [in *Cui Dongbi yishu* 崔東壁遺書 (rpt. Shanghai: Shanghai guji chubanshe, 1983), 536], inspired by a comment of Wang Anshi's 王安石 (1021–1086) quoted in Liu Jin 劉瑾, *Shi zhuan tongshi* 詩傳通釋 [Siku quanshu ed.], 1.35a–b) moves from the geographic locale to the temporal setting: since the area of the Ru River is in the vicinity of the Eastern Zhou capital at Luoyang, this should serve to date the poem to the Eastern Zhou period (771–256 B.C.). This dating of the poem then shifts both the general historical context and also the specific referent of the final stanza's burning "royal chamber" to the time of King You (r. 781–771 B.C.) of Western Zhou. Like Di Xin of Shang, King You was also regarded in traditional Chinese historiography as a paradigmatically evil last king, one whose capital was also overrun and burned. While this dating of the poem is closer to that accepted by most philologists, the use to which it is put does not seem to mark a significant departure from the traditional exegesis of the poem.

9. This dating of the *Nan* of Zhou poems is that of the traditional commentaries; there is now some consensus, at least among paleographers and philologists, that these poems could not have been created until the eighth or seventh centuries B.C.; see, for example, W. A. C. H. Dobson, "Linguistic Evidence and the Dating of the Book of Songs," *T'oung Pao* 51 (1964): 322–34. This could, of course, be reason to dismiss the traditional interpretation. I think such a response would be simplistic. While it is true that the traditional exegesis emphasizes specific historical contexts and referents, it is not necessarily the case that the creation of the poems had to come at those moments.

10. The verb *fa* 伐, "to cut, to chop," would suggest the cutting of firewood, but all three words used to describe the wood itself, *tiao* 條, *mei* 枚, and *si* 肄, refer to slender branches. Thus, it would seem most natural to see the woman gathering kindling, perhaps a not unusual activity for a woman. However, most commentaries stress that it is only in the absence of her husband that she must perform duties that would otherwise be his responsibility, suggesting that they envision her wielding an axe and chopping wood.

   The poetess's perceived chopping of firewood has also stimulated considerable discussion as to her social background: whether she is the wife of a high official or that of a commoner. Relevant comments are excerpted at great length in Gao Qiufeng 高秋風, "Shijing Zhounan Ru Fen pian yanjiu" 詩經周南汝墳篇研究, *Zhongguo xueshu niankan* 中國學術年刊 10 (1989): 83–84. Gao's conclusion to this discussion illustrates the lengths to which the literal interpretation of the *Classic of Poetry* has been taken:

> Based on the above survey, it is rather difficult to determine whether the poetess is the wife of a high official or that of a commoner. Those who hold her to be the wife of a commoner have two reasons: first, the wife of a great official would not personally cut firewood; second, the poem's description of her being hungry in the morning would apply to a low-placed woman. However, morning hunger is not necessarily to be attributed only to a low-placed woman. Also, it is hard to be certain whether the wife of a high official might not personally cut firewood. Especially since the setting of this poem is that the royal chamber is as if ablaze, and her husband has again gone off on campaign, perhaps there weren't enough hands at home or else she wanted to use going out to cut firewood as an excuse to go out and see whether her husband had returned, in which cases her cutting firewood would also be possible.

11. For this coloration of the fish, see Zhu Xi 朱熹, *Shi jizhuan* 詩集傳 (Sibu congkan ed.), 1.9a. For another comment on the color of the fish's tail, see n. 12.

12. Arthur Waley has sought to find support for this interpretation of the fish as a portent of the belabored state of a nation in a passage from the *Zuo zhuan* (Ai 哀 17), claiming "a fish with a bleeding tail, floating helplessly downstream, is the symbol of a ruined kingdom"; Arthur Waley, *The Book of Songs* (1937; rpt. New York: Grove Press, 1987), p. 152. This interpretation is rather too literal. In fact, the passage concerns a turtleshell divination that produced a crack in the shell:

> 衛侯貞卜，其繇曰：如魚窺尾，衡流而方羊。裔焉大國，滅之將亡。
>
> The Lord of Wei divined the crack. It *yao* said: "Like a fish with a red tail, Swimming carefree across the current: Coming to the end of the great state, being destroyed and about to perish.

The Eastern Han scholar Zheng Sinong 鄭司農 (1st c. A.D.) interprets this portent to symbolize the licentiousness of the Lord of Wei; quoted at

Chunqiu Zuo zhuan zhengyi 春秋左傳正義 (Sibu beiyao ed.), 60.5b. According to this explanation, the meaning of the portent is perhaps not inconsistent with the sexual symbolism perceived by Wen Yiduo. Wen's student Sun Zuoyun 孫作雲 adds the observation, based, he says, on "biology," that the tails of some fish redden in the spring in order "to attract the opposite sex"; Sun Zuoyun, *Shijing yu Zhoudai shehui yanjiu* 詩經與周代社會研究 (Beijing: Zhonghua shuju, 1966), p. 311.

13. In the *Lienü zhuan* 列女傳, Liu Xin 劉歆 (d. A.D. 23) cites this line writing the final word as *hui* 毀, "destroyed," certainly suggesting that this was how he saw the scene. On the other other hand, the earlier *Hanshi waizhuan* 韓詩外傳 writes the line with the word *hui* 焜, "fiery," as do the different textual traditions cited in the *Jingdian shiwen* 經典釋文, suggesting that the word was in fact originally understood to mean "fiery."

14. Sun Zuoyun, *Shijing yu Zhoudai shehui yanjiu*, 311–13; Chen Bingliang, "Shuo 'Ru Fen," 139.

15. Sun Zuoyun, *Shijing yu Zhoudai shehui yanjiu*, 311; Chen Bingliang, "Shuo Ru Fen," 139. In addition to these very similar readings, also worthy of note is the suggestion by Shirakawa Shizuka 白川靜 that the woman picked the plants in order to throw them into the river as an offering designed to cause her beloved to appear; Shirakawa Shizuka, *Shikyō kenkyū* 詩經研究 (Tokyo: Hōyū shoten, 1981), p. 511.

16. For Wen Yiduo's discussion of kindling as an evocation of sexual desire, see *Wen Yiduo quanji*, vol. 2, pp. 76–78, 123–24, 177–80.

17. Qian Zhongshu, *Guan zhui pian* 管錐編 (Beijing: Zhonghua shuju, 1979), p. 73. The translation of the "Heavenly Questions" given here is that of David Hawkes, *Ch'u Tz'u, The Songs of the South: An Ancient Chinese Anthology* (London: Oxford University Press, 1959), p. 49.

18. Pauline Yu, *The Reading of Imagery in the Chinese Poetic Tradition*; Stephen van Zoeren, *Poetry and Personality: Reading, Exegesis, and Hermeneutics in Traditional China* (Stanford: Stanford University Press, 1991).

19. I am not the first to arrive at such a conclusion regarding the traditional exegesis of the *Classic of Poetry*, though I would certainly not wish to go so far as C. H. Wang in describing it as "a manifest distortion of this classic anthology, a distortion both of its genetic character and of the original definition of *shih* [poetry] in general"; C. H. Wang, *The Bell and the Drum: Shih Ching as Formulaic Poetry in an Oral Tradition* (Berkeley: University of California Press, 1974), p. 1. The exegesis on the *Book of Poetry* has played an incomparable role in the history of literary criticism in China, and deserves to be appreciated within that tradition. The question is

whether that tradition extends back to the time of the *Book of Poetry's* creation. In the case of "The Bank of the Ru," I think it does not.

20. I certainly do not believe that the vacant ancestral temple suggestion proposed by Sun Zuoyun and Chen Bingliang in any way resolves this contradiction.

21. For both of these, see "Sunü jing," 素女經 in *Shuangmei jing'an congshu* 雙梅景闇叢書, ed. Ye Dehui 葉德輝, 3b and 3a.

22. A good example of just this variation is to be seen in comparing the Mawangdui "Zhanguo zonghengjia shu" 戰國縱橫家書 with corresponding texts of the *Zhanguoce* 戰國策. In the passage describing an audience between the Queen of Zhao 趙 and Chulong 觸龍, Commander of the Eastern State, whereas both the manuscript and the Bao Biao 鮑彪 text of the *Zhanguoce* (i.e., the Sibu congkan edition, 6.53a) read *wang ti* 王體, "royal body," the Yao Hong 姚宏 text of the *Zhanguoce* (i.e., the Sibu beiyao edition, 21.9b) reads *yu ti* 玉體, "jade body"; for this, see Yumiko F. Blanford, "A Textual Approach to 'Zhanguo Zonghengjia Shu': Methods of Determining the Proximate Original Word among Variants," *Early China* 16 (1991), 192.

23. Examples of such phonetic variation are too numerous to need demonstration here. To cite just one example, I have already noted (n. 14) that within the line "The royal chamber is as if ablaze," the word "ablaze" (*hui* 燬) is written with several different graphs in Han dynasty texts.

24. Fang Shanzhu (Pang Sunjoo) 方善柱, "Xi-Zhou niandai xue shang de jige wenti" 西周年代學上的幾個問題, *Dalu zazhi* 大陸雜誌 51.1 (1975): 17–23.

Selected Bibliography
of Secondary Works

Akatsuka, Kiyoshi 赤塚忠. *Chūgoku kodai no shūkyō to bunka: In ōchō no saishi* 中國古代の宗教と文化: 殷王朝の祭祀. Tokyo: Kadokawa, 1977.

Barnard, Noel. "Chou China: A Review of the Third Volume of Cheng Te-k'un's *Archaeology in China.*" *Monumenta Serica* 24 (1965): 307–442.

———. "The Nieh Ling Yi." *The Journal of the Institute of Chinese Studies of the Chinese University of Hong Kong* 9.2 (1978): 585–627.

Blanford, Yumiko F. "A Textual Approach to 'Zhanguo Zonghengjia Shu': Methods of Determining the Proximate Original Word among Variants." *Early China* 16 (1991): 187–208.

Chen, Bingliang 陳炳良. "Shuo 'Ru fen': Jianlun Shijing zhong youguan lianai he hunyin de shi" 說如墳: 兼論詩經中有關戀愛和婚姻的詩. *Zhongwai wenxue* 中外文學 7.12 (1979): 138–55.

Chen, Mengjia 陳夢家. "Xi-Zhou tongqi duandai" 西周銅器斷代, Parts I–IV. *Kaogu xuebao* 考古學報 1955.9: 137–75; 1955.10: 69–142; 1956.1: 65–114; 1956.2: 85–94.

———. *Yinxu buci zongshu* 殷虛卜辭綜述. Beijing: Kexue chubanshe, 1956.

Chen, Shou 陳壽. "Taibao gui de fuchu he Taibao zhu qi" 大保簋的復出和大保諸器. *Kaogu yu wenwu* 考古與文物 1980.4: 23–30.

Chen, Zungui 陳尊嬀. *Zhongguo tianwenxue shi* 中國天文學史. Shanghai: Shanghai Renmin chubanshe, 1980.

Chou, Fa-kao [Zhou Fagao]. "On the Date of the Chou Conquest of Shang." *Guoli Zhongyang tushuguan guankan* 國立中央圖書館館刊 19.2 (1986): 21–34.

Creel, Herrlee Glessner. *The Birth of China.* New York: Frederick Ungar, 1937.

Creel, Herrlee Glessner. *Studies in Early Chinese Culture: First Series.* Baltimore: Waverly Press, 1937.

———. *The Origins of Statecraft in China*, vol. 1: *The Western Chou Empire*. Chicago: University of Chicago Press, 1970.

Dobson, W. A. C. H. *Early Archaic Chinese*. Toronto: University of Toronto Press, 1962.

———. "Linguistic Evidence and the Dating of the Book of Songs." *T'oung Pao* 51 (1964): 322–34.

———. *The Language of the* Book of Songs. Toronto: University of Toronto Press, 1968.

Dong, Zuobin 董作賓. *Yin li pu* 殷曆譜. Nanqi, Sichuan: Academia Sinica, 1945.

———. *Zhongguo nianli zongpu* 中國年曆總譜, 2 vols. Hong Kong: University of Hong Kong Press, 1960.

Elman, Benjamin A. *From Philosophy to Philology: Intellectual and Social Aspects of Change in Late Imperial China*. Cambridge, MA: Council on East Asian Studies, Harvard University, 1984.

———. *Classicism, Politics, and Kinship: The Ch'ang-chou School of New Text Confucianism in Late Imperial China*. Berkeley: University of California Press, 1990.

Fang, Shanzhu (Pang Sunjoo) 方善柱. "Xi-Zhou niandai xue shang de jige wenti" 西周年代學上的幾個問題. *Dalu zazhi* 大陸雜誌 51.1 (1975): 17–23.

Fong, Wen, ed. *The Great Bronze Age of China*. New York: Metropolitan Museum of Art, 1980.

Gao, Heng 高亨. *Zhouyi gujing jinzhu* 周易古經今注. Shanghai: Kaiming shudian, 1947.

Gao, Qiufeng 高秋風. "Shijing Zhounan Ru Fen pian yanjiu" 詩經周南汝墳篇研究. *Zhongguo xueshu niankan* 中國學術年刊 10 (1989): 69–105.

Gao, Wence 高文策. "Shilun Yi de chengshu niandai yu fayuan diyu" 試論易的成書年代與發原地域. *Guangming ribao* 光明日報 2 June 1961, 4.

Granet, Marcel. *Fêtes et Chansons Anciennes de la Chine*. Paris: E. Leroux, 1919; translated into English as *Festivals and Songs of Ancient China*, trans. E. D. Edwards. London: George Routledge, 1932.

———. *Danses et legendes de la Chine ancienne*. Paris: Albin Michel, 1926.

Gu, Jiegang 顧頡剛. "Zhouyi guayaoci zhong de gushi" 周易卦爻辭中的故事. *Yanjing xuebao* 燕京學報 6 (1929): 967–1006. Rpt. in *Gushi bian* 古史辨, ed. Gu Jiegang. 1931; rpt. Shanghai: Shanghai guji chubanshe, 1982, vol. 3, 1–44.

———. "*Yi Zhou shu* Shi fu pian jiaozhu xieding yu pinglun" 逸周書世俘篇較注寫定與評論. *Wenshi* 文史 2 (1962): 1–42.

———. "Shangshu Da gao jin yi" 尙書大誥今譯, *Lishi yanjiu* 歷史研究 1962.4: 26–51.

———. "Wuwang de si ji qi niansui he jiyuan" 武王的死及其年歲和紀元. *Wenshi* 文史 18 (July 1983): 1–32.

———. "Zhougong zhi zheng cheng wang—Zhougong dong zheng shishi kaozheng zhi er" 周公執政稱王—周公東征史事考證之二. *Wenshi* 文史 23 (1984): 1–30.

———. "San jian ji dongfang zhuguo de fan Zhou junshi xingdong he Zhougong de duice" 三監及東方諸國的反周軍事行動和周公的對策. *Wenshi* 文史 26 (1986): 1–11.

———. "Zhougong dongzheng he dongfang gezude qianxi" 周公東征和東方各族的遷徙. *Wenshi* 27 (1986): 1–14.

Gu Jiegang 顧頡剛 *et al.* ed., *Gu shi bian* 古史辨. 7 vols. 1926–41; rpt. Shanghai: Shanghai Guji chubanshe, 1982.

Guo, Moruo 郭沫若. *Zhongguo gudai shehui yanjiu* 中國古代社會研究. 1930; rpt. Beijing: Renmin chubanshe, 1954.

———. *Liang Zhou jinwenci daxi kaoshi* 兩周金文辭大系考釋. Tokyo: Bunkyudo shoten, 1935; rev. ed. Beijing: Kexue chubanshe, 1956.

———. "Bao you ming shiwen" 保卣銘釋文. *Kaogu xuebao* 1958.1: 1–2.

Harper, Donald. "The Sexual Arts of Ancient China as Described in a Manuscript of the Second Century B.C." *Harvard Journal of Asiatic Studies* 47.2 (1987): 539–93.

Havelock, Eric A. *Preface to Plato.* Cambridge, MA: Harvard Belknap Press, 1963.

Huang, Peirong 黃沛榮. "Zhou shu yanjiu" 周書研究. Ph.D. diss., National Taiwan University, 1976.

Huang, Shengzhang 黃盛章. "Bao you ming de shidai yu shishi" 保卣銘的時代與史實. *Kaogu xuebao* 1957.3: 57–59.

Kaizuka, Shigeki 貝塚茂樹. "Shinshutsu Dan-haku Tatsu ki kō" 新出檀伯達器考. *Tōhō gakuhō* 東方學報 (Kyoto) 8 (1937). Rpt. in *Kaizuka Shigeki chosaku shū* 貝塚茂樹著作集. Tokyo: Chu'o koronsha, 1977, vol. 3, 171–214.

Karlgren, Bernhard. *The Book of Odes.* 1944–45; rpt. Stockholm: Museum of Far Eastern Antiquities, 1974.

Karlgren, Bernhard. *Glosses on the Book of Documents.* 1948–49; rpt. Stockholm: Museum of Far Eastern Antiquities, 1970.

Karlgren, Bernhard. *The Book of Documents*. Stockholm: Museum of Far Eastern Antiquities, 1950.

Keightley, David N. "Public Work in Ancient China: A Study of Forced Labor in the Shang and Western Chou." Ph.D. diss. Columbia University, 1969.

———. *Sources of Shang History: The Oracle-Bone Inscriptions of Bronze Age China*. Berkeley: University of California Press, 1978.

———. "The *Bamboo Annals* and Shang-Chou Chronology." *Harvard Journal of Asiatic Studies* 38.2 (December 1978): 423–38.

Kunst, Richard Alan. "The Original 'Yijing': A Text, Phonetic Transcription, Translation, and Indexes, with Sample Glosses." Ph.D. diss., University of California, Berkeley, 1985.

Lawton, Thomas. "A Group of Early Western Chou Period Bronze Vessels." *Ars Orientalis* 10 (1975): 111–21.

Legge, James. *The Chinese Classics*, vol. 3: *The Shoo King or The Book of Historical Documents*. 1865; rpt. Hong Kong: Hong Kong University Press, 1960.

———. *The Chinese Classics*, vol. 4, *The She King or The Book of Poetry*. 1871; rpt. Hong Kong: Hong Kong University Press, 1960.

———. *The Chinese Classics*, vol. 5: *The Ch'un Ts'ew with the Tso Chuen*. 1872; rpt. Hong Kong: Hong Kong University Press, 1960.

Li, Jingchi 李鏡池. *Zhouyi tanyuan* 周易探源. Beijing: Zhonghua shuju, 1978.

———. *Zhouyi tongshi* 周易通釋. Beijing: Zhonghua shuju, 1981.

Li, Xiaoding 李孝定. *Jiagu wenzi jishi* 甲骨文字集釋. Taipei: Academia Sinica, 1965.

Li, Xueqin 李學勤. "He zun xinshi" 何尊新釋. *Zhongyuan wenwu* 中原文物 1981.1: 35–39, 45.

Loehr, Max. "Bronzentexte der Chou-Zeit: Chou I (1)." *Sinologische Arbeiten* 2 (1944): 59–70.

Lord, Albert. *A Singer of Tales*. Cambridge, MA: Harvard University Press, 1960.

Ma, Chengyuan 馬承源. "He zun mingwen he Zhouchu shishi" 何尊銘文和周初史釋. In *Wang Guowei xueshu yanjiu lunji* 王國維學術研究論集, ed. Wu Ze 吳澤. Shanghai: Huadong shifan daxue chubanshe, 1983, 45–61.

Matsumoto, Masaaki 松本雅明. "Shū kō sokui kō" 周公即位考. *Shigaku zasshi* 史學雜誌 77.6 (1968): 1–37.

Moriyasu, Tarō 一森安太即. *Zhongguo gudai shenhua yanjiu* 中國古代神

話研究. Translated by Wang Xiaolian 王孝廉. Taipei: Dipingxian chubanshe, 1979.

Nivison, David S. "Royal 'Virtue' in Shang Oracle Inscriptions." *Early China* 4 (1978–79): 52–55.

———. "The Dates of Western Chou," *Harvard Journal of Asiatic Studies* 43.2 (1983): 481–580.

Pang, Huaijing 龐懷靖. "Ba Taibao yuge—jianlun Shaogong Shi de youguan wenti" 跋大保玉戈——兼論召公奭的有關問題. *Kaogu yu wenwu* 考古與文物 1986.1: 70–73.

Pang, Sunjoo. "The Consorts of King Wu and King Wen in the Bronze Inscriptions of Early Chou." *Monumenta Serica* 33 (1977–78): 124–35.

Pingxin 平心. "Bao you ming xinshi" 保卣銘新釋. *Zhonghua wenshi luncong* 中華文史論 1979.1: 49–79.

Qian, Zhongshu 錢鍾書. *Guan zhui pian* 管錐編. Beijing: Zhonghua shuju, 1979.

Qiu, Xigui 裘錫圭. "Shi 'wu' 'fa'" 釋勿發. *Zhongguo yuwen yanjiu* 中國語文研究 2 (1981): 43–44.

———. "An Examination of Whether the Charges in Shang Oracle-Bone Inscriptions Are Questions." *Early China* 14 (1989): 77–114.

Qu, Wanli 屈萬里. "Du *Zhou shu* Shi fu pian" 讀周書世俘篇. In *Qingzhu Li Ji xiansheng qishi sui lunwenji* 慶祝李濟先生七十歲論文集. Taipei: Qinghua xuebaoshe, 1965, vol. 1, 317–32.

Santillana, Giorgio de and Hertha von Dechend. *Hamlet's Mill.* Boston: Godine, 1977.

Saussure, Leopold de. *Les Origines de l'Astronomie Chinoise.* 1909–22; rpt. Taipei: Ch'eng-wen, 1967.

Schlegel, Gustave. *Uranographie Chinoise.* Leiden: E. J. Brill, 1875.

Schmitt, Gerhard. *Sprüche der Wandlungen auf ihrem geistesgeschichtlichen Hintergrund.* Deutsche Akademie der Wissenschaften zu Berlin, Institüt für Orient-forschung Veröffentlichung, Nu. 76. Berlin: Akademie-Verlag, 1970.

Schuessler, Axel. *A Dictionary of Early Zhou Chinese.* Honolulu: University of Hawaii Press, 1987.

Serruys, Paul L-M. "Towards a Grammar of the Language of the Shang Bone Inscriptions." In *Zhongyang yanjiuyuan guoji Hanxue huiyi lunwen ji* 中央研究院國際漢學會議論文集. Taipei: Academia Sinica, 1981, 313–64.

Shaughnessy, Edward L. "The Composition of the *Zhouyi*." Ph.D. diss., Stanford University, 1983.

———. "The Date of the Duo You *Ding* and Its Significance." *Early China* 9–10 (1983–85): 55–69.

———. "Zhouyuan Oracle-Bone Inscriptions: Entering the Research Stage?" *Early China* 11–12 (1985–87): 146–63.

———. "Extra-Lineage Cult in the Shang Dynasty: A Surrejoinder." *Early China* 11–12 (1985–87): 182–90.

———. "Historical Geography and the Extent of the Earliest Chinese King-doms," *Asia Major*, third series, 2.2 (1989): 1–22.

———. *Sources of Western Zhou History: Inscribed Bronze Vessels*. Berkeley: University of California Press, 1991, 134–55.

Shirakawa, Shizuka 白川靜. *Kinbun tsūshaku* 金文通釋. 56 vols. Kobe: Hakutsuru bijitsukan, 1962–84.

———. *Shikyō kenkyū* 詩經研究. Tokyo: Hōyū shoten, 1981.

Sun, Zhichu 孫稚雛, "Bao you mingwen huishi" 保卣銘文匯釋. *Guwenzi yanjiu* 古文字研究 5 (1982): 191–210

Sun, Zuoyun 孫作雲. "Shuo Tian Wang gui wei Wuwang mie Shang yiqian tongqi" 說天亡簋爲武王滅商以前銅器. *Wenwu cankao ziliao* 文物參考資料 1958.1: 57–64.

———. *Shijing yu Zhoudai shehui yanjiu* 詩經與周代社會研究. Beijing: Zhonghua shuju, 1966.

Tang, Lan 唐蘭. "Xi Zhou tongqi duandai zhong de 'Kang gong' wenti" 西周銅器斷代中的康宮問題. *Kaogu xuebao* 1962.1: 15–48.

———. "Xi Zhou shidai zui zao de yijian tongqi Li gui mingwen jieshi" 西周時代最早的一件銅器利簋銘文解釋. *Wenwu* 文物 1977.8: 8–9.

———. "Lun Zhou Zhaowang shidai de qingtongqi mingke" 論周昭王時代的青銅器銘刻. *Guwenzi yanjiu* 2 (1981): 3–162.

Waley, Arthur. *The Book of Songs*. 1937; rev. ed. New York: Grove Press, 1987.

Wang, C. H. *The Bell and the Drum: Shih Ching as Formulaic Poetry in an Oral Tradition*. Berkeley: University of California Press, 1974.

Wang, Guowei 王國維. "Shengpo sipo kao" 生霸死霸考. In *Guantang jilin* 觀堂集林, 4 vols. 1923; rpt. Beijing: Zhonghua shuju, 1959, vol. 1, 19–26.

———. "Yin Zhou zhidu lun" 殷周制度論. In *Guantang jilin* 觀堂集林, 4 vols. 1923; rpt. Beijing: Zhonghua shuju, 1984, vol. 2, 451–80.

Wen, Yiduo 聞一多. *Gu dian xin yi* 古典新義. 1941; rpt. in *Wen Yiduo quanji*, vol. 2.

———. "Shuo yu" 說魚. 1945; rpt. in *Wen Yiduo quanji* vol. 1, pp. 117–38.

———. *Wen Yiduo quanji*聞一多全集. 1948; rpt. Beijing: Sanlian shudian, 1982.

Wilhelm, Hellmut. *Heaven, Earth, and Man in the Book of Changes*. Seattle: University of Washington Press, 1977.

Xia, Hanyi 夏含夷 (Edward L. Shaughnessy). "Zhouyi Qiangua liulong xinjie" 周易乾卦六龍新解. *Wenshi* 文史 24 (1985): 9–14.

Xiong, Shili 熊十力. *Qian Kun yan* 乾坤衍. Rpt. Taipei: Xuesheng shuju, 1976.

Yang, Wuming 楊五銘. "Xi Zhou jinwen beidong jushi jianlun" 西周金文被動句式簡論. *Guwenzi yanjiu* 古文字研究 7 (1982): 309–17.

Yao, Xiaosui 姚孝遂. "Shangdai de fulu" 商代的俘虜. *Guwenzi yanjiu* 古文字研究 1 (1979): 337–90.

Yu, Pauline. *The Reading of Imagery in the Chinese Poetic Tradition*. Princeton, NJ: Princeton University Press, 1987.

Yu, Xingwu 于省吾. *Shangshu xinzheng*尙書新證. 1934; rpt. Taipei: Song-gao shushe, 1985.

Zhou, Fagao 周法高. *Jinwen gulin* 金文詁林. Hong Kong: The Chinese University of Hong Kong Press, 1975.

Index

agriculture: and dragon, 203, 205; and festivals, 222; and "Qian" and "Kun" hexagrams, 211–12

Airs of the States, 222–23

Airs of Zheng, 222

allegory, 222

anachronism, 41

ancestral sacrifice: liturgy of, 174–80

"Ancient" *Bamboo Annals* 古本竹書紀年, 69. See also *Bamboo Annals* 竹書紀年

annals, 8, 70. See also *Bamboo Annals* 竹書紀年

Announcement (*gao* 誥) chapters of *Shangshu* 尚書, 103. *See also under specific titles*

Antares, 201–2

apocrypha 緯, 207

appointments: records of, 5

archaeology, 10 n. 2

archaic script, 38, 52

archeoastronomy, 9. *See also* astronomy

archives, 4, 5

astronomy: historical, 9; imagery in, 203; and myth of battle between Yellow Emperor and Chi You, 210. *See also* constellations

Austin, J.L., 169

authenticity: criteria of, 70; determination of, 37; of received texts, 41

authority: of king vs. ministers, 102

Bai Wei 百韋, 34, 58 n. 13

Bamboo Annals 竹書紀年, 7; authenticity of, 70–73, 93; and chronology of Eastern Zhou, 95 n. 13; and date of Duke of Zhou's death, 124; and death of King Zhao, 92; and eclipse of 776 B.C., 233; historical value of, 69–70; and King Kang, 143; preconquest annals of, 99 n. 59; transposition of bamboo strip in, 81–93

bamboo strips: as medium for command documents, 3; mistakes in arrangement of, 81–93

Ban 班, Duke of Mao 毛, 72

"Ban 班 *gui*", 71–72, 94 n. 9

Bao Heng 保衡, 111–12

"Bao 保 *you*", 140–42

"Bao 保 *zun*", 140

bells, 182, 184. *See also* musical instruments

Bi 鼈 (Turtle) constellation, 20, 208–9

bi 幣 insignia, 114, 117, 133 n. 56

Bible, 2

Black Warrior, 208, 216 n. 23

Bo Qin 伯禽, 87

"Bo Xian 伯害 *ding*", 151 n. 9

Book of Changes. See *Yijing* 易經; *Zhouyi* 周易

Book of Documents. See *Shangshu* 尚書

bream, 227. *See also* fish

247

Index